Becc

the Lost Colony

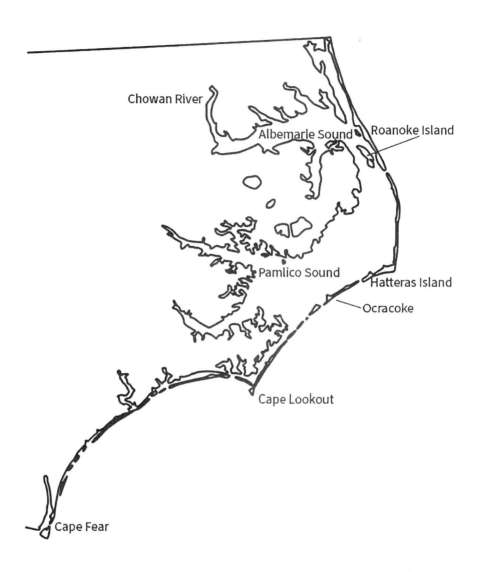

Chowan River

Albemarle Sound

Roanoke Island

Pamlico Sound

Hatteras Island

Ocracoke

Cape Lookout

Cape Fear

Becoming the Lost Colony

The History, Lore and Popular Culture of the Roanoke Mystery

CHARLES R. EWEN *and*
E. THOMSON SHIELDS, JR.

McFarland & Company, Inc., Publishers
Jefferson, North Carolina

Frontispiece: The Coastal Plain of North Carolina.

LIBRARY OF CONGRESS CATALOGING-IN-PUBLICATION DATA

Names: Ewen, Charles R., 1956– author. | Shields, E. Thomson, Jr., 1958– author.
Title: Becoming the Lost Colony : the history, lore and popular culture of the
    Roanoke mystery / Charles R. Ewen, and E. Thomson Shields, Jr..
Description: Jefferson, North Carolina : McFarland & Company, Inc., Publishers,
    2024 | Includes bibliographical references and index.
Identifiers: LCCN 2024010684 | ISBN 9781476694962
    (paperback : acid free paper) ∞
    ISBN 9781476652450 (ebook)
Subjects: LCSH: Roanoke Colony. | Colonists—North Carolina—Roanoke Island—
    History—16th century. | Roanoke Island (N.C.)—History—16th century.
Classification: LCC F229 .E936 2024 | DDC 975.6/17501—dc23/eng/20240306
LC record available at https://lccn.loc.gov/2024010684

BRITISH LIBRARY CATALOGUING DATA ARE AVAILABLE

ISBN (print) 978-1-4766-9496-2
ISBN (ebook) 978-1-4766-5245-0

Front cover images: *from top* 1590 map created by John White,
engraved by Theodor de Bry (New York Public Library);
Fort Raleigh National Historic Site earthwork (Zack Frank/Shutterstock);
scene from *The Lost Colony,* a historical outdoor drama
on Roanoke Island in North Carolina's Outer Banks
(Carol M. Highsmith, photographer, Library of Congress).

Printed in the United States of America

*McFarland & Company, Inc., Publishers
Box 611, Jefferson, North Carolina 28640
www.mcfarlandpub.com*

To Claire Shields and Gretchen Ewen,
for staying married to us
despite our interminable ramblings
about a subject in which
they had little interest.

Acknowledgments

The authors have several people to thank for their help in completing this book. And from the start, our apologies that the list is an incomplete one.

We want to thank Randy Daniel as well as several anonymous reviewers for reading earlier drafts, which helped improve the final draft.

The staff of the Joyner Library at East Carolina University, Jan Lewis, director, has been both encouraging and helpful with their expertise, especially Special Collections—Manuscripts and Digital Curation, Kelly Spring, head, and the North Carolina Collection, Jennifer Daughtery, head. Additional thanks to Brent McKee, for assistance with the 1936 WPA photograph of the log blockhouse and Virginia Dare Memorial. And thanks as well to Addison Siemon for his help with the figures.

The late Keats Sparrow needs to be recognized for dragging us into the Lost Colony Reality Distortion Sphere in the first place, as should be Andrew Lawler for asking questions that motivated our research along the way.

Finally, the convivial abuse and support of P7 as well as the Smith Roundtable has been greatly appreciated, as has been the assistance of Missy the White Dog, the White Doe's canine companion and the spirit animal of this project.

Table of Contents

Part I—What We Know

Part II—What We Think We Know

List of Figures

Introduction

What Was the Lost Colony?

For many people, the Lost Colony is a vague historical site which they know very little about. In fact, when we ask our students what they know about the Lost Colony, some smart aleck always replies, "They got lost." Asking about when it happened, we get the equally vague "a long time ago." And this is in North Carolina. If you stray too far across the state's borders, you have to recap the story before you can discuss the latest findings. Look at any press release concerning archaeology on the Outer Banks or at Fort Raleigh, and you will see a brief summary of the Lost Colony mystery, such as the following article from the Smithsonian's website discussing the investigation of a ring that supposedly belonged to one of the colonists:

> The settlers arrived from England in the summer of 1587, led by John White. They rebuilt an outpost on Roanoke Island, 50 miles north of Hatteras, abandoned by a previous band of colonists. White's group included his daughter Eleanor, who soon gave birth to Virginia Dare, the first child born of English parents in the New World. White quickly departed for England to gather supplies and additional colonists, but his return was delayed by the outbreak of war with Spain. When he finally managed to land on Roanoke Island three years later, the settlement was deserted. The only clue was the word "Croatoan" carved on a post, the name of a tribe allied with the English and the island now called Hatteras [Lawler 2017].

Even for those people who know something about the Lost Colony, this is about the extent of it. Early colonists were in North Carolina, and then they disappeared. The very fact that it's a mystery, one particularly vague on details, has drawn in many people. Different people for different reasons have been writing about the missing 1587 colonists for over 400 years.

So John White, the governor of the 1587 colony, returned in 1590

1

and found that the colony was gone. They didn't seem to have been massacred as no bodies are mentioned, and he assumed that they had moved to a better spot. "Croatoan" carved on a post suggested they had gone to the village of Croatoan on present-day Hatteras Island, but White's attempts to locate his family and friends were thwarted by bad weather and the impatience of the captain who had brought him over from England. Apparently, this was a detour from a privateering mission, and White was just a passenger. After a brief search of Roanoke Island and an unsuccessful attempt to reach Hatteras Island, White returned to England.

Sir Walter Raleigh, who put together the original venture, commissioned a couple more half-hearted attempts to check on the colonists, but the colony was a losing proposition, and Raleigh and his investors were unwilling to pour too much more money down that particular rathole. In late 1608 and early 1609, the colonists at Jamestown sent patrols into the Albemarle region to find any trace of the colonists, but returned with only vague rumors and second-hand accounts saying that perhaps there were people who looked like them in the hinterland. That no follow-up expeditions were sent out suggests that the Jamestown leadership thought the colonists were dead, but the Virginia Company still found it useful to keep the possibility of their existence alive to help bolster their land claims. The ensuing two centuries consigned the colonists to oblivion.

This should have been the end of the mystery, and it was, until historians and fiction writers of the nineteenth century rediscovered the story and embellished it, starting in the in 1820s and 1830s. The story of Virginia Dare growing up in savage wilderness while maintaining her innocence appealed to authors and their readership. This is when the lost colonists become *The* Lost Colony. Nineteenth-century archaeological attempts to investigate some low mounds on the north end of Roanoke Island provided no definitive evidence of the 1580s Roanoke colonies. That did not stop commemorations of the 1580s colonization attempts, especially the Lost Colony. In 1896, a granite monument was erected at the assumed site of Fort Raleigh, and in the 1930s, a presidential visit and an outdoor drama got the attention of the National Park Service, who agreed to take over the site despite the lack of authentication.

To remedy this lack of information, the National Park Service commissioned an historical study and some serious archaeology by pioneering historical archaeologist J.C. "Pinky" Harrington. The work lent credence to the claim that the newly created Fort Raleigh National Historic Site was located where the post with the word "Croatoan" carved on it had been, and so the ephemeral earthworks were completely reconstructed, though the actual settlement was not located. Subsequent work at the park has found only a handful of sixteenth-century materials, but it has been just enough to keep up public and scholarly interest, though the settlement remains elusive.

The search also looked to where the Lost Colonists might have gone. The initial focus was the North Carolina Outer Banks, a search for Croatoan. However, more recent archaeological and historical surveys have turned inland, looking for where John White said his people were prepared to move after his departure "50 miles into the main." Tantalizing clues have been found, but nothing definitive.

While scholars delved into the historical record, the popular culture surrounding the Lost Colonists continued to grow. Aside from the outdoor drama *The Lost Colony*, presented each summer since 1937, others were attracted to a story with all the elements of a made-for-TV melodrama: the treacherous Simon Fernandez, who may have stranded the colony at Roanoke; the romance of young Virginia Dare growing up in a trackless wilderness, fending off hostile and amorous natives; and conspiracy theories to tempt even the most skeptical of readers. Were they lost or purposefully forgotten? Were they located in a secret area to engage in clandestine commerce? Were they killed or enslaved by the local native peoples? Did the Spaniards find them and wipe them out? There is nothing that proves and nothing that rules out any of these hypotheses, letting them all lie at the intersection of popular culture and historical study.

The question of what happened to the Lost Colony may never be answered, but the story will live on. *The Lost Colony* outdoor drama performed every summer on Roanoke Island is the oldest continuously running outdoor drama in the nation. Thousands of tourists learn a version of the legend and take the story home with them. Fort Raleigh National Historic Site stands as a testament to the mystery and presents an historical antidote to the artistic license of the nearby outdoor drama. And to demonstrate the pervasiveness of the public perception, the massive bridge connecting Roanoke Island to the mainland, completed in 2002, was named after a North Carolinian who may not have survived her first year in the state, the Virginia Dare Memorial Bridge.

The authors of this book approach the Lost Colony from different perspectives. Charlie Ewen is an historical archaeologist focusing on the Early Contact Period (the sixteenth century) in what is now the United States. Tom Shields is an English professor with a specialty in early American and frontier literature. They found their interests (and personalities) complemented one another and were soon drawn into what might be called "The Lost Colony Reality Distortion Sphere." When examining the different hypotheses concerning the whereabouts of the colonists, Charlie tends to be Dr. No, a skeptic who needs solid evidence. Tom, on the other hand, while skeptical, also enjoys good stories and what those stories reveal about the people who tell them. Both are committed to understanding the search.

The Lost Colony may remain lost, but the fun is in the looking. Actually finding it might be somewhat bittersweet. It is also the people you meet along the way, from serious scholars to colorful fringe characters. When the little real data that exist are accessible to all, everyone can play, everyone has a "theory." And their theory is always right! Only a very foolish person wouldn't see the obvious truth. It is these people who are the real stars of books like Andrew Lawler's *The Secret Token: Myth, Obsession, and the Search for the Lost Colony of Roanoke* (2018) and Tony Horwitz's *A Voyage Long and Strange: Rediscovering the New World* (2008). So many hypotheses, so little data.

So how does this book differ from the myriad other Lost Colony books and articles published over the last century? Well, for one, it very purposefully does not present a preferred hypothesis about what happened to the Lost Colony. We provide the historical and archaeological background and then present the published hypotheses so readers have the data and the context to assess the various ideas about the fate of the colonists. We also attempt to separate the facts (such as they are) from the legends and folklore, again so readers can draw their own conclusions about the hypotheses as well as judge any future claims.

Spoiler alert, while almost all of the published hypotheses have some merit, none are wholly compelling. This is why no one can accurately state that the Lost Colony has been found—no matter what newspaper headlines about each new hint of possible Lost Colony evidence may declare. And that may be why Lost Colony mythology has influenced modern popular culture, from television programs to portrayals on the big screen, historical fiction, and even graphic novels. Indeed, the popular mythology has even influenced the scientific inquiry.

If what captivates people about the Lost Colony is trying to solve the mystery, why do we very purposefully not present a preferred hypothesis? In fact, as we sent out our manuscript to potential publishers, we were told on one occasion that we have a scholarly obligation, almost a moral duty, to tell what we believe most likely happened to the colonists. And another potential publisher found our manuscript well worth consideration, but their marketing department didn't think it could sell the book if we didn't include a new theory about the fate of the Lost Colony.

To begin, we don't promote one hypothesis over the others because of the importance of negative findings, understanding what is learned when the available evidence doesn't allow a hypothesis to be tested or when the evidence counters a hypothesis. If that ring, that ceramic sherd, that post hole *can* but does not necessarily indicate the 1587 colonists were in a specific place, how else might that ring, sherd, or post hole have gotten there? What do seeing the various valid explanations teach us about the history and culture of a location? Another reason not to promote one unproven hypothesis over others is that when hypotheses are repeated often enough, they start to be treated as proven, as being fact, which can then all too easily lead to extrapolating the next "fact" from the unproven first one, and so on.

John White says that "Croatoan" shows where the 1587 colonists intended to go becomes the colonists probably went there becomes the Lost Colony went to Hatteras Island—even though the same scattered bits of evidence allow for other equally valid and equally unprovable hypotheses. "Could be" becomes "was," usually accompanied by lines like "it all fits," "it's the only explanation that makes sense," "it all adds up."

Leaving the mystery unanswered leaves us open to examining all potential interpretations of the evidence. Pretty much everything after John White's 1587 departure from Roanoke Island is a blank slate that can be used to try out various ideas. This blank slate even provides a setting for writers to create literary accounts to explore a variety of topics—gender roles in society; loss and grief; what democracy means; just what is meant by *good* and *evil*. And fiction allows writers to explore hypotheses that can feed back into historical discussions. What if the 1587 colonists tried to sail away from Roanoke Island? What would their motivations for such an attempt be? What vessels would they have had available to sail in and what others might they have tried to build? Could they have attempted to sail back to England? And whether they tried to sail back to England or to Croatoan, to the Chesapeake, or to the western end of the Albemarle Sound, could they have capsized and drown? Fictional accounts can lead to new and interesting directions for further fact-based historical research. Not promoting one untested hypothesis over the others reminds us that the fun is in the looking.

Our goal, then, is to give readers the tools with which to assess all current and future claims concerning the Lost Colony, to provide examples of what might be learned even if the mystery is not solved, and in the end, to understand how a failed colonial venture became the epic drama it is today. So let us begin.

PART I

What We Know

1

The Background History

*What Do We Know
and How Do We Know It?*

As with all history, the Lost Colony isn't just a list of facts that tell what happened in the past. Investigating ideas about what led up to and what ultimately happened to the Lost Colony requires thinking about how histories are written. Evidence comes from archival documents, published accounts, material objects from archeological digs, folk traditions, and various other types of data. Rarely, if ever, are data complete. When people write histories, they can't help trying to fill in gaps in the record. How people have filled in the gaps is the historiography of the 1587 colony, the story of the Lost Colony.

As a basic definition, *historiography* is the study of how history is written—how writers' core beliefs and cultural influences affect what data are deemed important, the ways information is researched and presented, and the conclusions drawn from that information. Historiography is not only about the beliefs of and cultural influences on historians and their readers, but also how these affected the creation of the original, or primary, sources. In other words, historiography is "an exploration of the various contexts that affect historical thinking in any one time and place" (Andrews 2008).

The story of the 1580s Roanoke colonies can be, and often is, presented with the historical narrative foregrounded, while the historiography is given incomplete, perfunctory, or obscured attention—and is sometimes hidden or ignored altogether. However, especially because we don't know what happened to the 1587 colonists, the history of the Lost Colony *is* its historiography. In other words, the history of the Lost Colony is how various methods of historical scholarship have been applied to interpret the available data. The historical narratives and the historiography behind the narratives are worth examining together. The contexts of events, of how events were recorded, and of the interpretation of events over time make up the historiography of the Lost Colony. A good context to begin with for the Lost Colony is Sir Walter Raleigh's sending several English voyages to Roanoke Island in the 1580s prior to the 1587 colony.

The Adventure Begins (1584)

Raleigh was certainly not the first European who attempted to exploit North America. The Spanish had planted a successful colony at St. Augustine twenty years before Raleigh's first expedition to establish a foothold on the continent. In fact, Raleigh wasn't even the first Englishman to envision or to act on settling North America. For example, Raleigh's half-brother Sir Humphrey Gilbert received a patent from Queen Elizabeth in 1578 to conduct voyages to North America. However, Gilbert's attempts in 1578 and 1583 were unsuccessful, and after Gilbert was lost near the Azores on the return from Newfoundland in 1583, Raleigh obtained the patent to explore and colonize North America the following year. Specifically, Raleigh's patent permitted him to "discover search fynde out and viewe such remote heathen and barbarous landes Contries and territories not actually possessed of any Christian Prynce and inhabited by Christian people" (Quinn 1991[1955]:1:82). These "landes Contries and territories" he could exploit as he saw fit. Armed with this mandate from the Crown, Raleigh sent out his first exploratory venture in 1584.

Like so much concerning all of the 1580s Roanoke voyages, we know very little about the first expedition's leaders. Philip Amadas and Arthur Barlowe were both members of Raleigh's household, but beyond that the record is mostly silent. They each captained a vessel and together were charged with exploring the area between Norumbega [Newfoundland] and Florida. Virtually everything we "know" of this venture comes from a short report that apparently was written by Barlowe (the author is simply identified as "one of the said Captaines"). There are two editions of this report, the first published in 1589, the second in 1600, both edited by Richard Hakluyt for inclusion in his two editions of *The Principall Navigations, Voiages, Traffiques and Discoueries of the English Nation*. They are very nearly the same, but with some important additions and marginal editing.

According to the report, the expedition left from the west of England with two vessels on April 27, 1584. The type of vessels employed were a ship and a pinnace. David Beers Quinn, whose 1955 collection is the major source of primary and sixteenth-century secondary sources on the Roanoke colonization efforts, thinks the ship was the *Bark Raleigh* and the pinnace was the *Dorothy* (Quinn 1991[1955]:1:78, 91). Though the narratives initially refer to both as *barkes*, Barlowe later calls one of them a *pinasse* (Quinn 1991[1955]:1:98).[1] Amadas captained the larger of the vessels, and the expedition's pilot was Gilbert's former pilot, Simon Fernandez. John White, who became governor of the 1587 colony, appears to claim he was on this voyage as well.[2]

By May 10 the ships were in the Canary Islands. They took the long way to North America, through the Caribbean. Barlowe claimed they overestimated the effects of the currents, though later expeditions took this route in order to prey on Spanish shipping. In any event, Barlowe makes no comment on the time in the Caribbean. The next entry, on July 2, has the vessels seeing (or actually smelling) a land redolent with flowers. Historians debate whether Barlowe is referring to Cape Lookout or Cape Fear off the coast of North Carolina.

On July 13 the English established Port Ferdinando on Hatarask. Barlowe remarks about the lush vegetation and abundant game and waterfowl. After encountering the local natives, they met with Granganimeo, the brother of the chief Wingina, for several days of trading; they then visited Wingina's village at the northwest end of Roanoke Island.

There is some suggestion, based on 1586 testimony to the Spanish by an English castaway on Jamaica, that there was an earlier landing, but this is either uncorroborated or a mistake in the chronology of the 1584 expedition (Quinn 1991 [1955]:1:80–81). In any event, Amadas and Barlowe spent much of their time trading with the Indians and exploring the area of Pamlico Sound. They learned of the villages of Pomioc, Secotan, and Chowanoke on the mainland (figure 1.1),[3] and heard about a shipwreck near Secotan which Barlowe records the natives as saying happened some 26 years earlier. Barlowe adds that the natives said they tried to aid the castaways, though the sailors died three weeks later trying to return home in makeshift boats. The Secotan Indians also claimed they were able to salvage some of the metal from the ship (Quinn 1991[1955]:1:111), an interesting observation considering that any sixteenth-century European item found on the Outer Banks is assumed by most scholars to have come from the Lost Colony.

Barlowe then discusses his understanding of the region's politics. Wingina controlled as far inland as Secotan. Farther west were his mortal enemies, the Neusioc and the Ponouike, though alliances and conflicts shifted from time to time. Barlowe apparently learned most of this later from Manteo and Wanchese. Though Barlowe doesn't say how long

Figure 1.1: Theodor de Bry Map of Roanoke Island and Vicinity, "Anglorum in Virginiam adventus" or "The arriual of the Englishemen in Virginia," as published in the Latin edition of Thomas Hariot's *A Briefe and True Report of the New Found Land of Virginia* (1590a, 1590b). Most likely based on one or more of John White's watercolors, the map illustrates how sources even by the same person and based on the same information can differ. On John White's watercolor maps and another of Theodor de Bry's engraved maps, Secotan is further south along the coast rather than immediately behind Roanoke Island, with Pomioc closer to Roanoke Island than Secotan. And note that neither Pomioc nor Chowanoke is depicted on this map (Sloan 2007: 96–97, 104–106). For a discussion of issues with using the de Bry maps to identify and locate the Native American communities who encountered the 1580s English colonists, see Michael Oberg's "Tribes and Towns: What Historians Still Get Wrong about the Roanoke Ventures" (2020). Image courtesy of Special Collections, East Carolina University.

they explored eastern North Carolina, Thomas Hariot later states they were in country about six weeks, which would put their departure in late August. The return voyage was much quicker than the trip west, and the ships arrived in England by mid–September. The 1600 edition of Hakluyt adds the postscript, "We brought home also two of the

Savages being lusty men, whose names were Wanchese and Manteo" (Quinn 1991[1955]:1:116).

This first reconnaissance was successful in at least a couple of respects. It provided the English with a preview of the Mid–Atlantic region, and equally important, it convinced both Raleigh and the Queen that there was economic potential in the region, making it worthy of investment.

At the same time, the historiography of the 1584 voyage highlights the limitations of the sources about this and most of the other Roanoke colonization voyages. Here it is important to define terms, specifically what constitutes a source. Scholars differentiate between two types of sources, *primary* and *secondary*, but what these terms mean varies from one field of study to another. In historical study, a primary source is one that comes from the time being studied, while a secondary source comes from a later period and interprets the earlier events based on the primary sources. In literary study, primary sources are the texts (not only poems, plays, stories, etc., but also letters, reports, journals, etc.) being examined and interpreted, while secondary sources are any works aside from the primary sources used to help interpret the primary sources.

For an anthropologist, a primary source is something that presents a culture from a viewpoint within the culture itself—an oral tale, a written document, or for an archaeologist, a pot sherd, animal bone in a garbage pit, arrangement of postholes in the ground, or other pieces of material culture. What these definitions have in common is that primary sources are immediate to the subject being discussed while secondary sources are outside the immediate subject, a source used to help interpret the primary sources.

All of these definitions of primary and secondary sources are valid and useful within their different fields. However, because we are examining various hypotheses of what happened to the Lost Colony from a variety of disciplinary perspectives, we need a shared definition of *primary* versus *secondary source*. For our purposes, primary sources are those created by people engaged in the events they describe while secondary sources are second-hand accounts, histories of the period, theoretical works, and other sources used to help interpret the primary sources. This definition of primary and secondary sources is similar to the distinction in a courtroom between eyewitness evidence on one side and hearsay evidence, expert testimony, etc., on the other. The latter is often admissible and useful but not equivalent to eyewitness testimony.

Using these definitions, there is a paucity of primary sources about the events on and around Roanoke Island during the 1580s voyages. For the 1584 voyage, there is only Arthur Barlowe's narrative. Having a single source has various implications, most significant of all that while we tend to trust Barlowe's account about what happened, there is no corroborating evidence to verify his version of events.

First Colonization Attempt (1585–1586)

In contrast to sources on the 1584 voyage, the largest number of primary sources exist for the 1585 to 1586 voyages, including three main texts: the anonymous journal of the ship *Tiger*, which returned with Richard Grenville to England in the fall of 1585; Ralph Lane's report on the 1585–1586 expedition; and Thomas Hariot's *A Briefe and True Report of the New Found Land of Virginia*, describing the flora, fauna, and native peoples of the lands being colonized. In addition, there are several letters written by Lane and sent back to England with Grenville; a letter from Grenville to Sir Francis Walsingham written on his return to England in October of 1585; some reminiscences of Ralph Lane recorded in 1592; and three accounts by members of Sir Francis Drake's expedition that came to Roanoke Island and took Lane and his men back to England in the spring of 1586. Primary sources do not consist only of written records. John White painted watercolors which, like Hariot's *Briefe and True Report*, portray the flora, fauna, and native peoples of the region as well as two watercolor maps.

These sources tell how—after the success of the 1584 expedition resulted in a knighthood for Raleigh and after the Crown provided backing in the form of gunpowder and a large ship, the *Tyger*—a second expedition was sent. In fact, planning was underway even before Amadas and Barlowe returned. First, Parliament confirmed Sir Walter's original patent to "all suche lande being beyond sea out of the jurisdiction of any Christian kinge which he shall at costs discover and get, and to take such subjects with him to dwell ther" (Quinn 1991 [1955]:1:122). He was also granted ⅘ of all the gold and silver he should find (the Queen, of course, received the royal fifth). The land in question was called Wyngandacoia, though with the Queen's permission the English renamed it Virginia, in honor of the Virgin Queen, and Raleigh was given authority to rule over it as the Queen's representative.

With added data from the reconnaissance voyage, Raleigh assembled an ambitious expedition. The leader of this attempt would be Sir Richard Grenville, a well-respected leader of proven ability who was given the title of Admiral. Ralph Lane was named second in command with the title of Governor. Again, Simon Fernandez was employed as the chief pilot. It also appears that Amadas and Barlowe came along as captains of two of the vessels in Grenville's fleet. Although more than a dozen vessels were considered for the voyage, on April 9, we can account for only seven ships actually leaving England, including the *Tyger* (160 tons), *Roebuck* (140 tons), *Lion* (100 tons), *Elizabeth* (50 tons), *Dorothy* (50 tons), and two pinnaces. Sailing on the vessels were 600 people, half of whom Quinn claims were sailors (1991[1955]:1:159).

As with the previous voyage, Grenville's fleet followed the southern route, through the Caribbean, to reach North America. There were probably two equally important reasons for following this path. It took advantage of the prevailing winds and currents, and it provided opportunities to prey on Spanish shipping. Preying on the Spanish is a recurrent theme in all of the Roanoke voyages, and one has to wonder which was more important, the destination or the privateering journey?[4]

The expedition suffered adversity from the outset. Before it made the Canaries, a storm scattered the fleet and sank the pinnace attached to the *Tyger*. The *Tyger* sailed on to a small island off Puerto Rico, where Grenville stopped to consider his options. He was joined there by the *Elizabeth*, but the remaining ships are not mentioned in the narratives. Grenville and Lane built a surprisingly elaborate fortification and commenced building a pinnace to replace the one that sank. They negotiated with the local Spanish population for livestock and other supplies. These talks were tricky, especially after the English took two Spanish prizes. The Spanish governor was not pleased, but the local colonists were more than happy to trade with the English.

By the time the Spanish governor could muster forces enough to threaten Grenville's party, the English had already departed for points north. After negotiating the Bahamas, they arrived off the North Carolina Outer Banks on June 23. The Outer Banks, sometimes known as the "Graveyard of the Atlantic," nearly claimed the *Tyger* as one of its earliest victims. Fortunately for the colonists, the *Tyger* only ran aground on one of the shoals near Ocracoke Island. It was repaired and refloated, though the introduction of seawater into the hold resulted in the loss of most of the foodstuffs that the ship carried for the colonists. The *Tyger's* grounding was the beginning of another recurrent theme of the Roanoke voyages—the endangerment and sometimes loss of ships due to the hazardous currents and often dangerous weather along the Outer Banks.

The loss of the *Tyger's* cargo was offset by the reunion with the other vessels of the fleet. This was at Port Ferdinando, believed to be at an inlet along what came to be Bodie Island east of Roanoke Island. "Port" is probably too grand a word for a slipway/anchorage for their boats, though Lane later wrote that properly fortified with a sconce, it could not be entered by all the force of Spain (Quinn 1991[1955]:1:202). Quinn does not believe that any fortification was ever built, nor has any evidence of Port Ferdinando been found in the archaeological record. Once more, an historiographic issue is raised. How much do primary sources represent what actually happened and how much do they represent the image that the writers—and maybe their editors—want to portray about what happened?

Opposite and above: Figure 1.2: Theodor de Bry Engravings of Pomioc and Secotan, "Oppidum Pomeiocc" and "Oppidum Secota" ("The Towne of Pomeiooc" and "The Towne of Secota"), based on John White's watercolors "Secoton" and "The towne of Pomeiock..." (Hariot 1590a, 1590b; Sloan 2007: 111, 113). The depictions of the towns in both White and de Bry are stylized to show in one image activities that would have occurred at different times and to depict various parts of the towns and their surroundings in a limited space. For more on White's stylizing and de Bry's transformation of White's watercolors into engravings, see Chaplin (2007) and Kuhlemann (2007). Images courtesy of Special Collections, East Carolina University.

In any event, the expedition gathered its forces and took up most of July reconnoitering the region. Across Pamlico Sound, the English encountered the Indian villages of Aquascogoc, Pomioc, and Secotan; John White famously painted the latter two villages which Theodor de Bry turned into engravings for the 1590 edition of Hariot's *Briefe and Ture Report* (figure 1.2).

An incident over an allegedly stolen silver cup at Aquascogoc resulted in the destruction of that village by the English, which set the tone for future relations with the natives. At the end of July, Grenville met chief Wingina and established a settlement, presumably on the north end of Roanoke Island. Grenville then took the *Tyger* and left for England to update Raleigh on the state of the expedition and garner more supplies—pausing only to take another Spanish prize. He left Ralph Lane in charge, who used force and intimidation in his dealings with the local inhabitants.

At this point the historical narrative shifts from Grenville to Lane, and Lane's version of events are written more in the style of reminiscences than as chronological reporting. For example, he mentions only in passing that a fort and settlement had been established and really says nothing directly of their location. Quinn, himself, is frustrated at the lack of detailed information, saying: "We should like to have some clear account of conditions at the fort and the houses near it, of the day-to-day relations between Lane's men and Wingina's village nearby, and how White and Hariot proceeded with their task of surveying the ground and investigating the fauna and flora of the surrounding territory" (1991[1955]:1:244). We do have Hariot's *Brief and True Report*, but that looks outward at the natural and cultural environment, not inward at the colony itself except in its introduction, and then only in general terms.

Lane eschews the mundane activities of the colonists and, instead, discusses the politics of the region but, like Barlowe, only as he understood them. He opines wistfully how he would have built a series of forts northward to the Chesapeake if only he'd had the men and supplies. There are stories of riches that interest him: pearl beds to the north and a mine at a place called *Chaunis Temoatan*. He saw a few inferior pearls and small pieces of copper but was unable to visit the source of either of these commodities. Instead, his source was Menatonon, a Chawanoac chief he had imprisoned. Menatonon was also Lane's source for knowledge about the local geography and tribal politics.

Lane's men continued to explore the territory, especially north and west of Roanoke Island. This exploring had the advantage of providing not only greater knowledge of their surroundings, but also of lessening the burden on the main camp's supplies. As the imprisonment of Mena-tonon—and later his son, Skiko—demonstrates, Lane was heavy-handed in his negotiations with the groups he encountered. This caused the local inhabitants to quit supplying the colonists with food, which forced Lane to disperse his forces between Roanoke, Port Ferdinando, and Croatan.

The English spreading out further raised the level of unrest with the tribes in the immediate area and left the English vulnerable. Suspicions heightened on both sides. As Lane reported, "for in trueth, they, privie to their owne villainous purposes against us, held as good espial upon us, both day and night, as we did upon them" (Quinn 1991[1955]:1:286). In a preemptive move, Lane's men attacked the village of Dasemunke-peuc and, during the ensuing melee, killed and decapitated their chief, Wingina, who had changed his name to Pemisapan.

Whether killing Pemisapan would have resulted in open warfare will never be known as, shortly thereafter, Sir Francis Drake appeared off the coast on June 9 with a fleet of ships. Drake had just completed a successful privateering run through the Caribbean, culminating with the sacking of St. Augustine. He appeared with much needed supplies (though little in the way of food) as well as 100 African and 300 South American Indian slaves freed? captured? in his Caribbean raids. He also offered Lane several boats to continue his exploration of the coast. Before the English could accept this generous offer, a storm blew in, scattering or wrecking many of Drake's ships.

The loss of several vessels meant that Drake could afford to leave only one boat, the bark *Bonner*. At this point the colonists had truly had enough and pressed Lane to allow them to return with Drake to England. Lane reluctantly agreed, and on June 19, they bid a hasty farewell to their settlement—and three colonists who had not returned from exploring the interior. Their haste is made even more ironic in that a supply ship sent by Raleigh arrived less than a week later.

Here, another sort of historiographic question arises—how to reconcile facts given when they don't appear to add up. Drake's agreeing to take aboard Lane and his colonists raises an interesting question concerning passengers on the voyage back to England. Presumably with fewer boats in the fleet, space would have been at a premium. The 100+ extra passengers, that is, the colonists, would need to be put somewhere. Quinn notes that the 400 or so African and Indian slaves are not mentioned as being part of the cargo that arrived in Portsmouth (1991[1955]:1:254–255). Perhaps they were lost in the storm, or perhaps they were left behind along with the three colonists left upcountry. Were these the original "lost colonists"?

Meanwhile, back at Roanoke Island, the supply ship sent by Raleigh found no one and headed back to England. Grenville arrived with the bulk of the resupply fleet a few weeks later (his return somewhat delayed by the requisite prize-taking along the way). Taking a native captive, Grenville was able to determine what happened to the bulk of his colony. The three forgotten colonists were not recovered, and no mention was made of any marooned slaves. And Grenville was faced with a dilemma—what to do with the additional colonists and supplies he had brought? The decision, which Quinn found curious (1991[1955]:1:469), was to leave a small holding party of 15 or 18 men (depending on the source). They were to keep the settlement viable until Raleigh could send another venture. Then Grenville set off in search of more prizes. The holding party was, predictably, never heard from again.

Second Colonization Attempt (1587–1590)

Questions about what happened to the African and Indian slaves as well as what happened to the 15 or so men left by Grenville highlight how there are gaps in the history of the 1585–1586 colonization attempt even though the largest number of Roanoke colonization-related primary sources are about the 1585–1586 expeditions. This fact serves as an historiographic caution about interpreting the record of events most central to the Lost Colony question—the 1587 voyage that brought to Roanoke Island the people who would ultimately become known as the Lost Colony and the 1590 expedition that returned to Roanoke Island only to find the 1587 colonists gone. There is a single primary source for each: the 1587 account, seemingly based on a journal kept by White, and White's first-person narrative of the 1590 return to Roanoke Island. In other words, the only primary sources about leaving the 1587 colonists on Roanoke Island and about what was found three years later are from John White's point of view.

As with the 1585–1586 colonization efforts, preparations were underway for the 1587 effort even before the fate of the previous expedition was fully known. John White was appointed governor and given three ships. Simon Fernandez was, again, the pilot for the expedition and now raised to master of the fleet, much to White's dismay as conflict between the two characterized the passage across the Atlantic. White, in his retrospective writings about the expedition, claimed that the Chesapeake was the intended destination of the colony. They left Plymouth on May 8, and on May 16, White says that Fernandez "lewdly forsook our Flie boate, leaving her distressed in the Baye of Portingall"

(Quinn 1991[1955]:2:517). The other two ships made a relatively uneventful trip through the Caribbean, though White claimed Fernandez intentionally missed places where they had intended to take on salt and other supplies.

On July 22 the admiral, the *Lion*, along with the unnamed pinnace arrived at Roanoke Island, where White took forty of the colonists ashore to check on the men left by Grenville. They found the settlement deserted, except for a single skeleton, and the fort "razed down." It was not until later that White heard from the local Indians that Grenville's men had been attacked and fled in a small boat. Meanwhile, White tells us, Fernandez treacherously put the rest of the colonists ashore and refused to take them any further, claiming "the Summer was farre spent" and he needed to get back to England (Quinn 1991[1955]:2:523). This is another curious statement as Fernandez does not actually leave until a month later. On July 25, the flyboat that had become separated from the admiral and pinnace off the coast of Europe arrived with the rest of the colonists.

The colonists were left to make the best of their situation. Some settlers immediately set about repairing the houses and building new ones. Others gathered local resources to supplement their supplies. It was during this activity, while crabbing, that George Howe was ambushed and killed by some of the local Indians. White sent out envoys with their guide, Manteo, to assess the political situation. He found that most of the tribes in the area were arrayed against them except for the Croatoan, Manteo's people, who were based on Hatteras Island.

In an effort to turn the tables and make an example of their enemies, White's men carried out an ambush on an enemy village, Dasemunkepeuc, only to discover that their intended prey had already departed and the people they attacked were actually friendly Croatoan who were gathering up what the residents of Dasemunkepeuc had left behind. Manteo was pressed into service to smooth over the faux pas.

White relates little of what the English did at the camp other than that by Raleigh's order, Manteo was christened and proclaimed Lord of Roanoke and Dasemunkepeuc, and that five days later, on August 18, his daughter, Eleanor Dare, gave birth to Virginia Dare, who was christened that same day. However, there must have been some concern that the colony would need resupply within the year. John White was elected to plead their case in England, and he "reluctantly agreed." On August 27 he left with the *Lion* and the flyboat. The pinnace is not mentioned and was probably left with the colonists as White specifically mentions seeing no trace of it on his return (Quinn 1991[1955]:2:614–615). This is the last record of the 1587 colonists being seen by the English.

The passage home was difficult, and White didn't arrive in England until November 8. Upon his arrival in England, White immediately secured supplies and a ship, but before he was able to set sail, word came of a large armada being assembled in Spain to invade England. All fighting ships and sailors were pressed into service, and White lost his ships to the defense of England. In the spring of 1588, however, he was able to secure two small vessels with which to resupply his colony. Ironically, the privateering that financed much of the previous Virginia ventures was this expedition's downfall as they were driven back to port by a French privateer on May 22.

Soon there was both good news and bad for the White colony. By the end of July 1588, the Spanish Armada was defeated, releasing many ships that could be used by White for his colony. White applied to Raleigh for assistance and was told that he had the requisite licenses to proceed with the relief mission. Even so, no immediate action was taken.

Instead, it wasn't until March of 1590 that John White was able to take passage back to Roanoke Island, and then only as a passenger on a voyage primarily bent on taking Spanish prizes. They privateered their way through the Caribbean before arriving at the Outer Banks in mid–August. It was on August 18, after a brief search of Roanoke Island, that White found, first, a tree with CRO carved on it and then, farther inland, an abandoned fort with all the houses taken down and the word *CROATOAN* carved on a post without an added cross, the cross being an agreed-on sign of distress. For White, Manteo's village of Croatoan fit with the agreed upon plan made with the colonists to leave a sign of where they were going if they followed the intention to "remoue from Roanoak 50 miles into the maine" (Quinn 1991[1955]:2:613). Though his books, maps and other personal property he had left under the care of the colonists were disturbed, there were no overt signs of violence.

White returned to the ships, determined to go to Croatoan, but foul weather threatened the fleet, and a smaller boat had been capsized by waves and several men drowned. Because the ships were too large to navigate the sound and the season was getting late, the decision was made to go to the Caribbean to resupply and take prizes with the intention to return to Croatoan in the spring. However, the weather continued not to cooperate, pushing the ships toward home. Thus ended White's visible efforts to find his ill-fated colony.

The historiographic issues surrounding the 1587–1590 second colonization attempt begin with, but are not exclusive to, John White. Documents are never produced or read in a vacuum. It's important to think about the circumstances under which these two primary sources were written and published. It is the issue of *epistemology*, the study of how people know what they know. The context of the 1587 and 1590 narratives helps explore the questions underlying what is known, or what people believe they know, about both the 1587 and 1590 expeditions—the first narrative being the only eyewitness account of the colonists becoming "The Lost Colony" and the second the only account about the 1590 expedition's *not* finding the colonists.

The context of these documents begins with their author, John White. From the few extant records concerning White's life, because he was a painter and a skilled tradesman, he was likely from either the lower levels of the aristocracy or the upper end of the middle class.[5] Whichever, White lived on the cusp between the middle and upper classes, and his position as governor for the 1587 colony was his first as a government appointed leader. Therefore, these reports about what happened during each of the two voyages are not strictly objective presentations of facts but include the leader's explanation of why things happened as they did, good and bad.

Little has been written about John White as a writer. However, as Lorraine Hale Robinson (2003) has argued, White portrays himself in the 1587 and 1590 texts as the hero in a battle against Spanish colonial dominance in the New World. Michael G. Moran (2007) has highlighted how the 1587 narrative focuses more on defending White against accusations that had been or might be leveled against him than it focuses on the expedition's history. Both Robinson and Moran remind us that while we should ask "why would White lie?," we should also ask "why wouldn't White lie?," especially when his reputation and the fate of "his" colony were at stake.

Thinking about this question from both directions matters because among some researchers, there might as well be a bumper sticker reading, "John White said it, I believe it, that settles it." And when questioning what White writes, perhaps *spin* is a better term than *lie*. Information can be incorrect for several reasons: because a writer purposely gives misinformation; because a writer doesn't include all relevant information from a lack of knowledge or through a lie of omission; or because of the limitations of a writer's own biases. Writers interpret events from their own points of view, and those interpretations can differ from what others might emphasize about the same situation.

Take, for instance, a main clue often used to discuss where the Lost Colony went: the phrase *50 miles into the maine*. In 1587, White expressed his reluctance about his returning to England, including that the remaining colonists "intended to remoue 50. miles further vp into the maine presently, he being then absent, his stuffe and goods, might be both spoiled, and most of it pilfered away in the carriage..." (Quinn 1991 [1955]:2:533–34). This is the only place in the 1587 narrative that readers hear the colonists planned to relocate from Roanoke Island after not being left along the Chesapeake Bay. White never says where the spot fifty miles from Roanoke Island would be. Instead, White's fear of being accused that "he neuer meant to stay himself," but always intended "to leaue them behind him" (Quinn 1991 [1955]:2:533), along with the fear of losing his goods, become the focus in this part of White's narrative.

Effectively the same phrase, "remove fifty miles into the main," appears only once again, in the narrative of the 1590 voyage, when the landing party goes ashore to look for the 1587 colonists:

> [A]s we entred vp the sandy banke vpon a tree, in the very browe thereof were curiously carued these fair Romane letters C R O: which letters presently we knew to signifie the place, where I should find the planters seated, according to a secret token agreed vpon betweene them & me at my last departure from them, which was, that in any wayes they should not faile to write or carue on the trees or posts of the dores the name of the place where they should be seated; for at my comming away they were prepared to remoue from Roanoak 50 miles into the maine [Quinn 1991(1955):2:613].

When White describes the landing party's going into the empty palisade, at least one gap is filled when he tells about finding "CROATOAN" carved on a post "in fayre Capitall letters" (Quinn 1991 [1955]:2:614). To White, this means the colonists had gone to Manteo's village on Croatoan Island (the southern part of today's Hatteras Island). Neither narrative says that the colonists had a specific place in mind that was "50 miles into the maine" where they intended to move. White expresses a sense of relief at the end of this section of the 1590 narrative, writing, "I greatly joyed that I had safely found a certain token of their being safe at Croatoan" (Quinn 1991 [1955]:2:614). However, because the 1590 expedition never gets to Croatoan to see if the colonists actually went there and, if so, whether they were still there, White's certainty is never substantiated by facts on the ground, or on the sea.

Historiography needs to account for not only what a source says, but how that source was produced. The 1587 and 1590 narratives were both published by Richard Hakluyt, the late sixteenth- and early seventeenth-century clergyman, geographer, and editor who promoted English overseas ventures. His publications were primarily translations of works about exploration and colonization ventures by other European nations along with works about English exploration and colonization. The 1587 and 1590 narratives appeared in Hakluyt's *The Principall Navigations, Voiages, and Discoveries of the English Nation*, first published in 1589 and reissued in an expanded edition in 1598–1600. These same volumes included most of the other Roanoke-colonization primary sources.

Hakluyt's choice and arrangement of Roanoke-related texts in *The Principall Navigations* is discussed in the next chapter. But how an editor can affect the way a text might be read, an important historiographic issue, can be seen in how Hakluyt and later editors treat the 1587 narrative. The 1588 narrative of John White's attempt to resupply the colony and the 1590 account of White's return to Roanoke Island are both written in first person, generally using the plural *we* throughout, though at important points using the first person singular ("I my selfe was wounded twise in the head" in the 1588 narrative (Quinn 1991 [1955]:2:567) and "where I left our Colony" and "where I should find the planters seated, according to a secret token agreed vpon betweene them & me" in the 1590 narrative (Quinn 1991 [1955]:2:613]). There is little question of authorship for these two narratives; both are presented as John White's own words.

Authorship of the 1587 narrative is not so clear. As noted above, the 1587 text is presented in the form of a journal, but unlike the 1588 and 1590 texts, its voice switches back and forth between third person and first person plural. The story tells as much about "the Gouernour, with diuers of his companie" (Quinn 1991 [1955]:2:524) as it does about "our Flie boate, and the rest of our planters" (Quinn 1991 [1955]:2:525). Additionally, first person singular is used just twice in the narrative, neither time requiring that we assume the author is John White. Before transcribing the colonists' statement exonerating White from charges of abandoning the colony, the narrator states, "The copie of the testimonie, I thought good to set downe" (Quinn 1991 [1955]:2:534). And at the very end of the text, telling about men lost at sea on the return voyage to England, the narrator states, "The names of the chiefe men that dyed are these, Roger Large, Iohn Mathew, Thomas Smith, and some other saylers, whose names I know not at the writing hereof" (Quinn 1991 [1955]:2:538).

Both uses of the pronoun *I* are connected to how the narrative is being written or edited, not to events experienced by the narrator. While all the events described in the 1587 narrative come from John White's point of view, the text itself seems more like a rewriting of White's journal by Hakluyt than White's own writing, keeping some of White's own words but just as often being Hakluyt's words about what White had seen. How much Hakluyt kept in and how much he took out, how much his rewording revised the sense of White's original— and in what manner—there is no way to know. With the combination of White's original observations and Hakluyt's editing, it is ambiguous about whom to claim as the author of the 1587 narrative.

Modern editions of the Roanoke texts do not treat the question of authorship at all. While the standard edition of Hakluyt's *Principal Voyages*, the 1903–1905 Glasgow edition, follows Hakluyt's lead and does not give an author for the 1587 narrative, collections specifically devoted to documents from the Roanoke voyages follow Quinn's lead from his two volume *The Roanoke Voyages, 1584–1590* (1955; reprinted 1991). Quinn collected all the documents related to the 1580s expeditions known at the time and the collection has been an important research tool ever since. Just before giving Hakluyt's title for the narrative, "The fourth voyage made to Virginia with three ships, in yere 1587. Wherein was transported the second Colonie," Quinn gives his own title, "John White's Narrative of His Voyage" (Quinn 1991 [1955]:2:515). In his notes, Quinn states, "This is the earliest narrative of White's we have and it was evidently compiled by him ... before 25 March 1588, using his journal as a basis" (Quinn 1991 [1955]:2:515). Most discussions of the 1587 text follow Quinn, discussing the narrative as John White's writing.

Assigning authorship of the text to White reflects what has come to be called *the author function*, after the French historian and philosopher Michel Foucault's 1969 essay "What Is an Author?"[6] Readers often feel the need to credit a specific person as the creator of a text, someone to serve as the focus for discussion, including of the context in which the text was written. But if we honestly ask who the author of the 1587 narrative is, John White or Richard Hakluyt, we would have to say most likely neither and both. In fact, assigning the editorial role to Hakluyt is another version of the author function—what could be called the editor function.

Did Hakluyt or someone else revise White's journal? Did Hakluyt or someone else base the text solely on a single journal kept by White? The growing ambiguity behind such questions could easily stifle discussion about the content of the narrative, so we use the shorthand of "White's narrative" and "Hakluyt's editing." Even as we use this shorthand, we need to keep in mind the gaps in our understanding of the text and the authorial and editorial ambiguity that underlie them.

A second example of ambiguity moves from overarching concerns to specific word choices, the phrases "they intended to remoue 50. miles further vp into the maine" (1587) and "they were prepared to remoue from Roanoak 50 miles into the maine" (1590). Even a seemingly simple word like *main* (i.e., *maine*) is ambiguous. The *Oxford English Dictionary* entry for *main* shows that in the late sixteenth century, the word *main* could as easily be short for *main sea* as it could be for *mainland* ("main, n.1" 2019). Leaving alone the question of whether the colonists actually did "remoue 50. miles further vp into the maine" as the narratives say they intended to do, we can't be sure if the intention was to move inland—i.e., near the western end of the Albemarle Sound or along the Alligator River—or to move along the seacoast—i.e., to the Chesapeake Bay or to Croatoan, though White's 1587 narrative implies the latter.

Additionally, what distance was meant by a *mile* is not clear. In *A Briefe and True Report*, Hariot mentions distances measured in miles several times. Roanoke Island, he writes, is "fifteene miles of length, and fiue or six miles in breadth" (Quinn 1991 [1955]:1:328–329); in modern land miles, Roanoke is no more than eight or nine miles in length and two to two-and-a-half miles wide. Additionally, Hariot writes that the 1585–1586 expedition found Native Americans with copper plates "[a] hundred and fiftie miles into the maine" (Quinn 1991 [1955]:1:332) and, too, that "about 120. miles from our fort neere the water in the side of a hill was founde by a Gentleman of our company, a great veine of hard ragge stones" (Quinn 1991 [1955]:1:368), that is, good building stones. In Lane's report, there are no travels more than about fifty or sixty modern miles from Roanoke Island, so how do we deal with Hariot's distances? Were travels made further inland than those recorded by Lane? Was Hariot using a measure of distance significantly different from the modern mile? Or was Hariot just bad at measuring distances? And how does this affect the way we should read and measure "50 miles into the maine"?

Looking for the Lost Colony (1600–)

White's 1590 voyage was the last serious attempt to locate the colonists. After that it became more of an "if you're in the area" type of search. Raleigh sent Samuel Mace in 1602 with an expedition, but they spent most of their time harvesting medicinal herbs, particularly sassafras, on the southern Outer Banks, somewhere between Cape Fear and Cape Lookout. No trace of the colonists was reported. When the English established a foothold in the Chesapeake nearly twenty years later, exploratory parties were sent out from Jamestown. These efforts found no colonists, only rumors. (The primary sources for all of these efforts are discussed in the next chapter on the "First Retellings: The Roanoke Colonies in Print to the Early Seventeenth Century.")

Archaeologists and historians have been looking for the Lost

Colony for the past two centuries, but we are no closer to finding them now than Talcott Williams was at the end of the nineteenth century (see Chapter 3, "The Archaeology of the Lost Colony"). There really is very little that we can draw with any certainty from the historical record. We have Grenville's and White's reports, a letter from Lane and some miscellaneous sixteenth- and seventeenth-century correspondences that refer tangentially to the Roanoke venture. All can be combined in a paperback book of less than 200 pages, and that includes interpretive notes and bibliography (see Quinn and Quinn 1982). But if you were to total up the pages expended on hypothesizing about their fate (to say nothing of the fictional contributions) it would run into at least the thousands. The Cittie of Raleigh is North America's Atlantis. John White may have written more about the Lost Colony than Plato's scant dialog about the Lost Continent, but not by much.

These hypotheses engage us in a few more historiographical elements, ones that are at the heart of the search for the Lost Colony. One is the issue of ambiguity. As can be seen, the primary documents are filled with ambiguities. That is not necessarily a bad thing. For example, if we accept and foreground that ambiguity, it can remind us that there may not be a single solution about what happened to the Lost Colony. The fate of the 1587 colonists may have been determined by a single event with the group moving as a whole to a single place, or it may have been determined by several factors (some dying early, some moving to one place and some to another, etc.). Ambiguity may not be good for arriving at *the* answer; however, with so little extant evidence, it may be all we have to understand what happened to the Lost Colony. And ambiguity certainly helps us understand why the Lost Colony and its fate have played various roles in people's imaginations over the past four-hundred-plus years.

But people have hypothesized despite—probably even more because of—the ambiguity. How people hypothesize is affected by their assumptions about the way the world works, that is, their presumed *paradigms*. In the context of scholarship or research, *paradigms* are sets of assumptions about the way an academic discipline works, even about the way the world works. Often unspoken, and sometimes applied unconsciously, such presuppositions are necessary, but so is being conscious of them. And the paradigms in different fields affect the *methodology*, specifically *research methodology*, of each. We can define *methodology* as the examination of how the methods used to do research affect the data gathered and the conclusions reached.

Paradigms and their related research methodologies tell us what questions different researchers in different situations think are important. As an example, for many historians, one epistemological paradigm is that without obvious reasons to believe otherwise, we should assume historical records don't lie. In other words, assume a source is factually correct unless there is a reason to think otherwise. A second paradigm in much historical research assumes that what is most important is what events happened and why they happened. Finally, historians tend to believe that these motives are knowable.

What questions and what answers are thought of as being important define various fields of inquiry. These might be called the "So What?" questions for the various fields and subfields within academic disciplines. When looking at the Lost Colony, historians' "So What?" questions are what happened to the Roanoke colonists between August of 1587 and August of 1590 and why. For Tom, a scholar of literature and discourse, how texts about Roanoke colonization affect readers is a central "So What?" question. For Charlie, an anthropologically-trained historical archaeologist, core "So What?" questions are what material culture (physical objects) and historical records together tell about the human past and how cultures adapt to changing situations.

Of course, there is overlap among the disciplines. Understanding how texts affect readers can help explain the culture and the history of a particular time. In many ways, material culture can be read like a written text. Understanding what past events occurred and why depends on understanding how written texts reveal information to readers and on how material culture can reinforce and, sometimes, contradict the written record. When looking at hypotheses about what happened to the 1587 colonists, figuring out the "So What?" questions behind each hypothesis will matter.

Knowing the disciplinary paradigm—that is, knowing a field's assumptions and "So What?" questions—helps us understand the methodology a researcher is bringing to bear on the research being done. The assumptions a scholar makes affect the questions asked; the questions asked affect the kind of information sought; and the kind of information sought affects the answers found. A good example is David Beers Quinn who, aside from his 1955 collection of Roanoke-colonization related documents, published extensively about the Roanoke ventures starting in the 1940s, culminating with what became (and for many still is) the standard history on the subject, *Set Fair for Roanoke: Voyages and Colonies, 1584–1606* (1985).

As a historian, Quinn uses research methods that rely heavily on written documents and filling in the gaps in the written record using *historical imagination*, that is, using informed hypothesizing to fill in what is missing when there are gaps in the record. Quinn relies on the

1587 narrative, which in 1955 he labeled as "John White's Narrative of His Voyage," to discuss White's being pressured, and then agreeing, to return to England in 1587. As Quinn notes, the 1587 narrative says little about the time between White's agreeing to return to England and his departure. The narrative reads:

> The Gouernour being at the last through their extreame intreating, constrayned to returne into England, hauing then but halfe a daies respite to prepare him selfe for the same, departed from Roanoake, the seuen and twentieth of August in the morning: and the same daye about midnight, came aboord the Flie boate, who already had waied anker, and rode without the barre, the Admirall riding by them, who but the same morning was newly come thither againe [Quinn 1991 (1955):2:535].

This statement provides point A: with only a half day to prepare, White finally agrees to return to England. Then readers get point B: White departs from Roanoke Island on the morning of August 27 to be taken to the flyboat, the smaller ship of the two bound for England, already at sea (i.e., "withoute the barre," that is, beyond the sandbar that divided the ocean from the sounds). Explaining even this small moment in the narrative requires the use of historical imagination. The narrative does not say what sort of vessel took White to the flyboat. Our reading in other places and historical knowledge tell us this most likely would be a ship's boat and not, for example, a canoe. And that only the flyboat and the admiral are mentioned is why historical imagination implies that the smallest ship of the fleet, the pinnace, was probably left with the colonists.

Knowing what happened between points A and B matters to Quinn, whose "So What?" questions include the motives he sees expressed in the 1587 narrative. Using historical imagination, Quinn develops a picture of hurried preparations and sad goodbyes: "There is not even a word about the tender farewells that he must have had time for, even at the last long rush to reach the ship in time" (1985:292). Quinn's assumptions about family relationships fill in the gap, presuming sad goodbyes that are not recorded, to highlight what he sees as White's self-centered preoccupations.

In *A Kingdom Strange: The Brief and Tragic History of the Lost Colony of Roanoke* (2010), historian James Horn uses historical imagination differently, filling in the gap with governing arrangements: "He had little time to prepare for his departure and immediately threw himself into a flurry of activity. The first task was to make arrangements for the assistants to govern while he was away.... Then he and the assistants had to decide where the colonists would go when they left Roanoke Island" (2010:163).

Horn knows that the 1590 narrative tells about returning to Roanoke Island and not finding the colonists there, including plans for removing from Roanoke Island and giving signs about where they had gone. Horn, therefore, sees the time between White's agreeing to leave and his departure as the moment for settling on such plans. Both Quinn and Horn give valid explanations for what happened in the gap of time between points A and B, and they are not mutually exclusive of one another. But neither are they known events. Both historians use historical imagination to highlight what each sees as important—Quinn to explore John White's motives and Horn to set up his own hypothesis about the Lost Colonists' fate.

To examine how people have looked at the Lost Colony since the 1580s, keep in mind the ideas of *historiography, epistemology, methodology, paradigm, historical imagination, sources* (*primary* and *secondary*), and *ambiguity*. Whether addressed openly or not, they help test each step of the research process.

So there were three main expeditions that arrived on Roanoke Island: Amadas/Barlowe, Grenville/Lane, and White, and one rescue attempt. As for the Lost Colony, to examine how people have looked at and for it since the 1580s, keep in mind the terms mentioned above. Whether addressed openly or not, these ideas are used to test each step of the research process. Most important along these lines, we must rely almost completely upon John White for any information connected with the Lost Colony.

Many take him at his word: Why would he lie? Others are more skeptical. White left over one hundred people in his charge to the mercies of a hostile environment and failed to bring them relief. At the least, either he is incompetent or a victim of circumstances. White portrays himself as the latter. But how much of what we have is directly from White and how much was mediated by Richard Hakluyt or others? And what effects did White and/or Hakluyt want the narratives to have on readers? Did events truly transpire as the narratives say they did? All are important questions as we examine the search for the Lost Colony.

2

First Retellings

The Roanoke Colonies in Print to the Early Seventeenth Century

In 1908, Raleigh newspaperman Fred A. Olds used the now standard closing line about John White's 1590 voyage. "Oblivion fell like a pall upon the colony," wrote Olds, "and it came to be known through all the years as 'The Lost Colony of Roanoke'" (1908:3). However, the truth is that the 1587 colonists weren't lost until the early nineteenth century, at least not on paper. Before the nineteenth century, the 1587 colonists, though gone when White returned in 1590, were just Raleigh's colonists, not THE Lost Colony, capital *L*, capital *C*.

For 250 years after White's 1590 voyage, most writers presumed to know the fate of the colonists, even if the presumptions varied depending on the time, place, and type of writing being done. There were major shifts in the story. The first versions of the colonists' fate were written starting in the 1590s and continued through to reports from the Jamestown colony in the 1620s, portraying the colonists as still alive—probably. Starting in the mid–1600s, the story changed, with writers repeating two new assumptions about what happened to the 1587 colonists—they either starved or were killed by local Native Americans. William Byrd epitomizes these histories, writing in his 1730s manuscript *The History of the Dividing Line betwixt Virginia and North Carolina*, "These Wretches ... by some fatal disagreement, or Laziness, were either starv'd, or cut to pieces by the Indians" (2013:66). In other words, until the early nineteenth century, writers portrayed the colonists as separated from their English homeland, but their fate is not unexplained. They weren't lost.

Hakluyt's Principal Navigations *(1589 and 1598–1600)*

That the fate of the 1587 colonists has been portrayed in a variety of ways reminds us that all portrayals of the 1587 colonists after August 27, 1587, are speculative. These are imagined narratives of the colonists' fate rather than history, beginning with the narrative created by Richard Hakluyt in his *Principal Navigations*. Hakluyt's two editions, one published in 1589 and a second in 1598–1600, include the major primary sources about Raleigh's 1584–1590 attempts to establish a colony in eastern North America. The texts include Arthur Barlowe's narrative of the 1584 scouting expedition; four texts about the 1585–1586 Richard Grenville and Ralph Lane expedition, including Thomas Hariot's *Briefe and True Report*; and the narratives of the 1587 and 1590 voyages.

Though these are the major accounts of the 1580s Roanoke ventures, they do not provide information about what happened to the 1587 Roanoke colonists. At best, the narratives of the 1587 and 1590 voyages give a version of what the 1587 colonists intended to do, to move some fifty miles from Roanoke Island. Even the carving on the palisade post in 1590 is not definitive evidence that Croatoan is where the colonists ended up. However, Hakluyt's choices of what documents to include, and in what order, lead readers to fill in the gaps in the overall narrative in very specific ways. Hakluyt's editing would lead late sixteenth- and early seventeenth-century readers to the idea that the colonists John White left behind were alive, just waiting to reconnect with their English homeland. This speculative narrative, couched in the semblance of historical fact, first appeared in the 1589 edition of the *Principal Navigations*, then in a revised form in the 1598–1600 edition. Rather than by direct statement, Hakluyt portrays the survival of the 1587 colonists through the overarching narrative he creates through how he presents the sources.

Understanding Hakluyt's selection and presentation of sources is a form of textual analysis—an inductive form of analysis that starts with the details of the work, building to an overall idea the work communicates to readers. While not a major approach to studying Roanoke colonization, several critics have used textual analysis to understand Roanoke colonization-related writings, especially since the late 1970s and early 1980s. Whether looking at these texts through the lens of literary criticism, rhetorical analysis, cultural studies, or technical and professional communications, critics have seen these texts as not only sources of historical dates and actions, but also as sources to study how the Roanoke colonization story has come to mean what it has in the public imagination.

Hariot's *Briefe and True Report* in its various forms has been the most textually analyzed of all the Roanoke pieces, for example, by Stephen Greenblatt (1981; rept. 1988) and Ed White (2005) among many others. Some critics have examined other texts. As noted above, Michael G. Moran (2007) uses a rhetorical lens focusing on technical and professional communications, including an analysis of White's 1587 narrative as a form of apologia, and Lorraine Hale Robinson (2003) recognizes White's development of himself and others as characters in his story, allowing him to be the representative of Britain and the hero of his stories—both in 1587 and 1590—even as things seem to fall apart.

Other critics have read across several of the Roanoke-related texts. For example, Wayne Franklin (1979) defines three main forms of the earliest European American literature—discovery, exploratory, and settlement narratives, moving from idealized to realistic views of the New World—and uses Barlowe's 1584, Hariot's 1585, and White's 1590 narratives as examples of each.

More recently, Kathleen Donegan (2014) uses the lenses of historiography and cultural studies to examine how Ralph Lane's 1585–1586 and John White's 1587 narratives reflect a developing colonial identity. For Donegan, a colonial American identity was created when settlers expressed a sense of disconnection from England rather than emphasizing the imposition of European culture on the land and its people. In Donegan's analysis, as the Roanoke texts expressed more and more a sense of crisis and instability, the more they expressed a sense of colonial Americanness.

These textual analysis readings by modern scholars in various disciplines—rhetorical analysis, cultural studies, and technical and professional communications—highlight how the texts Hakluyt included in the *Principal Navigations* can be read as individual works and in relation to one another. The next step, then, is to understand Hakluyt's choice and arrangement of texts. Hakluyt's work as an editor created overall narratives about the 1580s Roanoke colonization efforts and, specifically, about the fate of the 1587 colonists.

Hakluyt's first version of the Roanoke colonization story appeared in 1589, towards the end of the first edition of *Principal Navigations*. This version was the first published overarching narrative of the Roanoke ventures, their first published history, coming after White had travelled to England to resupply the 1587 colonists but before he returned in 1590. In 1589, Hakluyt presents the following texts in the following order:

- Raleigh's 1584, six-year patent from Queen Elizabeth "for the discovering and planting of new lands and Countries";
- Arthur Barlowe's account of his and Philip Amadas's 1584 expedition to reconnoiter a possible location for Raleigh to attempt at a colony;
- a narrative of the 1585 voyage led by Richard Grenville to establish a settlement on Roanoke Island under the leadership of Ralph Lane, a narrative including Grenville's own brief explorations of the region, now being called Virginia, before returning to England;
- a list of the men left in Virginia from summer 1585 to summer 1586;
- Ralph Lane's report on the 1585–1586 Virginia colony, describing the land and what happened during the year, concluding with the English colonists' battle with Native Americans and their subsequent departure with Sir Francis Drake;
- a narrative of Raleigh's and Grenville's 1586 resupply voyages that arrived after Lane's departure with Drake and that left 15 men to hold Roanoke Island for the English;
- Thomas Hariot's *Briefe and True Report of the New Found Land of Virginia* describing the commodities and people of the region;
- the narrative of the John White 1587 colonization effort, including White's return to England for supplies;
- a list of the men, women, and children left on Roanoke Island in 1587; and
- the narrative of John White's 1588 failed attempt to resupply the Virginia colonists [1589:725–73].

Several pages later, Hakluyt inserts another Roanoke-related document, an excerpt of Ralph Lane's September 1585 letter to Hakluyt and his cousin (also named Richard Hakluyt) that opens with the line that "we have discovered the maine to bee the goodliest soile under the cope of heaven" (1589:793). Then, following materials about other English ventures, Hakluyt adds one last Roanoke-related document, the 1589 agreement between Raleigh and several investors in the Virginia project changing the structure of the venture (1589:815–817).

The Roanoke colonization texts can be read like a short story cycle. Each can be read separate from the others, telling of a specific expedition from a specific narrative point of view, but through Hakluyt's editing, they also work together, creating an overall narrative. As Hakluyt presents it in 1589, the overarching story of the Roanoke ventures begins with Raleigh being granted the right to explore and settle lands "not actually possessed of any Christian prince, nor inhabited by Christian people" (1589:725); so he sends out Amadas and Barlowe, who find a land not only worth settling, but worth being named after Queen Elizabeth, the Virgin Queen. Grenville and Lane are sent to the newly named Virginia,[1] and while their expedition doesn't work out as hoped, Hakluyt emphasizes the goodness of the land by including Hariot's *Briefe and True Report*. It is this wonderful land, well worth settling, that the 1587 planters now inhabit and that sustains them as they wait to reconnect with their homeland of England, even if the 1588 resupply did not reach them.

The final two documents, while inserted as seeming afterthoughts, end up reinforcing the positive narrative.[2] Lane's letter—with the line that North Carolinians have adopted as their own, "the goodliest soile under the cope of heaven" (1589:793)—ends up reinforcing the value of the colony and its commodities despite any difficulties in its settlement.[3] And with the new agreement at the end of his six years as patentee, Raleigh has joined with several men in London and the leading men in Virginia's City of Raleigh, a group that includes Richard Hakluyt and John White, giving them the right to gain from the colony as well as the responsibility to resupply it, an indenture lasting the next seven years. In Hakluyt's imagined 1589 picture, the Virginia colony continues to survive, even thrive, allowing its new backers to collect "all rents, subsidies, customs, toles, taxes, tallages, and all other charges, services, dueties, and demaunds ... for the trading, or transporting any commoditie or profite, into or from the sayde countrie of Assamacomock, alias Wingandacoia, alias Virginia..." (1589:816). Through his selection and order of documents included, Hakluyt creates a positive image of the Roanoke colony and the people left there.[4]

Even certain shared word choices among the different narratives enhance the idea of a thriving settlement. In the 1589 edition of his *Principal Navigations* and continued in the 1598–1600 edition, Hakluyt consistently calls Virginia a *colony* while using the term *planters* for the people settling the colony. *Colony*, according to the *Oxford English Dictionary (OED)*, was a newly recovered term, coming from the Latin *colōnia*, originally used to mean farms, landed estates, or settlements, especially in newly conquered lands. Sixteenth-century Neo-Latin and Italian writers began to apply the term to European settlements being founded throughout the world, including the Americas.

Introduced into English by Richard Eden in his mid-sixteenth-century translations of travel writings, the term *colony* was only just coming to mean a land settled by citizens of and under the control of another country ("colony, n." 2021). Instead, late-sixteenth-century con-notations of *colony* emphasized the idea of rural life—farming, plant-ing—done outside the normal bounds of a country's settled areas. Adding to the rural imagery, the narratives of the 1587 and 1590 expe-ditions refer to the people left on Roanoke Island as *planters*, not *col-onists*. *Colonist* did not come into use in English until the turn of the eighteenth century, while John White's 1587 narrative is the *OED's* ear-liest example of the word *planter* meaning of "[t]he founder of a col-ony; an early settler, a colonist" ("planter, n.," def. I.2.a 2021). Up to that time, *planter* had simply meant someone "who plants seeds, bulbs, etc.; (hence) a farmer, a cultivator of the soil, an agriculturist" ("planter, n.," def. I.1).[5] The same term, *planter,* was used to denote the Jamestown col-onists in the early 1600s. *Colony* and *planter* portray Raleigh's Virginia as an agrarian settlement—a community able to sustain itself, despite the difficulties it met with in its first days.

The turn of events on Roanoke Island in 1590, the year after the original publication of *The Principal Navigations*, forced Hakluyt to update the story of the Virginia colony and its planters when he revised *The Principal Navigations* in 1598–1600.[6] The same documents are reprinted in the same order, from the original "Letters Patents" up through the list of names of the men who remained on Roanoke Island with Ralph Lane (1598–1600:3:243–254). Then the extract from Lane's September 1585 letter is put in chronological order (1598–1600:3:254–255), right before Lane's "Account" of the 1585–86 expedition, the short narrative of Grenville's 1586 resupply, Hariot's *Briefe and True Report*, White's narrative of the 1587 expedition, and the list of 1587 planters left on Roanoke Island (1589–1600:3:255–286). But here the narrative changes. In 1600, Hakluyt omits the story of the 1588 failed resupply and the revised agreement of rights over the Virginia col-ony. In their place are a letter from John White to Richard Hakluyt (1589–1600:3:287–288), which serves as an introduction to Hakluyt's final Roanoke-related text, "The fift voyage of M. John White into the West Indies and parts of America called Virginia, in the yeere 1590" (1598–1600:3:288–295).

The 1600 version revises the story of 1587, adding to it the narra-tive of 1590, but taking out of the overall narrative two failures—the failed resupply attempt in 1588 and the description of the reorganized investment syndicate, whose seven years of rights had run out before 1600. With White's 1590 narrative, the Virginia colony's story is revised from 1589 but keeps the same general storyline of the 1587 planters inhabiting a wonderful land that can easily sustain them as they wait to reconnect with their homeland of England. Finding the word *Croatoan* carved on a post advances the optimistic storyline one more step, with the planters having safely moved, even if for unknown reasons.

Closely reading individual texts can easily complicate the story, as the examples of textual analysis above show. Even so, by concluding the 1600 version with White's 1590 narrative, Hakluyt presents an optimistic overarching Roanoke storyline implying that even some thirteen years after last being seen, the planters remain as farmers, sowing fields and growing what they need, not waiting to be found—for they are not lost—but instead waiting to reconnect with their countrymen. Hakluyt, through White's story of the 1590 expedition, implies that the English need a search and rescue mission to Virginia, not to rescue the planters from wherever they are, but to rescue the line of communication between the planters and England. Even though White's information about the meaning of *CROATOAN* would be labeled assumption and circumstantial evidence in a modern court of law, at the turn of the seventeenth century, Hakluyt's story of the Roanoke ventures, including White's 1590 narrative, could serve as inspiration for further settlement.

The Roanoke Colonies in Print, 1590–1606

The influence of Hakluyt's narrative, especially his portrayal of the 1587 colonists, can be seen in works from the 1590s until at least the 1620s. Most publications that mention the 1587 colony and its planters up until the early years of the Jamestown colony, founded in 1607, assumed the planters were alive—or at least that it was more than likely that they were alive.

It's not surprising that Raleigh published such an implication. In his *The Discouerie of the Large, Rich, and Beuutiful Empyre of Guiana* (1596), about his 1595 expedition to South America in search of the purported city of gold, El Dorado, Raleigh describes stopping at Port of Spain on the island of Trinidad, gathering as much information as he could from the Spanish about Guiana. He says that he was able to do so because he "bred in them an opinion that I was bound only for the reliefe of those english, which I had planted in *Virginia*" (5). Though he uses the Roanoke planters as cover for his secret voyage to Guiana, Raleigh adds he had fully intended to search for the Virginia planters on his return, "if extremity of weather had not forst [forced] me from the saide coast" (5). While Raleigh mentions his Virginia colony only in this one passage, he unequivocally portrays his planters as alive in 1596. He may have been saving face for not taking care of the Roanoke planters, but if the planters were alive, they effectively continued Raleigh's and his fellow backers' rights to Virginia, whose 1589 agreement was coming to its end during Raleigh's Guiana voyage.

Raleigh's *The Discovery of Guiana* is not the only published statement about aborted attempts to look for the 1587 planters. John Brereton's 1602 description of Bartholomew Gosnold's exploration of the New England coast, *A Briefe and True Relation of the Discouerie of the North Part of Virginia*, includes "A briefe Note of the sending another barke *this present yeere* 1602. *by the honorable* knight, Sir Walte [*sic*] Ralegh, for the searching out of his Colonie in *Virginia*" (Brereton and Haies 1966 [1602]:14). This one-page appendix states that Raleigh had attempted to resupply the planters "five severall times," but that these attempts "performed nothing." The 1602 attempt, headed by Samuel Mace, "fell fortie leagues to the Southwestward of *Hatarask* ... and having there spent a moneth; when they came along the coast to seeke the people, they did it not, pretending that the extremitie of weather and losse of some principall ground-tackle, forced and feared them from searching the port of *Hatarask*..." (14).

In other words, the 1587 planters were assumed to be alive, but that the expedition sent to find them did not follow through on its assigned task. Emphasizing the desire to continue settlement in the region, the "Briefe Note" ends with a list of the valuable commodities the Mace expedition brought back from where they landed, some forty leagues southwest of Hatteras.[7] Though Mace fails to connect with the planters, assuming they are alive would allow Raleigh and his fellow backers to argue for their continued rights to Virginia, including the right to exploit the region's commodities.

Other early published mentions of the 1587 planters emphasize their survival, though not as unequivocally as Hakluyt does. In *The Herball or Generall Historie of Plantes* (1597), John Gerard, a member of the Barber-Surgeon's Company in London and a well-known herbalist, writes about "Indian Swallow woorrt": "It groweth ... in the countries of Norembega, and now called Virginia by the H. sir *Walter Raleigh*, who hath bestowed great summes of monie in the discouerie therof, where are dwelling at this present English men, if neither vntimely death by murdering, or pestilence, corrupt aire, bloodie flixes [fluxes], or some other mortall sicknes hath not destroied them" (752).

Gerard appears to be one of the men assigned the rights to continue colonization of Virginia by Raleigh in 1589, the agreement included in Hakluyt's 1589 edition but dropped in 1598–1600 (Quinn 1991[1955]:2:570). And the woodcut used to illustrate the Indian Swallow-Wort is based on a John White watercolor. While Gerard's statement about the 1587 planters' fate came out before Hakluyt published White's 1590 account, as a 1589 assignee of Raleigh's original rights to settle Virginia, Gerard would have known of White's report. Though Gerard may equivocate about the 1587 planters' survival, he does not assume they are dead, and they are certainly not lost.[8]

A mixed message—and a mixed-up history—is found in George Abbot's *A Briefe Description of the Whole World*, first published in 1599 with seven subsequent editions published anonymously while Abbot was alive and an additional seven published with his name on them after his death in 1633. Abbot, appointed the Archbishop of Canterbury in 1611, was faculty at Balliol College, Oxford, when he wrote *A Briefe Description of the Whole World*, most likely as a textbook in general world geography (Fincham 2011). In Abbot's version of events, there were no planters left behind in 1587. Instead, all of the planters abandoned the venture.

In his original 1599 edition (and repeated in his 1600 edition), Abbot describes Virginia as "that part which lyeth betweene *Florida* and *Noua Francia*, was not inhabited by Christians, and was a land very fruitfull & fit to plant in" (1599:sig. H2v). About England's Roanoke colonization efforts, Abbot writes:

> [T]hey sent thither at two seuereall times, two seuerall companies, as *Colonies* to inhabit that part; which in remembrance of the virginity of their Queene, they named *Virginia*. But this voyage being interprised on the charge of priuate men, and not thoroughly being followed by the State; the possession of this *Virginia* is now discontinued, and the country at this present left to the olde inhabitants [sig. H2v].

For Abbot in 1599, Virginia had been abandoned by any Christian attempts to settle it—and presumably attempts to bring it into the Christian fold—leaving it "to the olde inhabitants," that is, to the Native Americans. No one dies. No one is left behind.

When the 1605 edition came out, the story was complicated by Abbot's method for revision in new editions. At least in his North America section, Abbot made few if any changes to what he had already written, simply inserting any new materials. Therefore, for the 1605 edition, immediately following the description of English colonization attempts in Virginia given above, Abbot added an expanded narrative of the same events:

> There were some *English* people, who after they had vnderstood the calmnes of the Climate, and goodnes of the Soyle, did vpon the instigation of some Gentlemen of *England*, voluntarily offer themselues, euen with their wiues and children, to goe into those partes to inhabite; but when the moste of them came there (vpon some occasions) they returned home againe the first time: which caused that second yeere, there was a greater

company transported thither, who were prouided of many necessaries, and continued there ouer a whole Winter, under the guiding of M. Lane: but not finding any sustenaunce in the Countrie (which could well brooke with their nature,) and beeing too meanely prouided of Corne & Victuals from *England*, they had like to haue perished for famine: and therefore thought themselves happie when *Sir Francis Drake* comming that way from the Westerne *Indies*, would take them into his shipping; and bring them home into their natiue Countrie. Yet some there were of these *English*, which beeing left behind, ranged vp and downe the Country (and hoouering about the Sea coast) made meanes at last (after their enduring of much miserie) by some Christian ships to be brought backe againe into *England*.

While they were there inhabiting, there were some children borne, and baptised in those partes; and they might well haue endured the Countrie, if they might haue had such strength as to keepe off the inhabitantes from troubling them in tilling the ground, and reaping of such Corne as they would haue sowed [1605:sig. S3v-(S4)r].

Abbot conflates the 1585–1586 Lane colony with the 1587 colony and adds elements to the history not found in the narratives of either. Families attempt to settle Virginia from the very start, there are children born, and in the end, Francis Drake saves them all, leaving the colony empty of Christian inhabitants (except for a few who wander along the coast until being picked up by some other fleet), reinforcing the idea that these lands were "left to the olde inhabitants." Abbot's 1587 planters abandon the colony and return to England. This version of the 1580s Roanoke colonization efforts is repeated in every edition of *A Briefe Description of the Whole World* from then on, up to the 1664 posthumous edition, even as new material is added, such as a description of the Jamestown colony that first appears in the 1617 edition.[9]

Repeating the idea that the 1587 planters were still alive in Virginia and putting that survival alongside images of Virginia's potential wealth—especially the commodities available for trade noted in Hariot and Brereton—turned the 1587 planters into a trope. David Clippinger's definition of *trope* in the *Encyclopedia of Postmodernism* is a good explanation of what happens to the image of the 1587 planters, starting with the 1589 first edition of the *Principal Navigations* on through the early seventeenth century: "A trope is a figure of speech that denotes or connotes meaning through a chain of associations. It employs a word or phrase out of its ordinary usage in order to further demonstrate or illustrate a particular idea" (2001:406–407). In other words, the planters became less important as actual colonists continuing to survive in Virginia than as symbols. As a trope, from 1589 into the early 1600s, the 1587 planters figuratively stood for continuing English claims on parts of North America, for the ability of English planters to live in those claimed areas, and for the potential worth of those claims, whether the planters were literally alive or not.

In 1605, on the eve of England's attempts to renew North American colonization at Jamestown, playwrights George Chapman, Ben Jonson, and John Marston's collaborative work *Eastward Ho!* was produced. A comedy, *Eastward Ho!* uses the 1587 planters' survival in Virginia as a satirical trope rather than a promotional one. In doing so, the play helps illustrate the wide range of attitudes toward American colonization in London at the time.

The plot centers around a London goldsmith whose older daughter is engaged to marry a bankrupt knight. While the knight promises her a castle, in reality he plans to take her money and run away to Virginia with another woman. *Eastward Ho!* satirizes, among other things, bought peerages, the desire for easy money, and usury. Even the play's title connects to its satirical aims, responding to Thomas Dekker and John Webster's 1604 play *Westward Ho!*, both titles referring to London's growth, mainly to the west, centered around the ambitions of the city's increasing middle class.[10] The ambitions of the Roanoke colonies, including the 1587 planters' becoming landowning gentlemen, play into *Eastward Ho!*'s satire of the growing middle class.

The Roanoke ventures first appear when Captain Seagull, the commander of a ship headed to Virginia, states, "A whole country of English is there, man, bred of those that were left there in '79" (III.iii.13–14).[11] While Chapman, Jonson, and Marston seem to get the date wrong or have a mixed-up history like Abbott (or the date may even be a transcription or typesetting error), they portray the planters as still alive, as Hakluyt did five years earlier, but with the added twist that the planters are in contact with England. The "historical" information about the planters being alive and in contact with England is used to help develop several satirical elements central in the play. Among these is that Virginia is a land of easy wealth. As Seagull states, the indigenous people of Virginia "are so in love" with the English planters "that all the treasure they have, they lay at their feet" (III.iii.16–17), the treasure being gold, which "is more plentiful there than copper is with us," in fact so plentiful that the Native Americans' "dripping pans and their chamber pots are pure gold" (III.iii.18–20).

In *Eastward Ho!*, Raleigh's Virginia is a satirical trope for greed. The trope intensifies with Sir Petronel Flash, the bankrupt knight. He is running away with his new wife's money, heading to Virginia for its purported riches and easy life. This same assumption about easy money motivates two other characters, with the suggestive names of Scapethrift and Spendall. Connected to this greed, *Eastward Ho!* satirizes excessive social ambition, including that Sir Petronel bought rather than inherited or earned his knighthood. Seagull brings the satire together when he says, "Then for your means to advancement there, it is simple, and not preposterously mixed: you may be an alderman there, and never be scavenger; you may be a nobleman, and never be a slave. You may come to preferment enough, and never be a pander; to riches and fortune enough and have never the more villainy nor the less wit" (III.iii.35–38). *Eastward Ho!* satirizes Virginia as a place of easy riches and easy advancement to the life of a noble, letting anyone be a town councilor rather than a street sweeper, a nobleman rather than a slave no matter who they are or where they come from.

Whether intended or not, *Eastward Ho!*'s satire of newly minted nobility could be applied to the 1587 Roanoke expedition's governor and twelve assistants. The goldsmith's daughter in *Eastward Ho!* marries a knight to move up the social ladder, and the peerage of the knight she marries was bought rather than being hereditary or earned. Similarly, the governor and his assistants—many of whom were guildsmen—immediately became landed gentry by participating in the 1587 Roanoke venture. As part of the inducement to the settlers, Raleigh awarded each male colonist five hundred acres of land, and in the process, the governor and his assistants were granted heraldic arms. *Eastward Ho!* uses Virginia to satirize the newly minted noblemen of England, but the satire of these newly minted knights and gentlemen also ends up satirizing the 1587 colonists and the Virginia ventures as a whole.

Eastward Ho! shows that by 1605, Raleigh's Virginia planters had become as much a trope as they were historical actors—a way to express desires and concerns about London and England as much as about the Virginia ventures themselves. People in late Elizabethan and early Jacobean London had many reasons to portray the 1587 colonists as alive and even thriving in Virginia. On one end, Raleigh and the English crown needed them as a symbol of continuous occupation since the 1580s to maintain a claim in the Americas. On the other end, Chapman, Jonson, and Marston keep them alive as metaphors to satirize dreams of easy money and social mobility.[12]

Early Jamestown Writings and the Roanoke Colonists (1606–1610)

The tropes of Raleigh's Virginia as both a place of continued English occupation and of riches (whether assumed to be real or as metaphoric objects of satire) took their next turn when the Virginia Company sent out the first Jamestown expeditions in 1606. Among the records of the first year in Virginia is John Smith's *True Relation of Such Occurrences and Accidents of Noate as hath Hapned in Virginia Since the First Plant-ing of that Collony*, sent by Smith to England in the late spring of 1608 and published in August of that year. As part of his narrative, Smith recounts what he has learned about the region from Native American sources, including two brief items people have connected with the 1580s Roanoke expeditions. In the first, Smith tells how Powhatan, identified as the Emperor of the region and who would later become known for being Pocahontas's father, "reported us to be within a day & a halfe of *Mangoge*, two dayes of *Chawwonock*, 6. frõ *Roonock*, to the south part of the backe sea." Smith continues that Powhatan "described a countrie called *Anone*, where they haue abundance of Brasse, and houses walled as ours" (1986[1608]:1:55).

The Mangoge (more often *Mangoaks*) were the Tuscaroran peo-ple of the present-day Virginia–North Carolina border region; Chaw-wonock (more often *Chowanoke*) was an Algonquian town on the Chowan River, and Roonock (that is, Roanoke) was the island in Algon-quian territory where the 1580s English expeditions had attempted to settle. However, the context is not Raleigh's planters, but information about a "backe sea," a saltwater sea mentioned by Powhatan and, ear-lier, the King of Paspahegh, the ruler of one of his towns. This saltwater sea seemed to be a possible passage from the Atlantic to the South Sea (that is, the Pacific Ocean), one of the objectives of both the Roanoke and Jamestown expeditions.

The second item in Smith's *A True Relation* people have connected to the 1587 planters tells about a non-event. The same King of Paspa-hegh "agreed ... to conduct two of our men to a place called *Panawicke* beyond *Roonok*, where he reported many men to be apparelled. We landed him at *Warraskoyack*, where playing the villaine, and deluding vs for rewards, returned within three or foure dayes after without going further" (1986[1608]:1:63). Warraskoyack was a town in the Powhatan Confederacy located in the area of present-day Smithfield, Virginia, from which the trip to Roanoke and beyond is *not* made.

Smith never mentions Raleigh's planters. Instead, at various points in *A True Relation*, Smith writes that his Native American informants report that there are people who are clothed like the Jamestown colo-nists, travel in similar ships, and in one case, build houses in the same manner as the English settlers. The first of these mentions comes at the same time the King of Paspahegh tells about salt water several days travel from Jamestown:

[T]he King [of Paspahegh] tooke great delight in vnderstanding the manner of our ships, and sayling the seas, the earth & skies and of our God: what he knew of the dominions he spared not to acquaint me with, as of certaine men cloathed at a place called *Ocanahonan*, cloathed like me, the course of our riuer, and that within 4 or 5 daies journey of the falls, was a great turning of salt water: ... [1986(1608):1:49].

A bit later, Smith describes travelling with the King of Paspahegh to meet Powhatan. Passing along the Tappahannock River, Smith tells why the King of Paspahegh attacked Smith and his men in the first place:

From hence this kind King conducted mee to a place called *Topahano-cke*, a kingdome upon another River northward: the cause of this was, that the yeare before, a shippe had beene in the River of *Pamaunke*, who having been kindly entertained by *Powhatan* their Emperour; they returned thence, and discoured the River of *Topahanocke*, where being recieued with like kindness, yet he slue the King, and tooke of his people, and they supposed I were hee ... [1986(1608):1:51].

Recounting his meeting with Powhatan at which the emperor tells about Mangoak, Chowanoke, and Roanoke to the south, Smith also writes how the emperor reinforced much of what the King of Paspahegh said:

[Powhatan] described people with short Coates, and Sleeves to the Elbowes, that passed that way in Shippes like ours. Many Kingdomes hee described mee to the heade of the Bay, which seemed to bee a mightie River, issuing from mightie Mountaines betwixt the two Seas, the people cloathed at Ocamahowan [1986(1608):1:55].

Without mentioning Raleigh's planters, Smith writes how the Native Americans of the Chesapeake Bay region have heard about and sometimes encountered Europeans in the region and beyond. Smith creates the trope of "just like us"—clothing, ships, houses—out of what he hears from the King of Paspahegh and Emperor Powhatan. Without ever stating it, "cloathed like me," "Shippes like ours," and "houses walled as ours" become stand-ins for Europeans. However, these are Europeans in general, not any one specific group, such as Raleigh's planters.[13] And at least one of these reported Europeans encounters identified by the "just like us" trope could not have been the 1587 planters—the ship that sailed up the Pamunkey River just the year before.

On the heels of Smith's *True Relation*, the Virginia Company published several pamphlets to promote its exploits in North America, some, unlike Smith, including specific mention of Raleigh's planters. One of the earliest of these was *Noua Britannia: Offring Most Excellent*

Fruites by Planting in Virginia. Exciting All Such as Be Well Affected to Further the Same (1609), by Robert Johnson. Johnson begins his discussion of the Roanoke colony by noting how "*Walter Raleagh* (then a Gentleman of worth) ... transported thether in *Anno 1587* ... above an hundred Men, Women, and Children at one time, and left them there to inhabite to this day" (1609:B2r). He continues, "It is now above twenty yeares agoe since these things were done, and yet ever since in all this time, we never sawe or heard of any good that hath come from thence, nor of any hope, that might encourage us anew to engage our selves therein" (1609:Br2).

In his role as a promoter for the Jamestown colony, Johnson does not blame the Powhatan or any other native people for this lack of success, let alone the land itself. Instead, blame lies in the fact that those charged with resupplying the colony "betooke themselves wholy to hunt after pillage vpon the Spanish coaste" (1609:B2r-B3v). In Johnson's version, "this most honourable enterprise so happily begunne, was by this occasion most vnhappily ended: neyther had our poore country-men left there, any meanes from thence to visite vs, nor in all this time to giue vs any light of their owne estate" (1609:B3).

Johnson mentions no people "just like us" to be found in Virginia and bemoans the loss of Raleigh's planters. But he doesn't focus on not knowing what has happened to the 1587 planters. Instead, he ends by saying, "whereas then, if those beginnings had beene followed as they ought, and as by Gods helpe we now entend that countrey had long since become a most royall addition to the Crowne of *England*, and a very nursery and fountaine of much wealth and strength to this Kingdome" (1609:B3v). It is the loss of the colony itself, not of the colonists, that matters to Johnson.

On the other hand, a variation of the "just like us" trope was picked up by the Virginia Company the next year, applying it specifically to Raleigh's planters. An anonymously authored pamphlet written for the Virginia Company of London, *A True and Sincere Declaration of the Purpose and Ends of the Plantation Begun in Virginia* (Virginia Company of London 1610), like Johnson's *Noua Britannia*, promotes continued investment in the Jamestown colony despite some setbacks. Along with reminders of the commodities that Virginia can supply, the pamphlet tells how, despite Jamestown's difficulties, the colony succeeded in gaining "*intelligence* of some of our Nation planted by Sir *Walter Raleigh* (yet aliue [alive]) within fifty mile of our fort, who can open the wombe and bowells of the country" (Virginia Company of London 1610:18). Knowledge of Raleigh's surviving planters "is testified by two of our colony sent out to seeke them, who, (though denied by the *Slauages* [sic] speech with them) found *Crosses*, & *Leters*, the *Characters* & assured Testimonies of *Christians* newly cut in the barkes of trees" (Virginia Company of London 1610:18).

As in *A True Relation*, the 1610 pamphlet tells how the King of Paspahegh agreed to and then reneged on an offer to take two men to find the surviving 1587 colonists. However, in *A True and Sincere Declaration*, the sign of Europeans in the region is not hearsay about "houses walled as ours" and "many men to be appareled." Instead, it is "obviously" Christian symbols—crosses and letters—that the two men see for themselves and that the pamphlet says must be signs of the 1587 colonists. Only these people could write on trees, "just like us." *A True and Sincere Declaration* changes the "just like us" trope. For Smith, the trope reminds readers—both in the early seventeenth century and today—that the Jamestown colonists were not the first Europeans in the Chesapeake Bay region or the wider Southeast. In *A True and Sincere Declaration*, "just like us" means a specific set of English colonists left some twenty years earlier, adding "just like us" to the trope that the 1587 planters are still alive. And it is gaining this intelligence of Raleigh's planters that lets *A True and Sincere Declaration* argue that the Jamestown colony is succeeding, despite its difficulties.

The definition of success in *A True and Sincere Declaration* reflects orders given to Governor Thomas Gates in early 1609 by His Majesty's Council for the Direction of Affairs of Virginia (The Royal Council for Virginia, predecessor of the Virginia Company). These "Instruccions Orders and Constitucions by Way of Advise Sett Downe Declared and Propounded" illustrate one possible story circulating in London about Raleigh's planters after the return of the Jamestown colony's first two resupplies. Gates is instructed to search for the Native American town of Ohonahorn, "Foure dayes Iourney from your forte Southewardes" (The Royal Council for Virginia 1969[1609]:264). The instructions then state that in going to Ohonahorn,

> you are neere to Riche Copper mines of Ritanoe and may passe them by one braunche of this Riuer, and by another Peccarecamicke where you shall finde foure of the englishe aliue, left by *Sir* Walter Rawely which escaped from the slaughter of Powhaton of Roanocke, vppon the first arrivall of our Colonie, and liue vnder the proteccion of a wiroane called Gepanocon enemy to Powhaton, by whose consent you shall neuer recouer them, one of these were worth much labour ... [The Royal Council for Virginia 1969(1609):265].

The instructions about Ohonahorn conclude by stating "if you finde them not, yet sea[r]ch into this Countrey it is more probable then towardes the north" (The Royal Council for Virginia 1969[1609]:265). For the Virginia Company in 1609 London, the majority of Raleigh's planters were killed by Powhatan when the Jamestown colonists first arrived. However, at least some of the 1587 planters were, without question, alive—though if they can't be found, it would be better, "more probable," to push further English settlement south of Jamestown, towards where the surviving colonists are, rather than to the north. But the sense of certainty that some of the 1587 colonists were alive at Ritanoe appears in manuscripts, not printed works. In print—that is, in public—only the suggestion of continued survival is given.

Smith, Strachey, and Purchas (1612–1626)

In 1612, soon after Jamestown's founding, two of the major sources people have used to discuss the fate of the 1587 colonists were completed. One was John Smith's second work on Virginia, *A Map of Virginia: With a Description of the Covntrey, the Commodities, People, Government, and Religion*, printed by Joseph Barnes in Oxford. The other was William Strachey's manuscript *The Historie of Travell into Virginia Britania*, of which three copies exist and which was not published until 1849.[14] Though contemporaneous, these works develop competing pictures of the 1587 Roanoke planters' fate.

Strachey, one of Jamestown's gentlemen settlers, travelled in literary circles—he was friends with Ben Jonson and at least acquainted with George Chapman and John Marston—but struggled financially. Strachey bought shares in the Virginia Company in order to get to Virginia with hopes of improving his financial situation. Leaving England in 1609, he was marooned in the Bermuda Isles for some ten months with the new governor, Thomas Gates, and some 150 others when the fleet's flag ship, the *Sea Venture*, was shipwrecked. After building two small boats, the castaways arrived in Jamestown in the spring of 1610. Soon after, Strachey was chosen to be the secretary of the colony's Council. We know very little about Strachey's year in Jamestown or why he returned to England in September of 1611.[15]

Strachey's *The Historie of Travell into Virginia Britania* is an incomplete manuscript history of Jamestown and Virginia which he appears to have started writing while in Virginia. The manuscript has two parts. The first is primarily descriptive, covering the geography and indigenous peoples of Virginia as well as its plants, animals, and minerals. The second part is a narrative history, running from the time of Columbus through the pre–Jamestown English expeditions of the early

1600s; this second part contains Strachey's story of the 1587 planters. After telling about John White's being sent back to England for supplies and making two thwarted attempts to get back to Roanoke Island, Strachey gives his version of White's 1590 return:

> [A]t breake of daie they landed and went through the woodes to that part of the Island directly over against Dasamanquepeuk and from thence returned by the water-side rownd about the northeren point of the Island vntill they came to the place where the Colony was leaft 1586 [*sic*].[16] Some tracts of Feeting they fownd and vpon a sandy banck on a tree curiously carved these romaine Letters *Cro*: which gaue them hope they might be removed to Croatan for their agreement was (indeed) to remove when Capt: White left them: howbeit Capt: White sought them no further, but missing them there and his Companie having other practices and which those tymes affourded they returned, covetous of some good successe, vpon the Spanish Fleet to returne that yeare from Mexico and the Indies, neglecting thus these vnfortunate and betrayed People, of whose end yet you shall hereafter read in due place in this Decade [1953(1612):149–150].

Strachey gives the standard narrative: White finds *CRO* carved on a tree (though not *Croatoan* carved on a palisade post) but can't search for them because the company goes after Spanish treasure. What Strachey doesn't include is the modern ending "and they were never heard of again." Instead, Strachey calls the planters "vnfortunate and betrayed People, of whose end yet you shall hereafter read in due place in this Decade." However, because he never completed his history, Strachey never does write the story of the 1587 colonists' end or tell how he came to learn about it.

Even so, Strachey includes passing references to the fate of Raleigh's planters scattered throughout the descriptive first part of the *History*. In his introductory "Praemonition to the Reader," Strachey notes that the 1587 planters, "as you shall fynd in this following Discourse came therefore, to a miserable, and vntymely destiny" (1953[1612]:15). Later, when telling about trading with native people in the area around Jamestown, Strachey states that even though the English gave "copper, hatchetts, and such like commodityes" for land, and did so "in all love and friendship," that "we shall fynd them practize vyolence, or treason against vs (as they haue done to our other Colony at *Roanoak*)" (1953[1612]:26).

In the first chapter of the first section, Strachey presents some specific details about the fate of the 1587 colonists, but it is a story told *in media res*, that is, starting in the middle of things. Writing about mountains some 200 miles west of the Chesapeake Bay up the James River, Strachey states:

> This high-land is, in all likelyhoodes a pleasant Tract, and the Mould fruictfull, especially what may lye to the South-ward, where at *Peccare-canick*, and *Ochanahoen*, by the Relation of Machumps, the People haue howses built with stone walls, and one story aboue another, so taught them by those English who escaped the slaughter at *Roanoak*, at what tyme this our Colony, (vnder the Conduct of Capt Newport) landed within the *Chesa-peack* Bay, and where the people breed vp tame Turkeis about their howses, and take Apes in the Mountayns, and where at *Ritanoe*, the Weroance *Eya-noco* preserved 7 of the English alive, fower men, twoo Boyes, and one young Maid, who escaped and fled (vp the River of *Chaonoke*) to beat his Copper, of which he hath certayn Mynes at the said Ritanoe, as also at *Pan-nawaick* are said to be store of salt stones [1953(1612):34].

Packed into a one-sentence paragraph is the claim that someone (identi-fied later in *The Historie* as the Powhatans) slaughtered most of Raleigh's 1587 planters in 1607 when the Jamestown colonists arrived, but two groups of colonists survived the attack. One group—of unspecified number—have taught some of the indigenous peoples to build two-story houses in the period following their 1607 escape, while another group— four men, two boys, and one maiden—serve a different indigenous leader "to beat his copper."

It is worth noting that Strachey presents second-hand information, that is, his manuscript fits our definition of a secondary source. The information doesn't come from Strachey's own experiences, but from Machumps (sometimes spelled *Matchumps*), a Powhatan who had gone to England in 1608 and returned to Virginia in 1609–1610 on the *Sea Venture*, the same ship Strachey was on. He was shipwrecked in Ber-muda with at least one other Powhatan, Namontack.

In 1624, John Smith related the second-hand information that Machumps and Namontack had a falling out while on Bermuda and Machumps killed Namontack. The veracity of this murder has been seriously questioned; even so, Machumps' relationship with Powhatan on his return from England is uncertain. Powhatan trusted Namontack enough to send him to England twice, and Machumps returned from this second trip while Namontack did not. Too, Strachey notes that Machumps "comes to and fro amongst vs, as he dares, and as Powhatan giues him leave, for yt is not otherwise safe for him, no more then yt was for one Amarice, who had his braynes knock't out for selling but a bas-kett of Corne, and lying in the English fort 2. or 3. Daies without Powha-tans leave" (1953[1612]:61–62).

It is possible that Machumps' story could have reflected preju-dice against Powhatan.[17] Or Strachey may have been predisposed to see the outlandish and the exotic in any tales about Virginia and its native people. After all, the "slaughter at *Roanoak*" comes alongside taking apes in the mountains, an exoticism, a point reinforced in one of the manuscripts with the marginal note, "Howses of stone, tame turkyes and monkyes, supposed at Peccartcanick" (1849[1612]: 26).[18]

Strachey adds other passing references to the "slaughter" of Raleigh's planters, now adding that it was Powhatan who had the planters killed. To tell why Powhatan should not be trusted, Strachey writes that Powhatan "doth often send vnto us to temporize with vs, awaiting perhapps but a fitt opportunity (inflamed by his bloudy and furious priests) to offer vs a tast of the same Cuppe which he made our poore Countrymen drinck off at *Roanoak...*" (1953[1612]:58). Strachey repeats his accusation that Powhatan slaughtered the 1587 planters when discussing religion. Strachey believes that the ordinary people under Powhatan's rule could be persuaded to follow Christianity if they came to understand what Powhatan did to the 1587 colonists. One approach would be

> making the comon people likewise to vnderstand ... that the men women, and Children of the first plantation at Roanoak were by practize and Comaundement of Powhatan (he himself perswaded therevnto by his Priests) miserably slaughtered without any offence given him either by the first planted (who 20. and od yeares had peaceably lyved and intermixed with those Savadges, and were out of his Territory) or by those who now are come to inhabite some parte of his desart lands ... [1953(1612):91].

By stating that the Roanoke colonists had lived peacefully near the Powhatans for some twenty years before his priests persuaded Powhatan to slaughter them, Strachey's version of events now adds that the slaughter occurred at the time of the Jamestown colonists' arrival in 1607.

Strachey repeats the charge that Powhatan killed Raleigh's planters after peacefully living near one another for twenty years, turning his story of a slaughter from a point of history into a trope. All he needs to do is mention "what Powhatan did to Raleigh's planters," and an image is invoked. For example, discussing the possibility of England's using violence to gain control over Virginia, Strachey writes:

> [Y]f wee should fynd cause nowe or hereafter to vse violence, there is no man among themselues so savadge, or not Capable of so much Sence, but that he will approue our Cause, when he shalbe made to vnderstand, that Powhatan hath slaughtered so many of our Nation without offence given, and such as were seated far from him, and in the Territory of those Weroances which did in no sort depend on him, or acknowledge him: ... [1953(1612):106].

Through repetition, Strachey turns Powhatan's presumed slaughter of all but the few surviving Roanoke colonists into a literary device which can be used to invoke a specific response in readers—we English are not naturally violent, but we will use violence to counter violence when necessary.

In 1612, as Strachey was sending his incomplete manuscript to potential sponsors, John Smith published his second work on the Jamestown ventures, *A Map of Virginia: With a Description of the Covntrey, the Commodities, People, Government, and Religion.* Like Strachey's manuscript *Historie,* Smith's *A Map of Virginia* was published with both a descriptive section and a narrative history, though with the addition of an engraved map of Virginia. The first part, titled simply "The Description of Virginia by Captaine Smith," includes a single reference to the Roanoke colonists. Telling about the various directions that had been explored from Jamestown, Smith states, "Southward they went to some parts of Chawonock and the Mangoags to search them there left by Sir Walter Raleigh; for those parts to the Towne of Chisapeack hath formerly been discovered by Master Heriots and Sir Raph Layne" (1986[1612]:1:150).

The second part of *A Map of Virginia* is a narrative history titled "The Proceedings of the English Colonie in Virginia since their First Beginning from England in the Yeare of our Lord 1606, till This Present 1612...." Authorship of this section is complicated. It is a compilation of narratives attributed to "Thomas Studly Cape-marchant, Anas Todkill, Doctor Russell, Nathaniel Powell, William Phetiplace, and Richard Pot" as well as "the laboures of other discreet observers, during their residences," all edited by W. S., identified by Philip Barbour as William Symonds, a clergyman with interests in the Virginia ventures (Smith 1986[1612]:1:200).[19] While not listed among the contributors, Smith was likely one of the "other discreet observers" because he would have had to provide the information about some of the events included. In fact, much of the text may be by Smith.[20]

In this narrative history of Jamestown, the first mention of the Roanoke planters comes after Smith has been elected president in September of 1608. The text complains about the instructions the Virginia Company gave to Christopher Newport: "How, or why, Captaine Newport obtained such a private commission as not to returne without a lumpe of gold, a certainty of the south sea or one of the lost company of Sir Walter Rawley I know not, nor why he brought such a 5 pieced barge, not to beare us to that south sea, till we had borne her over the mountains: which how farre they extend is yet unknowne" (Smith 1986[1612]:234). Most likely a reference to the 1609 instructions given to Thomas Gates rather than to Newport, "The Proceedings" expresses what became a regular complaint Smith had against the Virginia

Company—impossible tasks were assigned to measure the colony's success, including finding gold, finding a passage to the Pacific Ocean (the South Sea), or finding one of Raleigh's planters still alive.

"The Proceedings" include not only this dig at the Virginia Company, but at least a partial explanation of why the task of finding one of Raleigh's planters is impossible. "The Proceedings" tell how Smith set out on December 29, 1608, with several men to meet with Powhatan. They spend the first night at Warraskoyack, where Smith requests "guides to Chowanoke, for he would send a present to that king to bind him his friend. To performe this journey, was sent Michael Sicklemore, a very honest, valiant, and painefull souldier, with him two guids, and directions howe to search for the lost company of Sir Walter Rawley, and silke grasse ..." (Smith 1986[1612]:1:244).[21]

Several chapters later, a single sentence gives the results of Sicklemore's expedition along with the text's only mention of a second expedition sent to look for Raleigh's planters: "Master Sicklemore well returned from Chawonock, but found little hope and lesse certainetie of them were left by Sir Walter Rawley. So that Nathaniell Powell & Anas Todkill, were also, by the Quiyoughquohanocks, conducted to the Mangoages to search them there. But nothing could we learne but they were all dead" (Smith 1986[1612]:1:265–266). While Strachey unequivocally states that Powhatan had the 1587 colonists killed and that two groups of colonists escaped the slaughter, "The Proceedings" equivocates, stating that Sicklemore found no evidence about the colonists from the Chowanokes while Powell and Todkill found out that the colonists were all dead but with no indication of how they died. For Smith, finding "the lost company of Sir Walter Rawley" is a pipedream.

Little changes in the material about Raleigh's planters when it reappears a dozen years later in Smith's 1624 *The Generall Historie of Virginia, New-England, and the Summer Isles*, most famous for the first appearance of the Pocahontas story. While containing much of the same Jamestown-related Roanoke colonization material as the 1612 *A Map of Virginia*, *The Generall Historie* gives an extended relation of the 1580s Roanoke expeditions—condensed and sometimes directly lifted from the Roanoke texts in Hakluyt's 1598–1600 *Principal Navigations*.

For example, Smith's condensed version of John White's 1590 return voyage is given in two paragraphs. Smith includes how White "found three faire Romane Letters carved. C.R.O.," then found "in fayre capitall Letters CROATAN, without any signe of distresse," plus the information that "they intended to goe fiftie myles into the mayne," all the major clues about where the planters intended to go (1986[1624]:2:87). Smith also includes White's statement that weather prevented them from going to Croatoan and forced them to return to England. Switching from White's voice to his own, Smith concludes this section with the following, accompanied by the marginal note, "The end of the Plantation":

> And thus we left seeking this our Colony, that was never any of them found, nor seene to this day 1622. And this was the conclusion of this Plantation, after so much time, labour, and charge consumed. Whereby we see;
>
> Not all at once, nor all alike, nor ever hath it beene,
> That God doth offer and confer his blessings upon men [1986(1624):2:88].

For Smith, Raleigh's planters are gone because God does not always give people what they want.

Later, as part of the history of the Jamestown settlement, Smith includes the same materials about the Sicklemore and the Powell and Todkill expeditions' unsuccessful searches for the 1587 colonists as in "The Proceedings" section of *A Map of Virginia*. He also includes his satirical complaint against the Virginia Company's orders that made finding these colonists one of the impossible tasks to count the Virginia venture as successful. Reinforcing his satire of the Virginia Company, Smith adds a copy of a letter he sent to Jamestown's English backers in the autumn of 1608. Included in that letter is yet another repetition of how impossible the Company's goals are: "And ... at that time to find in the South Sea, a Mine of gold; or any of them sent by Sir Walter Raleigh: at our Consultation I told them was as likely as the rest" (1986[1624]:2:188). Smith's repeated theme is that the fate of Raleigh's planters is unknown and unknowable, God's will rather than a mystery to be solved.

Aside from Strachey's unfinished and unpublished manuscript and Smith's published histories, there is one other major early seventeenth-century source people have used to discuss the Roanoke planters, Samuel Purchas's 1625 *Hakluytus Posthumus or Purchas His Pilgrimes*. Purchas carried on in the tradition of Hakluyt, compiling narratives of European travelers and colonizers throughout the world. The first of these compilations was published in 1613 and then again in 1614 as *Purchas His Pilgrimage: Or Relations of the World and the Religions Observed in All Ages and Places Discovered, from Creation unto This Present*.[22] In the 1614 edition, Raleigh's colonies play only a small part, with Purchas instructing readers, ""For the description of the countrie, Mr. *Hakluyt* from others relations in his third Volume of voyages hath written largely of those parts, discouered for Sir *Walter Raleigh*" (1614:760).

The only other mentions of the 1587 planters are, first, in

connection with the 1602 Samuel Mace voyage: "In the yeare 1587, a second Colonie were sent under the government of Master *John White*. To their succour Sir *Walter Raleigh* hath sent five severall times, the last by *Samuel Mace* of Weymouth, in March, one thousand s[i]xe hundred and two; but he and the former performed nothing, but returned with frivolous allegations" (1614:755). Second, Purchas ends the section "Of the Religion and Rites of the Virginians" by telling how, for Powhatan, "[h]is will, and Custome are the Lawes," and that among the punishments he doles out are "broyling to death, being encompassed with fire, and other tortures" (1614:769). Purchas then adds the single line, "Some were sent to enquire for those which were left of Sir *Walter Rawleighs* Colony, but they could learne nothing of them but that they were dead" (1614:769).

In 1617, a new edition of *Purchas His Pilgrimage* appeared. Purchas repeats the same material about the Mace voyage (1617:938) and, in the conclusion of the Virginia section, the note that some men were sent out from Jamestown to look for Raleigh's planters, "but they could learne nothing of them but that they were dead" (1617:956). But Purchas adds a statement about Powhatan's power among his brothers:

> *Powhatan* was gone Southwards when our men came last thence; some thought for fear of *Opechacanough* his yonger brother, a man very gracious, both with the people and the English, jealous lest He and the English should conspire against him, thinking that he will not retum; but others thinke he will returne againe [1617:956].

Purchas does not explicitly connect Powhatan's fear of his brother's conspiring with the English with the English inability to learn about Raleigh's planters, and he makes no explicit connection between the inability to learn about the planters and Powhatan's violent tendencies, but the juxtaposition is there.

In 1625, Purchas published *Hakluytus Posthumus: Or Purchas His Pilgrimes: Contayning a History of the World in Sea Voyages and Lande Travells by Englishmen and Others*, an expanded version of the materials he had been working with in *Purchas His Pilgrimage*.[23] However, even before *Hakluytus Posthumus* was published, Purchas revealed his changing portrayal of what happened to the 1587 planters. Purchas provided one of the prefatory "Panegyrick Verses," laudatory poems, for Smith's 1624 *Generall History*. His was labeled "Samuel Purchas of his friend Captaine John Smith, and his Virginia." Purchas's fourth (and final) stanza reads:

> Haile S[ir] *Sebastian, Englands* Northern Pole,
> *Virginia's* finder; Virgin *Eliza* nam'd it,

Gave't *Raleigh*. (*Rut, Prat, Hore*, I not enrole)
Amadas rites to *English* right first fram'd it.
Lane planted, return'd, nor had *English* tam'd it:
Greenviles and *Whites* men all slaine; New Plantation
James founds, Sloth confounds, feare, pride, faction sham'd it:
Smiths Forge mends all, makes chaines for *Savage* Nation,
Frees, feeds the rest; the rest reade in his Bookes Relation
[Smith 1986(1624):2:48].

In this short poetic history, Purchas tells about England's discovery of, claims on, and colonization of Virginia, from the time of Sebastian Cabot's 1508–1509 expedition along the coast of North America to John Smith's part in founding Jamestown from 1607 to 1609. As part of this history, Purchas now openly states that Grenville's and White's colonists, those who were in Virginia between 1585 and 1587 and did not return, were slain. In *Hakluytus Posthumus*, Purchas would no longer write that "they could learne nothing of them but that they were dead." He would now put into print the assertion Strachey had made in his 1612 manuscript—that Powhatan had killed Raleigh's planters.

In the Virginia section of *Hakluytus Posthumus*, Purchas gives a brief overview of the Roanoke ventures, ending with, "Anno 1590. The said Master Iohn White put to Sea with Ships, and two Pinnaces, with purpose for Virginia, where they anchored at Hatorask in 36. 20. Aug. 15. They found some of the goods (such as the Sauages could not make vse of) and tokens as if they were at Croatoan; but the winds violence permitted no further search..." (1905–1907[1625]:18:300).[24] Purchas next adds materials about Bartholomew Gosnold's 1602 expedition, including the added paragraph from Brereton's 1602 *A Briefe and True Relation of the Discouerie of the North Part of Virginia* about Samuel Mace's unsuccessful voyage in search of Raleigh's planters that same year (1905–1907[1625]:18:322).

Later Purchas adds a narrative by Thomas Canner about Bartholomew Gilbert's 1603 voyage to Virginia, which included travel to the "Bay of Chesepian ... to seeke out the people for Sir Walter Raleigh left neere those parts in the yeere 1587" (1905–1907[1625]:18:334). However, recurring often enough in the context of early searches for Raleigh's planters to become its own trope, bad weather and dwindling supplies prevent the Gilbert expedition from achieving this goal.

Soon after, Purchas compiles a history of Jamestown from 1606 to 1610 using a good deal of material from the "Proceedings" section of *A Map of Virginia*, materials Smith had also repeated the year before in *A Generall Historie*. The complaint that Newport was sent with instructions that made success dependent on finding gold, a route to the South Sea, or "one of the lost Company of Sir Walter Rawley" is included (1905–1907[1625]:18:494), as is the story that "was sent Michael Sicklemore, a very honest valiant, and painfull Souldier, with him two Guides, and directions how to search for the lost company of Sir Walter Rawleigh" (1905–1907[1625]:18:504). And Purchas includes Smith's account used in both 1612 and 1624 about Sicklemore's lack of success as well as Powell and Todkill's failure to find out what happened to Raleigh's 1587 planters: "Master Sicklemore well returned from Chawonock, but found little hope and lesse certaintie of them which had beene left by Sir Walter Rawley. So that Nathaniell Powell and Anas Todkill, were also, by the Quiyoughquohanocks, conducted to the Mangoages to search them there. But nothing could we learne but they were all dead" (1905–1907[1625]:527).

However, one important difference from all other retellings of these events appears in a marginal note next to the passage about Sicklemore, Powell, and Todkill:

> Search for them sent by Sir W. Rawlew. Powhatan confessed that hee had bin at the murther of that Colone: and shewed to Cap. Smith a Musket barrell and a brasse Morter, and certaine peeces of Iron which had bin theirs [1905–1907(1625):18:527].

In his 1612 manuscript, Strachey asserts that Powhatan had killed the 1587 Roanoke colonists, not clearly giving his source but implying that it was Machumps. Like Strachey, Purchas asserts that Powhatan had Raleigh's planters killed, but adds assertions found nowhere else— that Powhatan made this confession to John Smith and that in doing so, Powhatan showed Smith English artifacts taken from the planters. While Smith says "nothing could we learne but they were all dead," Purchas says that Smith did learn more, that Powhatan ordered and was present at the slaying. While Smith promotes the view that Raleigh's colonists are dead and it is time to move on, Purchas promotes a very different view.

As the final chapter of his Virginia section in *Hakluytus Posthumous*, Purchas includes "Virginias Verger: Or a Discourse Shewing the Benefits Which May Grow to this Kingdome from American English Plantations, and Specially Those of Virginia and Summer Ilands" (1905–1907[1625]:19:218–267), a justification for English colonization in the Americas. Purchas's presumption that Powhatan slaughtered Raleigh's 1587 planters is one of the important justifications. The justification is not only that the English were the first Europeans to colonize the region but, as Purchas writes:

As for the former Plantations of Sir Walter Raleigh, some children were
borne to them there: and whether they live, they continued the possession; or if the Savages dealt perfidiously with them (as Powhatan confessed to Cap. Smith, that hee had beene at their slaughter, and had divers
utensils of theirs to shew) their carkasses, the dispersed bones of their
and their Countrey mens since murthered carkasses, haue taken a mortall immortall possession, and being dead, speake, proclaime and cry, This
our earth is truly English, and therefore this Land is justly yours O English
[1905–1907(1625):19:227–228].

Purchas first highlights that the 1587 planters gave birth to children
in Virginia—not only Virginia Dare, but the baby born to Margery and
Dyonis Harvie after Virginia Dare's birth, as well as others whom Purchas presumes were born after White left. Purchas suggests that some
of these children may still survive, "whether they live, they continued
the possession" of Virginia by the English. But even if they have all died,
especially at the hand of Powhatan, their murdered bodies possess the
lands, they "speake, proclaime and cry, This our earth is truly English,
and therefore this Land is justly yours O English."

Purchas goes on to tie the slaughter of Raleigh's planters to the
deaths of the fifteen men left on Roanoke Island by Richard Grenville in
1586 and to the deaths of Jamestown colonists at the hand of the Powhatan Indians. Purchas writes that, at first, "Temperance and Justice
had before kissed each other, and seemed to blesse the cohabitations
of English and Indians in Virginia" (1905–1907[1625]:19:229). Purchas
continues:

But when Virginia was violently ravished by her owne ruder Natives, yea
her Virgin cheekes dyed with the bloud of three Colonies (that of Sir R.
Greenevile, that of Sir W.R. both confessed by themselves, and this last
butchery intended to all, extended to so many hundreths, with so immaine,
inhumane, devillish treachery) that I speake not of thousands otherwise
mis-caring here and mis-carrying there, taking possession of Virginia by
their facts, and fates, by so manifold losses adding to the price of Virginias
purchase ... [1905–1907(1625):19:229].

For Purchas, the death of Raleigh's planters is not something to be gotten over, to move on from. They are part of the legal, moral, and spiritual
right of the English to Virginia, especially because Powhatan, leader of
Virginia's "unaturall Naturalls," spilled the blood that made the land
English.

These texts are the main written sources scholars have had available to explore what happened to the 1587 colonists. They are primarily
secondary sources, repeating what others have said. And even primary
sources, like the narratives of the 1587 and 1590 voyages, have been

mediated by Hakluyt's editing, and in the case of the 1590 narrative, tell what John White thought the signs meant. In other words, all the sources are based on secondhand information and guesswork.

For this reason, from the very start, Raleigh's colonists were more than just historical planters in England's Virginia colony. From the 1580s through at least the 1620s, above all else, they were symbols of possession—whether seen in a positive light or as a target for satire—because what actually happened to them was unknown. Raleigh assumed they were still alive—from the time of his intended search described in the 1596 *The Discovery of Guiana* to the various early seventeenth-century expeditions whose instructions included looking for the 1587 planters—but Raleigh's North American claims depended on continued settlement.

Aside from Raleigh's personal claims, any general British claims on North America were based at least in part on the presence of Raleigh's planters. Such claims are given up if one assumes the land has been abandoned, as George Abbot did. Even the satire in *Eastward Ho!* requires imagining the continued survival of Raleigh's planters. After the founding of Jamestown, it became more and more difficult to imagine the continuing survival of Raleigh's planters, so the texts kill them off—without knowing how they died, as in Smith, or by stating that Powhatan had slaughtered almost everyone except a few survivors held captive beyond the Jamestown's reach.

However, in all these early portrayals of Raleigh's 1587 planters, they were not lost, at least not in the sense of their fate being unknown and needing explanation. Even when John Smith writes of "the lost company of Sir Walter Rawley," it is in the context of satirizing the Virginia Company's orders. When Smith writes "nothing could we learne but they were all dead," the idea of the company being lost is about their death, the loss of loved ones, rather than being an open question about their fate. For Smith, God had taken them. For Purchas, Powhatan had taken them. By the 1620s, all that mattered was that they were dead. No one, to this point, sees the 1587 colonists' fate as an unsolved mystery.

3

The Archaeology
of the Lost Colony

The archaeology of the Lost Colony goes back nearly as far as the historical research into its disappearance. However, very little has actually been written about those archaeological investigations, and that little is mostly in grey-literature site reports or press releases. Even a professional archaeologist needs to know where to look or whom to ask to obtain the arcane manuscripts of past excavations. Unpublished surveys and site reports languish in the files of cultural resource management firms and government regulatory offices. There, one needs to know that they even exist before requesting a copy, and these are usually only available to professional archaeologists.

Ironically, it is the earliest archaeology that is most accessible. For instance, Talcott Williams's 1896 report can be found online by anyone with the patience and stamina to track it down. As we move closer to the present, the research conducted on private lands becomes more proprietary and jealously guarded by the investigators. This is especially curious because modern archaeology has not turned up any evidence that can unambiguously be associated with the Lost Colony. A ring, a gunlock, a rapier hilt, a scattering of early ceramics. All have been found in either post sixteenth-century contexts or on sites with ties to the Lost Colonists that are tenuous if not downright wishful thinking. With this caveat the following is what has been reported.

Early Searches

John White 1590

By any measure, the Lost Colony has been the subject of archaeological interest longer than just about any site in the United States.

60

If archaeology truly is the study of the past focusing on the material culture, then John White could be considered North America's first archaeologist. His was a reconnaissance survey, and his field report was the first to describe the abandoned site of the colony, though sadly not in the detail that subsequent archaeologists would desire. Below is how a modern archaeologist might have written White's report:

> Landed with crew on the shore of Roanoke Island and surveyed a transect through a wooded area across the sound from the previously recorded site of Dasamongwepeuk. Continued to the north forest parcel to revisit an intact site I had recorded in 1587. There were indications that others had been in the area, and I noticed that CRO had been carved on a tree trunk. My previous crew had promised to leave a sign of their final destination prior to their departure to another site, expected to be about 50 miles away. If there were problems with the project, they were to indicate that with a cross, but none was posted, so I assumed things went well.
>
> Upon arriving at the habitation site I noticed that much had changed. The previous crew had taken down the standing structures but enclosed the whole area with a log wall. One of the logs had the gang graffiti "CRO-ATOAN" written on it. I noted the following artifacts on the ground surface: several bars of iron, two pigs of lead, four iron fowlers, some iron sacker-shot and other unidentified large objects. Curiously, the falcons and small ordnance that I observed at my initial site visit were missing, as were the small boats at the creek.
>
> I was called back to the site by one of the crew who had found evidence of looting. Several pot-holes had been dug, and any artifacts not taken were broken and strewn about. Along with the artifacts were my earlier field-notes, pictures, and maps that the previous crew had left behind along with some protective field equipment (in poor shape). This really pissed me off! Clearly, this was the work of pothunters who had previously been found at the nearby site of Dasamongwepeuk. The looting of the site was unfortunate, but at least the crew had moved on to the next project area, near Buxton [with apologies to John White 1590 (Quinn 1991[1955]):2:613–616].

Though White may not have excavated the site, he does give later archaeologists a sense of what they are looking for: postholes denoting a palisade, personal artifacts and armaments dating to the late sixteenth century, and evidence of additional structures (e.g., postholes and nails).

Jamestown Expedition 1608–09

Nearly twenty years later, other early avocational archaeologists were contracted to undertake a site survey of Roanoke Island. Again, their efforts were perhaps not explicitly archaeology, but explorers from Jamestown were sent to search the island for evidence of the colonists.

William Strachey, as discussed in the previous chapter, related claims that the Powhatan had killed the colonists just as the Jamestown settlers arrived and that explorers into the interior had heard tales of European influence on the native inhabitants.

What can an archaeologist take away from these passages besides that Strachey had third-hand knowledge that Powhatan had had the colonists killed? Well, if true, the colonists had been living with local natives for two decades, that they still had armaments with them (the musket barrel, brass mortar, and pieces of iron Purchas says were shown to John Smith), and we should expect a fair amount of assimilation as trade with the native peoples was mentioned. We are later told that some of the colonists who survived the slaughter moved to high ground near the native sites of Peccarecamek and Ochanahoen (as yet unidentified archaeologically). There, Strachey writes, they built two-story stone houses and raised turkeys and mountain apes (which questions the reports' credibility). At the site of Ritanoe (also unknown archaeologically), several survivors of the massacre were engaged in working copper from nearby mines. Strachey adds that there are also rock salt deposits nearby.

These passages are as tantalizing as they are frustrating. They seem to indicate that there was a massacre of the settlers, but several survived, and seven survivors ended up at Ritanoe. This should be relatively easy to find as Strachey reports that salt and copper deposits were being worked in the area. But there is no such place that has these resources together, either in North Carolina or in Virginia. In fact, there is no workable copper outside of the Great Lakes region given the level of technology employed by the Native Americans of North America. Also, the "Europeanized" housing mentioned by Machumps is curious in that there was no construction of multi-story stone buildings in the coastal plain, or Piedmont for that matter, by Europeans until well into the eighteenth century.

Again, this is all hearsay. These nascent archaeologists didn't actually find the colonists or any of their gear. Rather, they gathered some secondhand rumors that would keep alive the hopes of maintaining England's claim on the region.

John Lawson 1700

John Lawson, who was certainly anthropological in his interests, can also claim a concern with the archaeology of the Lost Colony. In *A New Voyage to Carolina* (1709), he describes Roanoke Island in the early 1700s. Declaring it to be the place where Raleigh established the first colony of Carolina, he states that the "Ruins of a Fort are to be seen at this day, as well as some old English Coins which have been lately found; and a Brass-Gun, a Powder-Horn, and one small Quarter deck–Gun, made of Iron Staves, and hoop'd with the same Metal" (1967[1709]:68–69). Lawson also comments on the natives of Hatteras Island, whom he suggests were descendants of the Lost Colonists. He believed "that several of their Ancestors were white People, and could talk in a Book [read], as we do; the Truth of which is confirm'd by gray Eyes being found frequently amongst these Indians, and no others. They value themselves extremely for their Affinity to the English, and are ready to do them all friendly Offices" (1967[1709]:69).

Lawson speculated that Indian "treachery," as well as a lack of supplies, was responsible for the failure of the colony. This treachery took the form of assimilation, "for we may reasonably suppose that the English were forced to cohabit with them, for Relief and Conversation; and that in process of Time, they conform'd themselves to the Manners of their Indian Relations. And thus we see, how apt Humane Nature is to degenerate" (1967[1709]:96), an interesting observation from a man who supposedly held the native peoples in high regard.

It should be kept in mind that none of these early writers saw any actual colonists, though John White saw the artifacts left behind and Lawson saw what he believed to be materials from the 1580s colonists. The Jamestown investigators only heard tell of "people like them," and it is not entirely clear whether Lawson actually saw any of the grey-eyed Indians or was just passing on stories told to him, as he did elsewhere in his book (e.g., the global myth of animals fishing with their tails [1967(1709):126]). A century later all that remained to be investigated were legends and the low mounds of a "fort."

Edward Bruce 1860

The active search languished for a hundred and fifty years until Edward Bruce, a writer for *Harper's New Monthly Magazine*, undertook an investigative report to retrace the footsteps of the first English colonists in North America, "Loungings in the Footprints of the Pioneers: II.—Raleigh and His City" (1860). By the early 1800s, the Roanoke colonies were becoming more and more a part of the literature and lore of the recently formed United States, to the extent that when President Monroe was brought to the area in 1819 to support work on re-opening Roanoke Inlet, he was taken to see what his local hosts identified as the remains of the 1580s fort (*Columbian Centinel* 1819:1; Powell 1965:23–25). Bruce's quest took him to the same area on the north end of Roanoke Island, as that much continued to remain in the historical memory of the area's residents.

Bruce was directed to the spot believed to be the colonists' old fort and reported along with an illustration titled "Site of Roanoke" depicting a hunter shooting at a deer, that "the trench is clearly traceable in a square of about forty yards each way. Midway of one side ... another trench, perhaps flanking the gate-way, runs in some fifteen or twenty feet. This is shown. And on the right of the same face of the enclosure, the corner is apparently thrown out in the form of a small bastion. The ditch is generally two feet deep, though in many places scarcely perceptible.... A fragment or two of stone or brick may be discovered in the grass, and then all is told of the existing relics of the city of Raleigh" (Bruce 1860:734–735). How this description jibes with those made later by Talcott Williams and J.C. Harrington would be a point of some contention.

Talcott Williams 1887, 1895

In 1887, Bruce was followed by another journalist, Talcott Williams, the son of missionaries proselytizing in the Middle East. He was educated in America, however, and upon graduation worked for three decades at the *Philadelphia Press* before becoming the first head of the Columbia School of Journalism. The Lost Colony was to hold a particular fascination for Williams throughout his career, and his investigations into its disappearance went beyond just reviewing the documents, but actually engaging in some archaeological excavation as well. He had read Bruce's article and found its depiction of the area to be less credible than John White's drawings of nearly three centuries earlier. Williams also remarked that, to the best of his knowledge prior to his survey and test excavations, the site had been disturbed only once: "During the occupation of the island by Federal soldiers in 1863 holes were dug in the embankment at the eastern angle and on the southeastern face" (Williams 1896:58). He stated that Union officers were notified and put a stop to the looting. He then opined that this was probably when an ax he had been shown was found.

Williams decided to revisit the site and see firsthand what was there. He noted that the brick and stone Bruce had seen were gone, but the earthworks were otherwise unchanged. It is worth quoting Williams' description at length to compare with what was later reconstructed based on subsequent excavations:

> It is a quadrangular embankment whose angles lie due north and south and east and west, so that the faces front southeast, northeast, northwest,

southwest. The mound, which is perfectly clear around the entire inclo-sure [*sic*], is two feet four inches high above the ditch at its most promi-nent point. The eastern angle has a slope of 23 feet on the angles and about 15 feet on the curtains and is broken by what was apparently a sally port crossing the southwest angle.... The four faces measure: The southeastern, 84.3 feet; the southwestern, 77.6 feet: the northwestern, 63.3 feet, and the northeastern, 73.9 feet. As the mound is irregular, these measurements are necessarily approximate. By measuring from points on the irregular slope farther in or farther out, different dimensions would be secured, but it was probably originally a square of 25 yards.

The eastern angle is a right angle, without any signs of a bastion

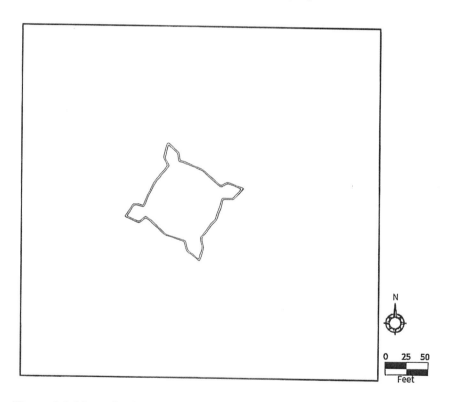

Figure 3.1: Map of Talcott Williams' 1895 Excavation. An approximate out-line of the earthworks on northern Roanoke Island as Talcott Williams described them: "It is a quadrangular embankment whose angles lie due north and south and east and west, so that the faces front southeast, north-east, northwest, southwest. The mound ... is two feet four inches high above the ditch at its most prominent point. The eastern angle has a slope of 23 feet on the angles and about 15 feet on the curtains and is broken by what was apparently a sally port crossing the southwest angle..." (1896:57). Each of the four sides is approximately 25 yards long. (From Keel 2003:121.)

whatever. Each face is broken by an angle about 15 to 18 feet across and pro-
jecting from the embankment line about 5 to 7 feet. The southern, western,
and northern angles are bastioned [1896:57–58].

So, where Bruce saw a 40-yard square earthwork, Williams saw a more
irregular series of embankments about 25 yards on a side (figure 3.1).
Much of this would be obliterated by Williams' subsequent excavations
and early attempts at reconstruction before a professional archaeologist
could view them.

Williams returned to Roanoke in 1895 and dug thirteen trenches
at the fort, most within the enclosure, though at least one outside the
western ditch. These were generally 5 feet long and 3 feet wide and dug
to an astonishing depth of 9 feet in places, although he claims to have
hit sterile sand by 4 feet below the surface. He was surprised at how few
artifacts were encountered, having only recovered a corroded nail and
some iron fragments as well as some native lithics and net-impressed
ceramics (Williams 1896:59). He tested the earthworks and found
them made of "heaped sand, the dark ashy layer curving over its slopes"
(Williams 1896:60). His excavations outside the earthworks revealed
nothing else and left him determining that the site must have been thoroughly looted in the distant past and not disturbed since, except for the
aborted looting by Union soldiers. At the conclusion of his excavations,
the earthworks were resurveyed and outlined with stone markers. Both
Bruce and Williams did not take their investigations any farther. They
accepted local lore that the earthworks were associated with the Roanoke colonists, and when they failed to find much in the way of corroborating evidence, simply rationalized that there was not much left to find
rather than calling the identification into question.

National Park Service

As mentioned previously, the earthwork at the north end of Roanoke Island has been associated with Raleigh's colonists since at least
the nineteenth century. Efforts to actively promote the site in the
national consciousness would begin in earnest by the end of that century, building off the attention that Williams had brought with his
excavations.

In 1894 the property containing the earthwork was owned by the
Dough family (longtime Roanoke residents), when the Roanoke Colony
Memorial Association acquired 260 acres that included what had come
to be known locally as Fort Raleigh. A monument, made from North

Carolina granite on a base of Virginia granite, was later erected in the center of the earthen enclosure, commemorating the colonists, specifically Virginia Dare. However, subsequent efforts to raise the visibility of the site, including the making of a 1921 silent movie concerning the Lost Colonists, were not very successful, and by 1934 all but a little over 16 acres were sold back into private ownership. In 1934 the remaining acreage was donated to the State of North Carolina to develop into an historic site.[1]

No further fieldwork had been undertaken since the conclusion of Williams' excavations at the end of the nineteenth century, but with the 350th anniversary of the Roanoke colonies looming between 1934 and 1937, statewide efforts to commemorate the 1580s colonies redoubled.

Figure 3.2: 1930s Log Structures Built to "Replicate" the 1580s Roanoke Colony Site. These were built on the remnant earthworks at Fort Raleigh, and the commemorative monument to Virginia Dare can be seen in front of the blockhouse, built using labor provided by the Civilian Conservation Corps, Civil Works Administration, and Works Progress Administration (CCC, CWA, and WPA). This photograph was taken September 15, 1936, by the WPA (1936, National Archives). For more pictures of Fort Raleigh in the 1930s, see "A New Deal for Fort Raleigh" (2017) at the *New Deal of the Day* website.

By 1937, the outdoor drama *The Lost Colony* was commissioned, and a fanciful recreation of the fort had been erected. The recreated site included "a palisaded, bastioned fort, with log blockhouse; several log cabins and a log chapel, all with thatched roofs; a palisaded enclosure around the entire tract, with log gatehouse at the entrance" (Harrington 1962:4; figure 3.2). The public relations campaign paid off. Negotiations with the Federal government coupled with the announcement that the nearby Cape Hatteras National Seashore would be created brought another presidential visit to Roanoke Island, this time by Franklin D. Roosevelt.

A.R. Kelly 1938

As the mechanism for the Federal acquisition of the property ground forward, historical and archaeological research into the site was re-instigated. The noted southeastern archaeologist A.R. Kelly undertook a small archaeological survey in 1938, but the results were inconclusive (Keel 2003:122). Meanwhile, the Fort Raleigh "reconstruction" had become a source of concern for the National Park Service as the kind of log-style construction used was inappropriate based on their own historical research. Fortuitously, a hurricane blew down the stockade posts in 1944, and the remaining log structures were removed as they began to fall apart. Unfortunately, subsequent archaeologists would have to deal with the footprint left by these reconstructions which had been sited over the original earthworks.

J.C. Harrington

SURVEYS 1947–49

Although World War II delayed the physical development of the new national park—officially coming under National Park Service administration as Fort Raleigh National Historic Site in 1941—historical research moved ahead. The findings of National Park Service historian Charles Porter III, which exposed the fanciful nature of the earlier reconstruction, prompted the National Park Service to engage J.C. "Pinky" Harrington to conduct archaeological research to inform an accurate reconstruction of the fortification and, if possible, to locate the main settlement. Aided by Porter's 1943 historical research, Harrington set forth to test the earthworks to see what remained of the original construction. This work would stand him in good stead as later he would conduct similar investigations at Fort Necessity in Pennsylvania.

There, as at Fort Raleigh, he was called upon to re-examine a conjectural reconstruction of a palisaded earthwork only to find a completely different configuration (Harrington 1957).

There were hurdles to be overcome. As Harrington wrote, "Throughout the work, interpretation of soil conditions was complicated by tree roots and the excavations for the [reconstructed] 1936 stockade and blockhouse, and to a lesser extent by the pits dug by Talcott Williams and the trench prepared for the 1921 movie" (Harrington 1962:9). Specifically, along with the thirteen trenches he had dug, Williams had set out stone markers along the earthwork to mark what he surveyed. Four decades later this outline was roughly followed when the log stockade was erected. Williams' excavations disturbed the deposits and had to be accounted for, and the recreated stockade was a trench dug into the site and posts placed within, further confusing the original deposits. To top it off, the set for the silent movie apparently impacted the site with a ditch as well. All this previous activity made Harrington's work of interpreting features in sandy soil that made soil color differences ephemeral extra challenging.

Harrington spent two years cross-trenching the by-then barely visible ditch and excavating into the area to the west of the earthworks, where he presumed the settlement to have been. In 1947 he gathered data to authenticate the site because there had been a suggestion that the earthwork was unrelated to the English colonists (Harrington 1962:49). Harrington also assessed the soil conditions and site formation processes in planning for the larger reconstruction project. The second year he had a better understanding of the stratigraphy and sediments and was able to better document Talcott Williams' excavations and to detail the shape and construction of the fort (Keel 2003:122).

It is interesting to note that what Harrington found did not exactly match what Williams saw a half century earlier (which was different from what Bruce saw decades before that). Williams mapped a four-sided fort with triangular bastions in the corners. Harrington saw a somewhat different configuration: two triangular bastions, to the north and east, a rounded bastion to the south, and an opening to the west. This was not unlike John White's watercolor of Ralph Lane's earthwork built in Puerto Rico in 1585, which historians had uncovered and was made known to Harrington (Sloan 2007:103; figure 3.3).

FORT EXCAVATION 1950

At the conclusion of his exploratory trenching, Harrington had determined to his satisfaction that the earthwork was associated with the Roanoke colonists, Ralph Lane's 1585–86 expedition to be precise,

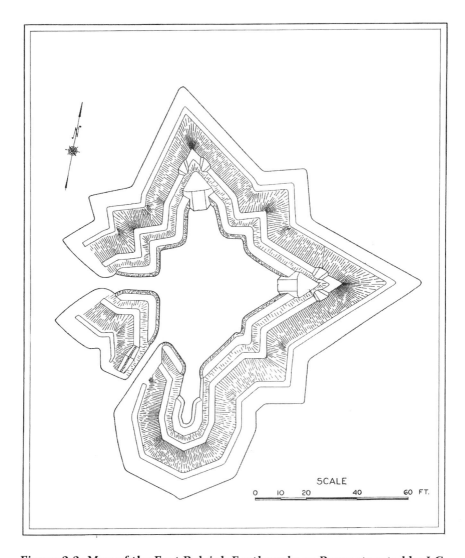

SCALE

0   10   20   40   60   FT.

Figure 3.3: Map of the Fort Raleigh Earthworks as Reconstructed by J.C. Harrington. The map shows how J.C. Harrington interpreted the earthworks at the Fort Raleigh National Historic Site following his 1947 excavations and rebuilt in 1951–1952. Compare to Talcott Williams' interpretation of the earthworks following his 1895 excavations as shown in Figure 3.1. (From Porter 1952: 34.)

and the Park Service made the decision to reconstruct the fort. To facilitate the reconstruction, "a complete excavation was carried out in 1950. First of all, the area inside the fort and beneath the parapet was excavated carefully, working alternate 10-foot trenches.... The ditch fill was removed very carefully, following the original slopes" (Harrington 1962:12–13). Harrington was unable to really determine what had been originally placed in the interior of the earthwork due to the disturbances created by a commemorative monument to Virginia Dare, the replica blockhouse, numerous tree roots, and Williams' previous test pits. Still, the earthworks were reconstructed in 1951–1952 based on Harrington's interpretations.

Harrington found very few artifacts within the confines of the earthwork. "These objects," Harrington wrote, "include one nearly complete iron sickle and possible fragments of a second, a carpenter's auger, several large wrought-iron spikes, a few wrought-iron nails, three latten casting counters, two copper nuggets, one glass bead, several fragments of Spanish olive jars, a portion of a majolica jar, one brick fragment, and a small piece of roofing tile" (Harrington 1962:17). It was hoped that excavations west of the earthwork (the entrance to the reconstructed earthwork was along its western wall) would turn up evidence of the "Cittie of Raleigh" where the colonists would have actually lived. It should also be noted that when White returned to Roanoke in 1587, they repaired and reused the houses that Lane's colonists had left. This would have been the palisaded town that White saw in 1590 with "Croatoan" carved on one of the posts, palisades that weren't there when he left in 1587.

Elizabethan Gardens 1953

An opportunity to test outside of the earthworks came the following year when the privately-owned Elizabethan Gardens was being developed. In 1953, Harrington put in 5' wide trenches of varying length in all directions around the earthworks, an impressive 3,320 linear feet in all. The test trenches were excavated as far away as the grounds of the Elizabethan Gardens. Few artifacts were found, but Harrington was able to gain a good understanding of the stratigraphy of the area: "It was soon discovered that almost the entire area was covered by a moderately recent deposit of wind-blown sand. This deposit is several feet deep in the dune area paralleling the shore, but even the thinner deposit successfully sealed off the older original topsoil" (Harrington 1962:35). After the sand level had been removed, Harrington went over the trenches with a metal detector, but found little other than a few nails. The Roanoke settlement remained elusive.

Outwork Excavation 1965

It was another dozen years before more excavations were done. The accidental discovery of old brick during the installation of a waterline to the fort prompted Harrington to return for a final season at Fort Raleigh in 1965. Excavations just outside the west entrance to the earthen enclosure revealed a rectangular structure with interior pits. European and native ceramics and bricks were recovered. Harrington interpreted this as an English structure of some kind and that one of the pits may have been associated with a forge (Harrington 1966). Park historian Phil Evans would later notice the resemblance of this "structure" to flankers at the 1619 fort at Martin's Hundred in Virginia (Evans et al. 2016:24).

Later NPS

In 1982, under the direction of John Ehrenhard, National Park Service archaeologists used remote sensing (proton magnetometer, resistivity, and aerial & infrared photography) to determine if the "outwork" was part of a larger structure. The archaeologists discovered several anomalies, suggesting parallel rows of houses. Unfortunately, none of these anomalies panned out during ground-truthing excavations. Phosphate analysis also proved inconclusive. The following year, Ehrenhard, and later Jack Walker, expanded the survey, but further digging (1120 sq. ft.) found very little (Keel 2003:123).

Meanwhile, while walking the north shore of the island, Evans spotted two interesting features in the surf. He interpreted both as wells—one was lined with a barrel, the other formed from a hollow log. Radiocarbon dates placed their use as the late sixteenth century (National Park Service 2011). This discovery would cause many to believe that the settlement had been lost to erosion off the north shore of the island, though repeated underwater surveys have failed to confirm this hypothesis.

Virginia Company Foundation

Even after two additional decades of fruitless NPS archaeology at the site, the enigmatic "outwork" still beckoned archaeologists. In 1989, Audrey and Ivor Noël Hume reanalyzed artifacts recovered by Harrington in 1965 and concluded they had been misidentified. What had originally been classified as eighteenth-century types were reinterpreted as sixteenth-century utilitarian wares associated with metallurgy (Noël Hume 1994:76, 1996:107). In 1991, Noël Hume, operating under the auspices of the Virginia Company Foundation, opened a trench and three units near Harrington's 1965 excavations to follow up on the "outwork."[2] Based on the artifacts previously recovered and reidentified, Noël Hume had doubts about the interpretation of the structure as part of the fortifications. Despite encountering many instances of modern disturbance, additional sixteenth-century artifacts were recovered, such as crucible fragments, sherds of Normandy flasks and native ceramics, as well as evidence of a forge, e.g., charcoal deposits and shaped bricks (Noël Hume 1994:79, 1996:109).

By the end of 1992, Noël Hume was convinced that the earthwork was *not* Ralph Lane's fort nor had it anything to do with the Lost Colonists. This was based on the stratigraphic position of sixteenth-century material underneath the fortification and that the ditch surrounding the fort cut through the "outwork." The fort also appears on two late eighteenth-century maps, but not on two earlier maps of the region (Noël Hume 1994:86, 1996:109). While suggesting that the earthworks themselves were built in the eighteenth-century, Noël Hume reinterpreted the "outwork" as an early science center, used by Joachim Ganz during the 1585–1586 expedition to assay ore samples in the colonists' quest for precious metal.

The Virginia Company Foundation, now under the direction of William Kelso, undertook its final work at Fort Raleigh in 1994–1995. Further excavations outside the earthwork revealed nothing of interest. A survey of the eastern woods next to the Hariot Nature Trail recovered two sherds of Spanish olive jar, a crucible sherd, English pipe bowl fragments, and numerous sherds of Colington type native ceramics in a deeply buried stratum (Luccketti 1996:23).[3] No features were uncovered, though, and work ceased—and the Virginia Company essentially ceased as well.

First Colony Foundation

A decade later a couple of the core constituents of the Virginia Company reconstituted as the First Colony Foundation (FCF). Their first Roanoke undertaking was by underwater archaeologist Gordon Watts west of the Prince House Woods on the east end of Fort Raleigh National Historic Site in 2005 and in Shallowbag Bay in 2007. The aim was to find evidence of the settlement if it had fallen victim to erosion. However, the surveys only recovered prehistoric as well as some post–sixteenth-century historic ceramic sherds (Watts 2008).

In 2008 the FCF archaeologists returned to the Hariot Nature Trail to reexamine the buried sixteenth-century land surface. The first year they were accompanied by the PBS television program *Time Team America*.[4] Even the celebrated Time Team failed to find definitive evidence of the Cittie of Raleigh. Three seasons of work produced little in the way of features, but did recover some historic artifacts, including

Venetian glass beads, two copper aglets (lacing tips), and sherds of Martincamp flask and Olive Jar. The prize find was fourteen copper squares which appear to have been strung into a necklace. The FCF archaeologists found this to be "persuasive evidence that this area of the Thomas Hariot Nature Trail Woods was the site of some type as yet unidentified activity by Raleigh's Roanoke colonists" (Evans et al. 2016: iii). Yet work ceased there at the end of the 2010 season. Since that time, there have been small excavations conducted by NPS archaeologists, mainly for cultural resource management (CRM) compliance purposes,[5] but no compelling evidence beyond a few small artifacts possibly dating to the sixteenth century has been recovered.

So where does that leave us? No settlement site has been found—connected with Ralph Lane's 1585–1586 colony and/or with the 1587 planters. The property owned by the Park Service, certainly the area immediately surrounding the earthwork, has been thoroughly excavated, and while sparse signs of sixteenth-century activity have been found, no remains of a settlement. Perhaps a different strategy is in order? If archaeology hasn't shown where the Lost Colony left from, can it find where they went?

Site X

In early 2012, a First Colony Foundation board member, Brent Lane, noticed that John White's *La Virginea Pars* map had been patched in two places. Curious as to what the patch covered, he requested that the British Museum place the map on a light table to see if there was anything underneath to be revealed. The southern patch appeared to be a simple redrafting of the coastline, but the northern patch concealed a symbol that looked like it might be a fort. This fort-like symbol was located at the west end of the Albemarle Sound at the confluence of the Cashie River and Salmon Creek (Ambers et al. 2012; Lawler 2018).

FCF archaeologists mobilized on the information and revisited a site that archaeologist Nick Luccketti had recorded in 2007 in the vicinity of the "patch." The site had yielded both prehistoric and historic artifacts. Although some of the historic artifacts were clearly post–sixteenth-century, there were some green-glazed coarse earthenwares that might date to the Elizabethan Period. This ceramic type, known as Surrey-Hampshire Border Ware, had also been found at Jamestown. It declines in popularity during the late sixteenth century and disappears from the archaeological record by the mid–seventeenth century.

Excavations at the site from 2012 to 2014 yielded over two dozen sherds of the Border Ware, a couple of tenterhooks (for stretching hides), and various other artifacts of uncertain age: an aglet (lacing tip), a priming pan (for a musket), a buckle fragment, and a bale seal. And though no evidence of structures was found, the assemblage clearly spoke of prolonged residence in the area. However, as at the Cape Creek site on Hatteras Island (discussed below), there appear to be two components at Site X, an early prehistoric occupation and a later historic presence. Whether a sixteenth-century component can be defined depends upon the acceptance of the Surrey-Hampshire Border Ware as a marker for this time period. Though the State of North Carolina acquired the property as a state nature preserve, partly for its historic value, the FCF made the decision to suspend further excavation. Their interpretation was that Site X may have represented a small outpost for the Lost Colonists who later continued up Salmon Creek (Evans et al. 2015; "Salmon Creek State Natural Area" n.d.).

In 2019 the FCF archaeologists revisited a nearby previously recorded site and reinterpreted some of the ceramics as dating to the late sixteenth and/or early seventeenth centuries. Further investigation turned up more early European ceramics but no structural features. Dubbed Site Y, this has been interpreted as a small group of Lost Colonists living perhaps in temporary quarters (Evans et al. 2020).

Meanwhile, other archaeologists have been looking elsewhere.

Archaeology of Hatteras Island

John White claimed the 1587 colonists left him a clue when they carved "Croatoan" on a post of their palisade, and the territory of the Croatoan Indians has been identified by historians as the southern end of Hatteras Island (Quinn 1991[1955]:616). Yet surprisingly little archaeology has taken place on Hatteras Island. Even less has been published. The lack of archaeological research may be due to the fact that much of the island is transitory, with numerous inlets opening and closing over time, making the presence of archaeological sites fleeting. On the southern portion of the island, the area known as Buxton Woods is one of the few geographically stable areas along the Outer Banks.

The Outer Banks became a serious contender in the Lost Colony derby in 1938. It was just after the 350th anniversary celebrations of Roanoke Colonies, including the first production of *The Lost Colony* in 1937. This was followed by the discovery of the Dare Stones, which allegedly told the tale of the Lost Colonists' demise (discussed in depth in Chapter 6). Popular and scholarly interest in the Lost Colony was as high as it had ever been. When it became evident that there was serious interest in establishing a National Seashore on Hatteras Island, preliminary archaeological investigations were initiated by the National Park Service. These investigations, although limited in scope, gave some indications of the archeological content of the region. Joffre Coe, who founded the Laboratory of Anthropology at the University of North Carolina at Chapel Hill, conducted a minor survey near Buxton on Hatteras Island. It was at this time that the Cape Creek site was found and recorded as 31DR1 (Heath 2012).[6] Cape Creek was the first site recorded for not just Hatteras Island, but all of Dare County. This later became identified as the village of Croatan. Curiously, no further investigation was undertaken for over a decade.

Haag Survey

Beginning in 1954, William Haag of Louisiana State University undertook an archeological program on the Outer Banks that had two purposes. The first was to delve into the Indian past and reconstruct an occupation of the region from the earliest times until what he termed "the dispersal of Indian culture by white men." Second, evidence of the Lost Colony was to be sought. Haag plainly stated in his report that "in this latter endeavor there was no success" (Haag 1958:155). He did, however, revisit the Cape Creek site and claimed it was the best midden found on the Outer Banks. Despite the seemingly meager deposits (the midden was about a foot thick, but overlain by 1 to 5 feet of sand), the extensiveness of the site suggested a large population. But at that time, he saw no evidence for contact with the Lost Colonists or, indeed, any Europeans (Haag 1958). Another thirty years passed before archaeologists returned to this area.

Croatan Project

Following up on Bill Haag's work, David Phelps, professor of anthropology at East Carolina University, tested the Cape Creek site in 1983. Phelps' research focused on the Carolina Algonquian peoples encountered by English explorers in 1584–1585 as part of an "America's 400th Anniversary" research project. He re-confirmed that a buried stratum with rich archaeological material evidence of early Croatan habitation activities still remained partially intact on the eroding eastern end of the site (Phelps 1996–1998).

A decade later, after hurricane Emily exposed more of the site in 1995, local residents Fred Willard and Barbara Midgett were able to entice Phelps back out for three weeks. He observed the intact Coling-ton period (AD 800–1600) midden on this brief visit and felt the site warranted further work. With the support of East Carolina University students, numerous volunteers, local landowners and various businesses, formal excavations began in 1995 (Heath 2012). Phelps established the Coastal Archaeology Office at ECU to serve as the administrative center for the project and, after securing emeritus status, decided to devote his retirement to this project.

Work continued during the summer of 1997. Among the more interesting finds was what Phelps called a "workshop area." In addition to fire pit features, a number of artifacts were found near the workshop, including eight tiny rings seemingly made from bird bones. "I've not found anything like this," Phelps is quoted saying in the *ECU Report*. "They were probably ornamental, but they are totally unusual" (Gray 1997). The recovery of a partial bust of a male figure made of copper was interpreted to be an example of the Croatoan Indians using European materials for their own purposes.

Another interesting find was two copper farthings. One was complete and the other cut in half. Both had holes drilled in them, which could have meant they were meant to be suspended from a cord and worn as a necklace. The surface of the complete coin was worn; however it was possible to make out the word CAROLUS on the other, referring to Charles II of England. This would indicate that the farthings were minted in the 1670s, during Charles II's reign. Peach pits were also recovered from the midden and may indicate trade with other Native Americans in the region or with the Spanish, who introduced peaches to the Americas and were growing them in Florida as early as the seventeenth century. Another area of the site revealed post molds, where it was suggested that fish smoking or food storage occurred (Heath 2012).

Though at the time Phelps did not publicly state that the Cape Creek site was where the Lost Colony went after it abandoned the fort on Roanoke Island, he did believe the Croatan inhabitants were in contact with the settlers. "The Native Americans of this area were at least trading with the English—if not living with some of the Lost Colonists," the June 15 *Virginian-Pilot* quotes Phelps as saying. "This is certainly part of the Lost Colony story" (DeGregory 1997:A1).

According to Charles Heath, who supervised much of the work as an ECU graduate student, the Cape Creek site midden is clearly separated into two distinct occupations. The uppermost stratum contained both Native-produced artifacts and objects of European origin (Heath 2012) as well as plant and animal refuse. The artifacts that could be securely dated placed the occupation in the early Colonial Period (ca.

AD 1670–1720). The lower stratum, which was separated from the upper stratum by sterile sand, also contained animal bone, but only prehistoric Indian pottery and artifacts. The earlier occupation appeared to have accumulated over an extended period of time. Radiocarbon dating placed that stratum between AD 870 and 1445. There is no occupation layer that can be solidly dated to the sixteenth century.

Heath (2012) notes that "of particular interest is the quantity of European-origin artifacts from the upper midden stratum and several fire pits features, which include, lead musket shot in various calibers, native-made gunflints and English-made gun spalls, glass bottle fragments and ceramic sherds (English, Dutch, German), cut brass and cut copper artifacts, and various iron tools (awls, chisels, punches, wedges)." Many of the European-produced objects, some which Heath thought were salvaged from shipwrecks, "were modified and used by Hatteras Indians for their own purposes."

The datable artifacts recovered by Phelps include glass trade beads (a review of bead sequences for the Northeast and Southeast regions indicates that the bead sample from the Cape Creek site is post–1650), English copper coins (Charles II Farthings, ca. 1672–1679), seventeenth-century European pottery sherds (delft, slipware, Rhenish stoneware, etc.), mid–seventh- to early-eighteenth-century clothing buttons, lead bale seals associated with the reign of Charles II (1660–1685), as well as a Lluellin Evans pipe bowl fragment which was produced ca. 1661–1688 (see, e.g., Noël Hume 1969; Magoon 1999). It is important to note that these artifacts were actually produced during the seventeenth century and could not have arrived at the site any earlier.

Two European artifacts have garnered the most attention due to their believed connection to the Lost Colony. A gunlock recovered at the site in 1999 is an English snaphance mechanism (Godwin 2006), likely representing, in Heath's view, one of the earliest European guns traded to Coastal Algonquian Indians in eastern North Carolina. Since no other identifiable gun parts were recovered in the excavation unit where the lock was found, Heath believed the mechanism must have been removed from the original weapon sometime before it was discarded in the activity area associated with the midden. In other areas of the site, the upper midden has consistently yielded a diverse array of mid- to late seventeenth and early eighteenth-century European-origin artifacts.

In early October of 1998, Phelps recovered the other artifact, the one that became for many people the smoking gun evidence connecting the Cape Creek site to the 1587 colonists. Phelps's excavations recovered what he believed to be a signet ring from Cape Creek. The shank of the ring had been broken, and the edges were turned under after the shank was either damaged or purposely cut. On the ring's face was a side view of an English lion (figure 3.4). The ring was buffed clean and shown to a local jeweler, whose casual assessment led Phelps to suggest that the artifact was 10+-carat gold and manufactured in the late

Figure 3.4: The Brass "Signet" Ring. Found at the Cape Creek site on Hatteras Island by David Phelps in 1998, it was originally assumed to be a gold ring bearing a signet—a personal seal—belonging to one of two men associated with the English expeditions of 1585–1586. Later testing showed it to be a brass ring used for trade rather than being associated with any specific English family and making it less likely to be associated with the 1580s Roanoke expeditions than originally assumed (Special Collections, East Carolina University 1600–1650). Image courtesy of Special Collections, East Carolina University.

sixteenth century (Phelps 1996–1998). Because many such designs were based on coats of arms, it was hoped that the ring's original owner could be traced. Signet rings had been found at Jamestown and elsewhere, but most of those were made of brass. Because this ring was thought to be gold, it was hypothesized that it was most likely originally owned by a gentleman. Perhaps the ring was given to a Native American who lived at Croatoan or was left there by an English settler.

The following year, research by a local avocational historian connected the ring to the Kendall family. An article in the *Virginian-Pilot* related, "[T]he probable owner of a 16th-century gold ring unearthed in October has been narrowed down to one of two men who came to the Outer Banks before the infamous Lost Colony arrived on Roanoke Island. Even though the ring's wearer almost certainly had nothing to do with the 1587 settlement that mysteriously vanished, the rare personal link to American history is still considered an important Elizabethan artifact" (Kozak 1999).

It was proposed that the rampant lion crest was most likely associated with the Kendall family. According to historical documents, there were two Kendalls associated with the Roanoke voyages. The first was a "Master Kendall" with the 1585–1586 Lane expedition. The second, Abraham Kendall, was one of Sir Francis Drake's officers, with the fleet that came to resupply the Grenville colony in 1586. Neither of these Kendalls was part of the 1587 Lost Colony settlement group (Quinn 1991[1955]; "Family Crest on Sixteenth-Century Gold Ring Tentatively Identified" 1998; "Croatan Fall Season Uncovers Important Finds" 1999). There were several other Kendalls in early colonial America, including one at the Jamestown settlement as early as 1607. Whoever owned the ring, it was recovered in refuse deposits stratigraphically-associated with late seventeenth- and early eighteenth-century European trade artifacts.

For all the speculation, later research disproved the earlier claims. Science writer Andrew Lawler, who was working on his own book about the Lost Colony (Lawler 2018), asked Charlie to re-examine the ring using an XRF device, which determined it to be brass, not gold. Further research on the crest indicated that the ring was unlikely to be associated with the Kendall family. Especially because the image was cast, not engraved, it appears likely that the ring was intended for trade and not associated with any noble family (Ewen and Farrell 2019).

Following Phelps's digs in the 1990s, Charles Heath and Clay Swindell were contracted in 2006 by Fred Willard of the Lost Colony Center for Science and Research (a private research group) to explore beyond the confines of Phelps' previous excavations. With permission from several landowners, the search team conducted a six-site survey, gridding possible locations, shovel testing as deep as possible, and recording what they recovered. Two sites yielded significant evidence of prehistoric activity. At one, several large sherds of late Colington pottery were found. From the second, archaeologists recovered late seventeenth-century material from a shell midden. At this second site, archaeologists also uncovered evidence of a brick house built around 1700. The remaining sites produced no artifacts and were deemed "culturally sterile" (Charles Heath: Personal communication 2006).

Heath felt that the midden area at the Cape Creek site was not a habitation, but rather a trading station, because there was no real evidence of structures. Posts identified at the first site could not be plotted in any recognizable shape. Most likely the Croatoan were living in Buxton Woods and that the shoreline site was used seasonally.

University of Bristol

Several years would pass before another archaeologist resumed investigations at Cape Creek. At the behest of Andy Powell (then mayor of Bideford, England—a town with historic ties to the Lost Colony) and local Buxton historian Scott Dawson, University of Bristol students and many local volunteers under the supervision of Dr. Mark Horton excavated for annual three-week seasons from 2010 through 2017. As with much of the previous work, there are no formal publications and descriptions of the work, and findings come from newspaper accounts, websites, and personal observation.[7]

As an archaeologist, Charlie's personal observations based on site visits suggest that the same two components that Heath discerned were present at Horton's site (i.e., a late prehistoric and a seventeenth- to eighteenth-century historical component). More artifacts manufactured in the sixteenth and seventeenth centuries but deposited no earlier than the seventeenth have been recovered, including a rapier handle, a drawing slate and pencil, a seventeenth-century Nuremburg token, several beads, copper fragments, a seventeenth-century coin weight, and seventeenth- and eighteenth-century European ceramics fragments (Croatoan Archaeological Society 2020; Lawler 2018). This was accompanied by a large amount of Colington type pottery and faunal remains. Again, these sixteenth-century artifacts were mixed with mid–seventeenth-century artifacts in the upper stratum, which means they could have been deposited no earlier than the mid–seventeenth century.

Horton's interpretation was that a number of the colonists left

Roanoke Island and gradually assimilated with the local Croatoan: "They are living as Native Americans, but we're finding material culture to suggest they are wearing clothes and living a partly European lifestyle.... If you can explain the social context, then it suddenly makes sense. The things we are finding are not those they would be trading from Jamestown anyway!" (Lawler 2018:195–197). Clearly there is some form of contact between Natives and Europeans going on at the Cape Creek site. But is it the Lost Colonists or is it later?

Invoking Occam's Razor, a more parsimonious explanation is that the European items are trade items from the ships passing up the coast. The Gulf Stream was used by every ship returning from the Caribbean or Florida to Europe. North Carolina is where the ships would turn east. Ships preparing to head back to Europe would, no doubt, stop to resupply with food and fresh water. Trade with the native inhabitants at this time would be advantageous to both sides. What the altered artifacts represent may not necessarily be the integrated colonists slowly being assimilated into the native culture, but could show the native people repurposing the European artifacts for their own uses.

Without any significant find of artifacts that could at best possibly—and not even probably—be connected with the 1587 colonists, the question archaeologists should be posing prior to investigating a Lost Colony site candidate is, "What, exactly, would be good archaeological evidence for the colonists? What should we be looking for?" There are a couple of good indicators that archaeologists have used investigating other contact period sites. Evidence of European-style structures—rectangular rooms with evidence of sawn timbers (flat bottoms of posts) and iron fasteners. An array of sixteenth century or earlier European artifacts. And probably most definitive, European, Christian-style, individual burials (extended in an east-west orientation) that can be positively dated to the sixteenth century. This kind of evidence has been elusive, but given the sparse and ambiguous nature of the historical record, archaeological evidence such as this will be the only way to test and confirm the hypotheses presented in this volume. As such, this evidence is entirely lacking.

PART II

What We Think We Know

4

From Histories to Stories
Becoming The *Lost Colony*

By the mid–1620s, the main texts from which people have drawn clues about the fate of the 1587 colonists had all been written, and most had been published. Belief that the colonists had survived and moved to Croatoan as expressed in the narrative of the 1590 voyage had changed. By 1624, John Smith had killed off the colonists, stating, "was never any of them found, nor seene to this day" (1986[1624]:2:88). Meanwhile, by 1625, Purchas had also killed off the 1587 colonists, but attributed their demise to Powhatan, adding the complicating twist that Smith, who had once again written that he didn't know how the colonists had died, was the source for information about their slaughter.

As for clues from material culture about the 1587 colonists, nothing has brought the colonists back to life from the death blows dealt by Smith and Purchas. No evidence of European-style structures or recovered non-trade item artifacts unambiguously datable to the sixteenth century have been found beyond Roanoke Island. And yet to be found is the almost ironic main archaeological evidence to show if the 1587 colonists survived, and if so where they went—signs of death, i.e., European Christian–style burials in a sixteenth-century context. Therefore, instead of solid history, discussions of what happened to Raleigh's planters after August of 1587 are speculations based on the limited, questionable, and sometimes contradictory evidence.

Starting in the late seventeenth century, most writers who addressed the ultimate fate of Raleigh's planters (and many who wrote about the 1580s Roanoke expeditions did not address the issue) followed Smith's and Purchas's leads until the early nineteenth century. With a few exceptions, histories killed off the colonists sometime between 1587 and 1607, presenting two main scenarios to explain what happened to the 1587 colonists—they either starved for lack of resupply or were killed by Native Americans. Only rarely did a writer suggest the colonists had integrated with Native Americans. In the seventeenth and eighteenth centuries, if a writer addressed the issue at all, the ultimate fate of the 1587 planters was presented with a sense of certainty. Not until the first half of the nineteenth century did Raleigh's 1587 planters become *the* Lost Colony.

"Starved or Killed by Indians": Seventeenth-, Eighteenth- and Early Nineteenth-Century Histories

Interestingly, one of the only seventeenth-century histories of British colonization in the Americas to mention the 1587 colonists doesn't use any of these three scenarios. Instead, in his 1670 *A True and Faithful Account of the Four Chiefest Plantations of the English in America* (i.e., Virginia, New England, Bermuda, and Barbados), Samuel Clarke opens with Virginia and the 1580s Roanoke expeditions. Clarke wraps up by writing, "This *Manteo* was afterwards Baptized, and by Sr. *Walter Rawleigh* was made Lieutenant of *Roanock*. Here also Mrs. *Dare* the Governours Daughter was delivered of a Daughter, that was Baptized by the name of *Virginia. Aug.* the 27. they departed and returned into *England*" (4). Similar to, maybe even borrowing from, George Abbot's *A Briefe Description of the Whole World* (the latest edition of which had come out in 1664), Clarke has Raleigh's 1587 planters returning to England rather than being left behind. Still, as in most seventeenth- and eighteenth-century accounts, Clarke saw no mystery about what happened to Raleigh's 1587 colonists.

Two early eighteenth-century works illustrate the more typical presentations of the 1587 colonists' non-mysterious fate: Robert Beverley's *The History and Present State of Virginia* (1705) and John Oldmixon's *The British Empire in America, Containing the History of the Discovery, Settlement, Progress and Present State of All the British Colonies, on the Continent and Islands of America* (1708).

Beverley's history of Virginia opens with the story of Raleigh's 1580s colonization efforts, from the Amadas and Barlowe expedition to John White's 1590 return and even to the early 1600s pre–Jamestown voyages. Beverley tells about John White's finding the Croatoan carvings but being unable to look for the colonists because of the storms. Beverley then adds what was becoming a standard explanation of the colonists' fate: "And it is supposed, that the *Indians* seeing them forsaken by their Country, and unfurnish'd of their expected Supplies, cut them off: For to this Day they were never more heard of" (2013[1705]:19).

Similarly, in *The British Empire in America*, Oldmixon writes about the Croatoan carvings and the storms making it impossible to travel to Croatoan. As for what happened to the colonists, Oldmixon writes: "There were no more Attempts to find and relieve the 115 Men Mr. *White* left at *Roenoke* for sixteen Years following; and what became of them God only knows, for they were never heard of to this Day. 'Tis suppos'd the Indians seeing them forsaken by their Countrymen, fell upon them and destroy'd them" (1708:1:217). The parallels in language imply that Oldmixon used Beverley as his source about the colonists' fate (though differing details in other parts show Beverley was not Oldmixon's only source).[1] And both admit the hypotheses they give for what happened to the 1587 colonists are suppositions without proof—that they died because the local Indians, seeing them cut off from England, starved them out by not supplying the colonists themselves or attacked and killed them—but no other possibilities are given, and discovering what really happened doesn't seem to matter.

Even so, by repeating Beverley's idea that the Native Americans brought about the ruin of the 1587 colony—either starving out the colonists or physically attacking them—Oldmixon starts the historiographic process of turning a possible explanation into accepted historical "fact." An important historiographic issue is reification, when a supposition is repeated frequently enough that it starts being treated as fact. A brief Roanoke colonization example of reification comes from Hariot's *Briefe and True Report*. The first item Hariot lists as a marketable commodity is "Silke of grasse or grasse Silke" (Quinn 1991[1955]:1:325). In a footnote to his 1955 edition of Hariot's work, David Beers Quinn discusses the type of plant Hariot would have meant by silk grass, concluding that "*Y[ucca] filamentosa* appears the most likely species in this instant" (Quinn 1991[1955]:1:325, n.4).

One common name for *Yucca filamentosa* is *spoonleaf yucca*, and that is how some people have identified Hariot's silk grass since. Included among these identifications is the National Park Service on their signage along the Thomas Hariot Nature Trail in the Fort Raleigh National Historic Site. And that is where Tom saw the identification and began repeating it in some of his own writing, including his PhD dissertation (Shields 1990:138) as well as a later essay on exploration literature (Shields 2005:360). Through repetition, what Quinn *thought* Hariot meant reified to become what Hariot *did* mean.

As discussed in Chapter 2, repetition of an idea not only gives it the chance to become reified as a truth but at the same time allows it to become a trope. Repetition of the statement that Native Americans either cut off any assistance or else openly attacked the 1587 colonists when no English resupply arrived implies Native Americans are not to be trusted. The implication matters not only because it explains what happened to the 1587 colonists but because both Beverley and Old-mixon were involved in the continuing English colonization of early eighteenth-century North America. Oldmixon promoted colonization from England and Beverley from his position as a colonist, "a *Native* and *Inhabitant* of the *Place*," as given on the title page of *The History and Present State of Virginia.*

Aside from the "attacked by Indians" trope, both works develop a second Roanoke colonization-related trope. After describing the 1602, 1603, and 1605 voyages to North America sent by the English, Beverley writes:

> In all these latter Voyages, they never so much as endeavour'd to come near the Place where the first Settlement was attempted at Cape *Hattoras*; nei-ther had they any Pity on those poor Hundred and Fifteen Souls settled there in 1587 of whom there had never since been any Account, no Relief sent to them, nor so much as any Enquiry made after them, whether they were dead or alive.... So strong was the Desire of Riches, and so eager the Pursuit of a rich Trade, that all Concern for the Lives of their fellow Chris-tians, Kindred, Neighbours and Country-men, weigh'd nothing in the Comparison; tho' an Enquiry might have been easily made, when they were so near them [2013(1705):20].

According to Beverley, the pre–Jamestown voyages failed the 1587 colo-nists because of avarice, because of greed. Using comparable language, Oldmixon writes about the 1605 George Weymouth expedition: "They had forgot the 115 Men whom Mr. *White* had left at *Roenoke*: Their Pity was too weak for their Avarice, Trade and Profit was all they thought of..." (1708:1:220). Like Beverley, Oldmixon turns the failure of these expeditions searching for Raleigh's planters on Hatteras Island into a symbol of greed, of people's inability to put aside personal desires to help those who came before. Though in a different form than in *East-ward Ho!*, these early eighteenth-century histories also use pre–James-town Virginia as a trope for avarice. And, interestingly, neither Beverley nor Oldmixon discuss the Jamestown attempts to find out what hap-pened to the 1587 colonists.

Beverley and Oldmixon illustrate the basics of how the Roa-noke colonies were seen from the mid-seventeenth to the early nine-teenth centuries. The colonists died because Native Americans of the region saw that the colonists had been abandoned. The cause of death was either that the Native Americans abandoned the colonists as well, leaving them to starve, or else they attacked the colonists outright. From White's 1590 final return to Roanoke Island to the 1607 founding of Jamestown, any purported attempts to find the Roanoke colonists are portrayed as half-hearted at best, turning them into tropes about human avarice.

To illustrate, three British histories of the 1730s repeat one or both of these tropes. About dying from a lack of supplies and harsh treatment by Native Americans, John Brickell writes in his 1737 *The Natural History of North-Carolina*, "The first Settlement of this Country was made in Queen Elizabeth's time, by Sir *Walter Raleigh* and others, at *Roanoke*, in *Albemarle* County; but continued not long, either by Sickness or other Misfortunes, or by the Barbarity of the *Indians*, who were very numerous and powerful in those Days..." (9). And in 1735, Fayrer Hall's *A Short Account of the First Settlement of the Provinces of Virginia, Maryland, New-York, New-Jersey, and Pennsylvania by the English* states, "Hence we may suppose that the Indians thus seeing them forsaken and neglected by their Country, cut them off; for to this Day were never more heard of" (5). Hall then goes on to write about the early seventeenth-century voyages' not searching for Raleigh's planters: "During all these Voyages, not the least Search or Enquiry was made after those poor People that were left by Mr. *White*, which might easily have been done, considering how near they were to them; but so much did private Interest prevail over the Love of, or Concern for our Countrymen" (6).

Most fully, in 1737, Thomas Salmon published Volume 30 of his *Modern History; or, the Present State of All Nations* (1725–1738), the volume that covers Virginia. Salmon treats everything from Raleigh's original patent to John White's return in 1590, noting that the 1590 expedition "found, by some Inscriptions cut on the Trees and Beams of the Houses, that the Colony was remov'd to the Island of *Croatan*" (1724–1738:30:411), but that because of dangerous weather, "they sail'd directly to *England*, and left the Colony to shift for themselves; and whether they were famish'd, or cut in pieces by the *Indians*, or perish'd in attempting to get home by Sea, I could never learn, for they have not been heard of from that Day to this" (1724–1738:30:412). Salmon amplifies the tropes found in Beverley and Oldmixon by repeating them and then adding a new possibility—a failed attempt to sail back to England.

Salmon does not puzzle about the fate of the colonists—one of these three options *must* be what happened. More important to Salmon is the second subject of Roanoke colonization tropes—assigning blame for the 1587 colony's failure. For Salmon, the blame rests solidly on what he sees as the courtier Raleigh's avaricious shoulders. After writing that the planters were starved, killed in an Indian attack, or drowned, Salmon states, "This must render People exceeding cautious how they engage in such Enterprizes on the Faith and Promises of Courtiers to support them. The Safety of the State, a Project of more Importance, or the Prospect of gaining greater Treasures another way, are too often thought sufficient Reasons for abandoning our distressed Friends..." (1724–1738:30:412). Salmon continues by saying that as soon as the threat of the Spanish Armada was over, Raleigh

> might, surely, have re-inforc'd his Colony, or brought them back, considering the Figure he then made in the Court of *England* and the royal Navy: But I doubt, the Capture of the Galleons, the plunder of *Cades*, and the Gold Mines of *Guiana*, which he went in search of soon after, put the *Virginian* Colony too much out of his Head, after he found himself disappointed in his principal View of possessing Mountains of Gold in *Virginia* [1724–1738:30:412].

Making sure readers don't miss the point, Salmon adds, "Thus it appears but too evident, that Sir *Walter Raleigh*'s expectations of discovering immense treasures in *Guiana* were in a great measure the ruin of our first attempts to settle colonies in *Virginia*" (1724–1738:30:414). The question of the eighteenth century was not what happened to Raleigh's 1587 planters, but why it happened.

A sense that what happened to the 1587 planters was not a mystery can be seen in many of the histories that followed, published in a variety of places. From Williamsburg, Virginia, William Stith wrote in *The History of the First Discovery and Settlement of Virginia* (1747) that the group who took over Raleigh's rights to the Virginia colony "made no farther Search, nor gave themselves any other Trouble about the Matter; but these poor Souls were basely deserted by them, and left a Prey to the barbarous Savages, neither were they ever seen or heard of afterwards" (28).

Six years later, from Boston, William Douglass wrote in his 1753 second volume of *A Summary, Historical and Political, of the First Planting, Progressive Improvements, and Present State of the British Settlements in North-America*, about "the poor Settlers, to whom no Visit was attempted for the 16 following Years, and perhaps cut off by the Indians, being never heard of afterwards" (1749–1753:2:386). In the London-published *A Concise Account of North America* (1765), Robert Rogers states that "it is presumed, they all either perished with hunger, or were destroyed by the savages, as none of them was ever heard of afterwards..." (94–95).

Again from London, John Huddleston Wynne writes in his 1770

A General History of the British Empire in America, "The settlers were left to themselves, and perished to a man, by famine, or the sword of the enemy" (1770:1:30). Published in 1799 Philadelphia, William Robertson's *The History of America* states, "The unfortunate colony in Roanoke received no supply, and perished miserably by famine, or by the unrelenting cruelty of those barbarians by whom they were surrounded" (51).

And William Grimshaw, in his *History of the United States* (Philadelphia, 1820), repeats what had clearly become both a standard trope and an accepted theory, "Receiving no supply, its inhabitants perished miserably by famine, or by the hands of their surrounding enemies" (23). Too, whether the blame is put on the sailors of the 1590 expedition or on the colony's backers in England, several of these early histories add to the trope what Grimshaw does, "This atrocious desertion of their duty proved fatal to the colony" (23).

The "starved or killed by Indians" trope is passed on to young readers in works such as Noah Webster's 1823 *Letters to a Young Gentleman Commencing His Education: To Which Is Subjoined a Brief History of the United States* (New Haven, Connecticut) and Hosea Hildreth's 1831 *An Abridged History of the United States of America* (Boston). In his 1831 *History of the United States, Containing All the Events Necessary to Be Committed to Memory* (Philadelphia), Bishop Davenport has, as the answer to a study question about whether the 1587 colonists were more successful than those in 1585–1586, "No: they all perished, either by famine, or the hands of the natives" (12).

And in his 1837 *A History of the United States, on a New Plan; Adapted to the Capacity of Youth* (New Haven, CT), Jesse Olney does not posit a specific fate for the 1587 colonists; however, he adds the following study questions: "What was done in 1587? What probably became of those left by Grenville? What did White do? How long before supplies were sent to the colony? What had become of the settlers in the mean time?" (32). Immediately before this, Olney had said about the men Grenville left in 1586, "They probably had been killed by the Indians" (32). Olney implies the 1587 colonists either starved because of the lack of resupply or, by parallel to the assumed fate of Grenville's men in 1586, they were attacked by Native Americans.[2]

A less common explanation of the 1587 colonists' fate appeared in some eighteenth- and early nineteenth-century histories—the possibility that the colonists cohabited with Native Americans. Despite suggestions found in some Jamestown materials, the idea that any of the Roanoke colonists joined with any Native American peoples—whether by choice or by force, whether at Croatoan or elsewhere—didn't have the traction of the "starved or killed by Indians" trope.

The suggestion that at least some of the 1587 colonists lived and intermarried with a Native American tribe appeared as early as John Lawson's 1709 *A New Voyage to Carolina*. Lawson writes about "the *Hatteras Indians*, who either then [in the 1580s] lived on *Ronoa*k-Island, or much frequented it." Lawson continues:

> These tell us, that several of their Ancestors were white People, and could talk in a Book, as we do; the Truth of which is confirm'd by gray Eyes being found frequently amongst these *Indians*, and no others. They value themselves extremely for their Affinity to the *English*, and are ready to do them all friendly Offices [1967(1709):69].

For Lawson, the prevalence of grey eyes among the Hatteras Indians as well as stories of literate ancestors meant one thing—that the Roanoke colonists left behind in 1587 had abandoned Roanoke Island to live among and ultimately integrate with the Native American people on Hatteras Island. Just as important to Lawson—and what makes cohabitation a trope, something that works figuratively not just literally—is the explanation Lawson gives for their cohabitation as well as its effects on the colonists. Starting with the standard explanation of the 1587 colonists' fate, Lawson writes:

> It is probable, that this Settlement miscarry'd for want of timely Supplies from *England*; or thro' the Treachery of the Natives, for we may reasonably suppose that the English were forced to cohabit with them, for Relief and Conversation; and that in process of Time, they conform'd themselves to the Manners of their *Indian* Relations. And thus we see, how apt Humane Nature is to degenerate [1967(1709):69].

For Lawson, the colonists ended up living with the Hatteras Indians for the same reasons given through the standard tropes—the violent nature of Native Americans and/or lack of European supplies. However, rather than starve for either food or society, Lawson's imagined colonists are willing to live with the Indians, even though the end result is that they lose their European identity or, in Lawson's word, they degenerate.[3]

The idea that Raleigh's colonists may have ended up living with Native Americans is repeated only a few times in the eighteenth and early nineteenth centuries, and with much less certainty than in Lawson's *A New Voyage to Carolina*. Thomas Jefferson writes in *Notes on the State of Virginia* (Paris, 1785; London, 1787), "What was the particular fate of the colonists he [Raleigh] had before sent and seated, has never been known: whether they were murdered, or incorporated with the savages" (178). In *The History of North Carolina, from the Earliest Period* (New Orleans, 1829), François-Xavier Martin writes of the "the unfortunate colonists," that "They were never heard of. Lawson, who lived in

North Carolina, during the first year[s] of the eighteenth century, sup-
poses; they were forced to cohabit with the natives for relief and conversation" (36). The possibility that Raleigh's planters went to live with the
Hatteras Indians is presented only as a supposition by Lawson. Martin
himself never endorses the idea.

Even George Bancroft, often credited with making the history of
the Roanoke colonies an important first step in U.S. history, equivocates in a manner similar to Martin. In the first volume of *A History of
the United States, from the Discovery of the American Continent* (1834),
Bancroft writes:

> An inscription on the bark of a tree pointed to Croatan; but the season
> of the year and the dangers from storms were pleaded as an excuse for
> an immediate return. Had the emigrants already perished? Or had they
> escaped with their lives to Croatan, and, through the friendship of Man-
> teo, become familiar with the Indians? The conjecture has been hazarded,
> that the deserted colony, neglected by their own countrymen, were hospi-
> tably adopted into the tribe of Hatteras Indians, and became amalgamated
> with the sons of the forest. This was the tradition of the natives at a later
> day, and was thought to be confirmed by the physical character of the tribe,
> in which the English and the Indian race seemed to have been blended.
> Raleigh long cherished the hope of discovering some vestiges of their exis-
> tence; and though he had abandoned the design of colonizing Virginia,
> he yet sent at his own charge, and, it is said, at five several times, to search
> for his liege-men. But it was all in vain; imagination received no help in its
> attempts to trace the fate of the colony of Roanoke [1834:1:123].

While Bancroft allows for the possibility that Manteo saved the colonists by taking them to his village of Croatan, like Martin, Bancroft
undercuts the probability of this scenario. Bancroft implies that like
Raleigh's post–1590 searches, any conjectures about the colonists' fate
are "all in vain," that "imagination received no help in its attempts to
trace the fate of the colony of Roanoke." For Bancroft, even the most
educated guesses cannot be tested because there is no real evidence of
what happened after they carved CRO and CROATOAN on Roanoke
Island.

Probably because there is no hard evidence concerning the fate of
the colonists, many writers don't speculate about that fate at all. A good
example would be John Marshall, whose *The Life of George Washington*
(Philadelphia, 1804–1807) includes, as noted on its title page, "an Introduction, Containing a Compendious View of the Colonies Planted by
the English on the Continent of North America, From Their Settlement,
to the Commencement of That War, Which Terminated in Their Independence."[4] After describing the 1590 expedition, Marshall writes, "The

company made no other attempt to find this lost colony; nor has the time, or the manner of their perishing, ever been discovered" (1804–1807:1:20). Marshall does not use any of the tropes of starvation, attack, or cohabitation. Instead, he simply says no one knows what happened without speculating further.[5]

The Early Nineteenth Century: A Growing Sense of Mystery

Despite the sense that the 1587 colonists were starved out, attacked, or cohabited with Native Americans—or even a sense that what happened to these colonists didn't matter—a new trope began to develop in the early nineteenth century. When Marshall wrote about "this lost colony" in 1804, he was not giving the 1587 colonists the name they have come to be known by, but he was leading in that direction. The first part of his line places him in the camp of those who do not speculate about what happened to the 1587 colonists, "The company made no other attempt to find this lost colony...." However, adding "nor has the time, or the manner of their perishing, ever been discovered" begins to push the idea that the colonists' disappearance is a mystery that should have been—and perhaps should still be—explored.

At the same time Marshall starts to move his historical thinking about the 1587 colonists' fate as a mystery, imaginative literature picked up on the same point. In 1805, John Davis's *The First Settlers of Virginia, an Historical Novel*, about John Smith and Jamestown, includes an aside on the 1580s Roanoke colonization attempts.[6] In Davis's work of historical fiction, Michael Sicklemore is "sent to the south to look for the long lost company of Sir Walter Raleigh" (1805b:140). In the novel, John Smith is "[n]ot satisfied with the expedition of Mr. Sicklemore to learn the destiny of the unfortunate men," so he sends Nathaniel Powell and Anas Todkill to the Mangoags (or Mangoaks). Like Sicklemore, "they could obtain no tidings of the Colony, nor find a single trace of them" (1805b:146). As a novelist, Davis uses the action of the narrative—the unsuccessful searches sent from Jamestown to look for the 1587 Roanoke colonists—to indicate that the colonists' fate is a mystery that still remains unsolved.

Over the next thirty years, a few other works began to build on the idea that the fate of the 1587 colonists was a mystery. Sometimes these works used the term *lost*, but just as often did not. In his 1819 *A History of the United States before the Revolution: With Some Account of the Aborigines*, Ezekiel Sanford describes what the 1590 expedition found, or didn't find: "Not a vestige remained of the settlers, who had been left there three years before," except "[t]he word, CROATAN, was found upon one of the chief posts" (8). Sanford concludes by writing, "*Croatan* was an Indian town, on the north side of Cape Lookout: they set sail for it the next day; but, meeting with a storm, they returned to the West Indies; and when, or where, or how the colonists had perished, remains, to this day, undiscovered" (9). Like Marshall's use of *ever* ("nor has the time, or the manner of their perishing, ever been discovered"), Sanford's use of "to this day" makes the fate of the 1587 colonists not just a mystery of the past, but one of the present. Raising the question of the colonists' fate without providing an answer—especially by not repeating the "starved or killed by Indians" trope—highlights the question as something important.

Similarly, when Frederick Butler published his 1821 chronology *A Complete History of the United States of America, Embracing the Whole Period from the Discovery of North America, Down to the Year 1820*, his 1590 entry read, "This year Governor White brought out supplies and recruits for his colony at Roanoke; but to his surprise they were all lost, and not a vestige of them was to be found" (57). Even without *ever* or *to this day*, "they were all lost, and not a vestige of them was to be found" takes on the air of an unsolved mystery, especially because Butler doesn't mention the *Croatan* carving or speculate about what he believes happened. Aside from these American works, James Grahame's 1827 London publication, *The History of the Rise and Progress of the United States of North America, Till the British Revolution in 1688*, states, "An expedition conducted by White ... found the territory evacuated of the colonists; and no further tidings of their destiny were ever obtained" (1:35).

However, it is William Darby in his 1828 *View of the United States, Historical, Geographical and Statistical* who pushes the idea the furthest that the fate of the 1587 colonists is a mystery without actually naming the planters the Lost Colony. Curiously, Darby ends his narrative with White's 1587 departure, "On the 27th of August 1587, the governor sailed to England in quest of supplies; but of the wretched people left behind, no trace was ever since known" (22). Darby also tells about Bartholomew Gilbert being unsuccessfully sent out "in search of the lost colony of Sir Walter Raleigh" (25). Writing geography rather than history, Darby comes back to the Roanoke colonies in his overview of North Carolina. About the 1587 colonists, he writes that "they sunk from the reach of all attempts to ascertain their fate" (579). While most writers continued either to accept the assumption that they had starved, been killed, or even integrated with the local Native Americans—if the writer didn't ignore the fate of colonists all together—the conditions for seeing the colonists' fate as an unexplained mystery had been created.

As noted, the 1834 first of the ten volumes in George Bancroft's *A History of the United States, from the Discovery of the American Continent* (1834–1874) is often cited as the first history to promote the idea that the Roanoke colonization efforts were an important starting point for U.S. history.[7] Bancroft's inclusion of Lawson's "conjecture" about the colonists cohabiting with the Hatteras Indians is undercut by labeling it as *conjecture*. However, the term *conjecture* ends up building on the sense of mystery already seen in Darby, especially when Bancroft adds that "imagination received no help in its attempts to trace the fate of the colony of Roanoke" (1:123). And Bancroft promotes a sense of mystery about the colonists in other ways, such as when he writes about Gilbert's 1606 voyage: "Bartholomew Gilbert, returning from the West Indies, made an unavailing search for the colony of Raleigh. It was the last attempt to trace the remains of those unfortunate men" (1:130). In addition, the header for the page describing the 1590 expedition reads, "THE ROANOKE COLONY IS LOST" (1:123). Bancroft does not give the 1587 colonists the title of the Lost Colony, but he comes close.

Virginia Dare and Becoming The *Lost Colony*

Along with promoting the growing sense of mystery about the 1587 colonists' fate, Bancroft brings out a new, significant element in the colonists' history. While earlier writers sometimes mentioned Virginia Dare's birth, including mention of Eleanor Dare as her mother and/or John White as her grandfather, Bancroft is one of the first historians, if not the first, to make Virginia Dare's being John White's granddaughter a motivating force in the historical narrative.

From the seventeenth through the early nineteenth centuries, mention of Virginia Dare is inconsistent at best. Histories that mention Virginia Dare follow the pattern in "The Fourth Voyage Made to Virginia, With Three Shippes, in the Yeere, 1587," from Hakluyt's *Principal Navigations*, which connects Virginia Dare's birth to Manteo's being baptized and dubbed a knight:

> The 13. of August, our Sauage Manteo, by the commandment of Sir Walter Ralegh, was christened in Roanoak, and called Lord therof, and of Dasamongueponke, in reward of his faithfull seruice.
> The 18. Elenora, daughter to the Gouernour, and wife to Ananias Dare, one of the Assistants, was deliuered of a daughter in Roanoak, and the same was christened there the Sunday following, and because this childe

was the first Christian borne in Virginia, she was named Virginia [Quinn 1991(1955): 531–532].

For these histories, the conversion of a Native American plus the birth and baptism of an English child strengthen England's claim on the land because it is now native-born and blessed by the Church of England.

The earliest histories—Clarke in 1670, Beverley in 1705, Oldmixon in 1708, and Salmon in 1737—all use the same basic form as Hakluyt: Manteo is baptized and made Lord of Roanoke and Dasemunkepeuc, then the Dare child is born and baptized as Virginia. The differences come in how Virginia's family is identified. Clarke identifies Virginia's mother as "Mrs. *Dare* the Governours Daughter" without mentioning Ananias (297). Beverley calls Virginia "a Daughter of Mr. *Ananias Dare*" with no mention of John White or Eleanor (21). Similarly, Oldmixon identifies Virginia as "the Daughter of Mr. *Ananias Dare*," again with no mention of White or Eleanor (1:216).

Only Salmon gives the complete lineage: "Mrs. *Eleanor Dare*, Wife of Mr. *Ananias Dare*, one of the Court of Assistants, and Daughter of Governor *White*, was deliver'd of a Daughter, afterwards baptiz'd by the Name of *Virginia*" (1724–1738:30:410). Ten years later, Stith (1747) tells about Manteo's baptism and knighthood, then writes, "And on the 18th, the Governor's Daughter, Wife to *Ananias Dare*, one of the Council, was delivered of a Daughter, which, being the first Child born there, was called *Virginia*" (24). There is no consistency about whether Virginia Dare's baptism matters as much as Manteo's or about what relationships matter between Virginia, Eleanor, and Ananias, as well as John White.[8]

In contrast to these earlier writers, Bancroft adds familial concerns and parental worries to the story. Describing the scene as John White leaves in 1587, Bancroft writes:

> Yet previous to his departure, his daughter, Eleanor Dare, the wife of one of the assistants, gave birth to a female child, the first offspring of English parents on the soil of the United States. The child was named from the place of its birth. The colony, now composed of eighty-nine men, seventeen women and two children, whose names are all preserved, might reasonably hope for the speedy return of the governor, who, as he sailed for England, left with them, as hostages, his daughter and his grandchild, Virginia Dare [1:120].

Then, as the transition between White's 1589 failed attempt to return to Roanoke and the 1590 expedition, Bancroft writes, "More than another year elapsed before White could return to search for his colony and his daughter; and then the island of Roanoke was a desert" (1:122–123). Before Bancroft's *History*, no one seems to have mentioned John White's feelings about leaving his daughter and granddaughter on Roanoke Island. Now Governor John White is also John White the father and, to a lesser extent, grandfather.

Bancroft's bringing together the historical themes of mystery and family were important, but the ultimate step of the 1587 colonists becoming *The Lost Colony* happens in imaginative literature. As noted above, John Davis included the Jamestown searches for the 1587 colonists in his 1805 novel about Jamestown, *The First Settlers of Virginia*. And earlier, Joel Barlow referenced the colonists in his 1787 epic poem *The Vision of Columbus*:

> That feeble train, the lonely wilds who tread,
> Their sire, their genius in their Raleigh dead,
> Shall pine and perish in the frowning gloom,
> Or mount the wave and seek their ancient home [146].

Even as he revised and enlarged his poem, retitling it *The Columbiad* in 1807, Barlow doesn't portray the fate of the colonists as a mystery. For Barlow, they either wandered off into the wilderness or unsuccessfully tried to sail back to England.

However, a major shift in how the fate of the colonists was portrayed happened when a story appeared in which one of the 1587 colonists has survived. In 1825, the Virginia lawyer and politician John Robertson anonymously published *Virginia: Or, the Fatal Patent*, a pamphlet-length narrative poem, "A Metrical Romance, in Three Cantos," as described on its cover page.[9] The poem is set in the Chesapeake Bay region at the time of Jamestown's founding, with the main characters being John Smith, Pocahontas, Powhatan, and a man named Tressillian, borrowed from Walter Scott's 1821 novel *Kenilworth* (where his name is given as Edmund Tressilian, with one *l*).

In Scott's novel, set in Elizabethan England, Tressilian is unable to save the woman he loves and so heads off to Virginia with Walter Raleigh. There are obvious historical inaccuracies in the novel. For example, the novel is set in about 1575, a decade before Raleigh would begin to send expeditions to North America—not to mention that Raleigh never made any Virginia voyages himself. However, Scott's *Kenilworth* is one of the first uses of the 1580s Virginia ventures in a fictional setting since *Eastward Ho!* in 1605. When the novel ends tragically, Scott's Tressilian "embarked with his friend Raleigh for the Virginia expedition, and, young in years but old in grief, died before his day in that foreign land" (2000[1821]:595). Robertson takes this brief element from Scott's *Kenilworth* to develop a central character for his Jamestown poem.

The first canto of Robertson's *Virginia* begins with Tressillian seeing the arrival of the Jamestown fleet. As Tressillian slips off, Robertson describes the colonists in unflattering terms, mainly as greedy for gold, but distinguishes John Smith from the rest as someone who watches over the Jamestown colony "with a parent's care" (16). Several months after the colonists' arrival, Smith fall asleep in the woods and dreams about the beautiful new lands. Pocahontas comes across the sleeping Smith and sings a warning to watch out for Powhatan; just as the song wakes Smith, Pocahontas slips back into the woods and Powhatan's men capture Smith. Pocahontas again sneaks near Smith, now singing a song of encouragement. As Pocahontas slips off, Tressillian appears disguised as an Indian, letting Smith know that while he can do nothing, Pocahontas is working to gain his freedom.

Robertson brings out the Roanoke connection most fully in the second canto. When Smith is brought before Powhatan, the backstory—including the fate of the Roanoke colony—is revealed. Powhatan is overjoyed to see Pocahontas, who, it turns out, had been captured by the Allegheny Indians. Tressillian had saved Pocahontas from the Allegheny and taken her to Analostan Island in the Potomac River, his hermit's hideaway.[10] Powhatan, though happy Pocahontas is safe, recognizes Tressillian:

> ... [T]hou art the last of those
> Whom Raleigh left to perish on our shore.
> Far to the south I march'd in fight to close,
> And dyed my arrows in their Christian gore [44].

Having admitted to killing the 1587 colonists, Powhatan reveals his deepest fear: "'Has Pocahontas,'—his voice was deep, and low, / 'Has Pocahontas learnt your God to adore?'" (44). Because Tressillian introduced Pocahontas to Christianity, Powhatan threatens that "thou shalt die the death my nation's deadliest foe" (44), the same as his fellow Roanoke colonists did.

The rest of the poem tells how Smith, Pocahontas, and Tressillian escape from Powhatan and his men. The poem ends with the trio in sight of Tressillian's Analostan Island retreat and with Tressillian, now identified as "the aged man" (58), having a prophetic deathbed vision. Tressillian explains the fatal patent of the title is the charter for Jamestown, a patent from James I, a "Dreaming despot" (59). James would cause Raleigh to be beheaded, and his patent for Jamestown would inevitably lead to the Revolutionary War, fatal to Britain's ambitions. The last stanza has Tressillian "see my Indian Maid array'd in white; / I see her blessed with every Christian rite" (62). With that, Tressillian and the Roanoke colony's beginnings of Christian America die, leaving the next step with Smith, Pocahontas, and Jamestown.

Two elements that become common in the literary Lost Colony appear in Robertson's poem. One is that the colonists have died at the hands of Native American attackers, with only a few survivors (in this case, a lone survivor). The survivors' role is not to tell the tale of the colonists' fate, but to be the focus of their own story.

Second, Robertson (like Scott in *Kenilworth*) plays loose with the known history. This is not surprising considering the zeitgeist of 1820s Romanticism. In the prefatory "Advertisement" to *Virginia: or, The Fatal Patent*, Robertson asks whether or not "the achievements of Captain Smith are sufficiently mellowed by the flight of time, to render them subservient to the purpose of romance" (7). Distancing fictional characters from historical fact is reminiscent of James Fenimore Cooper, who writes in the introduction to his 1823 novel *The Pioneers*:

> As this work professes, in its title-page, to be a descriptive tale, they who will take the trouble to read it may be glad to know how much of its contents is literal fact, and how much is intended to represent a general picture.... [R]igid adhesion to truth, an indispensable requisite in history and travels, destroys the charm of fiction; for all that is necessary to be conveyed to the mind by the latter had better be done by delineations of principles, and of characters in their classes, than by a too fastidious attention to originals [2014(1823):3].

Robertson turns the historical John Smith, Pocahontas, and Jamestown into a literary legend and, by extension through Tressillian, does the same for the Roanoke colonies. It is the ideas expressed more than the historical facts that are important.

Bancroft and Robertson are important immediate precursors to the full-blown fictionalization of the Lost Colony. The actual full-blown fictional versions come in a pair of short stories written by two women, both publishing in the growing sphere of nineteenth-century periodicals and include the story's (and for some people, the history's) main tropes—the colony destroyed through Native American attack with only a few survivors, usually saved by Manteo's people; a focus on Virginia Dare; and naming the 1587 colonists *The Lost Colony*. The earliest of these short stories is "Virginia Dare; or, the Lost Colony: A Tale of the Early Settlers," by Eliza Lanesford Cushing. The story was first published in the December 1837 issue of *The Ladies' Companion*, then revised and republished as "Virginia Dare; or, the Lost Colony" in the June 1840 issue of *The Literary Garland*. The second is Cornelia L. Tuthill's "Virginia Dare: Or, the

Colony of Roanoke," published in the September 1840 edition of the *Southern Literary Messenger.*[11]

Cushing was the daughter of novelist Hannah Webster Foster, best known for *The Coquette; or, The History of Eliza Wharton* (1797), and the sister of novelist Harriet Vaughan Cheney.[12] Originally from Brighton, Massachusetts, Cushing married in 1828 and moved with her husband to Montreal in 1833. "Virginia Dare; Or, The Lost Colony" was first published anonymously in the New York–based *The Ladies' Companion* four years after she had moved to Montreal and the revised version appeared in the Montreal-based literary journal *The Literary Garland*, this time using her initials, E.L.C.

Cushing tells her story in three parts. The first follows John White from the arrival of the 1587 colonists on Roanoke Island to his 1590 return, finding *Croatan* carved on a tree. White dies on the homeward voyage, being spared the pain of learning the fate of his daughter and the other colonists. The second part of the story gives that fate. Virginia Dare's mother dies from the strain of wilderness life, and her father is shot by a poisoned arrow soon after. Later, when Manteo tries to get the other colonists to Croatoan to escape a hostile Native American attack, he is only able to save Virginia and her nursemaid, Rachel. Even as Virginia grows up playing among the Croatoan Indians, Rachel uses books recovered from the ruined Roanoke Island settlement by Manteo to teach Virginia to read and to appreciate her European heritage.

In the last part of the story, Virginia is sixteen years old. Okisko, the Croatoan king, who admires Virginia, promises her in marriage to his son Orinka, but Virginia, while appreciating what the Croatoans have done for her and Rachel, does not want to marry Orinka. At this point, a band of Croatoan hunters returns with Ferdinand Velásquez, a young Spaniard who had been taken captive by English sailors. When Velásquez came ashore with an English exploration party, hostile Native Americans captured him, then handed him over to the Croatoan hunters.

Of course, Velásquez and Virginia fall in love. Meanwhile Manteo, in search of the English ship Velásquez had been on, finds instead a Spanish ship. Because of Orinka's jealousy, Manteo arranges for Virginia, Velásquez, and Rachel to escape along with Manteo and his son, Ensenore. Almost stopped by Orinka, they get away and sail to Spain, where Virginia and Velásquez marry and live on his family's estate. The story ends with Velásquez trying to contact Virginia's relatives in England, but his letters go unanswered. Cushing concludes by writing, "and thus perished from the page of history, all memorial of the *Lost Colony of Roanoke*, for there was none to pen the record, that one individual still survived, who could have told its fate" (1837:92).

In this line, Cushing appears to be the first to name the 1587 planters as "The Lost Colony." Her 1840 revision doesn't use the same capitalization and italics, but the story's title, "Virginia Dare; or, The Lost Colony," gives the 1587 planters that same name. And Cushing's revised last line in the 1840 version highlights the idea of the mystery even more than the 1837 version. When Velásquez does not receive any replies from Virginia's relatives in England, "He therefore, forebore again to address them, and thus from the page of history that record, which had it been written, would have solved to posterity, the mystery that now involves in its impenetrable folds, the fate of the lost colony of Roanoke" (1840:324). While in 1834 the historian Bancroft may give the page about the 1590 expedition the header "The Roanoke Colony Is Lost," Cushing actually christens them "The Lost Colony."

Bancroft's and a few other historians' use of the phrase *lost colony* highlights that the shift in how the 1587 colonists were being viewed was part of the zeitgeist, the spirit of the time, rather than any single writer's creation. Tuthill's "Virginia Dare: Or, the Colony of Roanoke" highlights the point further.[13] When Tuthill wrote her story, she almost certainly did not know of the second version of Cushing's story, which came out in a Montreal magazine only three months before Tuthill's story appeared. Tuthill could have read the 1837 version—the letter prefacing her story is datelined from Hartford, Connecticut. However, that same letter states, "It is a wonder that no one has before paid a tribute to the memory of 'Virginia Dare,' the first offspring of English parents born on the soil of America. The historian alone has done justice to the inhabitants of 'the City of Raleigh'..." (1840:585). Tuthill specifically references Bancroft but states there are no fictional works that precede hers. Even so, like Cushing, Tuthill focuses on Virginia Dare, who is saved by Manteo, and she allows Virginia to grow to womanhood and marry a stranded European rather than a Native American. While the stories have significant differences, Cushing and Tuthill share several important plot elements, reflecting the Romantic literary zeitgeist of the period.

Tuthill's story opens with Eleanor Dare pushing her way onto the 1587 expedition by putting the thought into Raleigh's mind that families, rather than just men, could make his New World colony successful. Roanoke Island seems an Edenic place, but the new colonists also find the bones of the fifteen men left a year earlier and the fort is in ruins. After several months, and before John White returns to England for resupply, Eleanor Dare's husband dies from overexertion and her newborn daughter is baptized—a child and ceremony so beautiful that Manteo promises to watch over the child.

The first half of the story ends with John White returning to Roanoke, finding the colonists gone, and being unable to go to Croatoan. Overwrought, White dies soon after returning to England. The second half reveals that Manteo had saved the colony's sole survivors—Virginia, Eleanor, and the colony's clergyman, Dr. Carson—from an Ocracoke Indian attack eighteen years earlier. Manteo also saved some of Eleanor's and Dr. Carson's books, which they have used to educate Virginia. Tuthill writes that Arcana, Manteo's son, is enamored of Virginia, but she loves him only like a brother. Virginia cannot imagine marrying Arcana, not because he is an Indian but because he is not her intellectual superior, someone who could provide her with even greater education than the wilderness has provided to Arcana.

As the story continues, as Virginia is out hunting one day, she accidentally wounds Henry Johnstone, a lost member of the Jamestown settlement, with whom she falls in love. Arcana realizes he cannot marry Virginia, so he marries the best of the Indian maidens, Criana, and Eleanor realizes her life's work is done, having prepared Virginia for womanhood. Eleanor can now die. The spring after Eleanor's death, Virginia falls sick but recovers. Following her recovery, Virginia and Henry become closer. Dr. Carson marries them, but only a year later, Henry becomes ill and dies. The story ends with Virginia showing the strength that her mother taught her, accepting Henry's death and living out her life with the Indians. Virginia is cheerful in the Indians' companionship and, more, in knowing that she will see those she loves in heaven.

The parallels between Cushing's and Tuthill's stories illustrate what elements of the early nineteenth-century zeitgeist have entered the general Lost Colony story. In both stories, the infant Virginia survives because Manteo saves her along with a female caretaker. She grows into young adulthood with the possibility she will marry a Native American young man but is spared that possibility when an eligible European young man with whom she falls in love chances along. Through these plot elements, both stories reflect the idealized vision of women described by Barbara Welter in "The Cult of True Womanhood: 1820–1860" (1966), especially that a woman should embody "piety, purity, submissiveness and domesticity" (152). While in both works there is no Native American who is morally or intellectually advanced enough to be a proper soulmate for Virginia, she recognizes an innate goodness in Native Americans that can lead these people to Christianity, even if some Native Americans, like Orinka, are inextricably attached to the wilderness.

In the early eighteenth century, John Lawson had suggested that the 1587 colonists "were forced to cohabit" with the Hatteras Indians "for Relief and Conversation," and that over time, had degenerated "to the Manners of their *Indian* Relations." In the three early nineteenth-century narratives, only the most ideal colonists are seen living alongside Native Americans—John Smith and Virginia Dare. These idealized colonists improve the Native Americans (in early nineteenth-century terms) rather than degenerating themselves (again in early nineteenth-century terms).

Robertson's John Smith can marry Pocahontas, but Virginia cannot marry a Native American man because, as Tuthill's Virginia explains from the viewpoint of an idealized nineteenth-century woman, "When I think of a husband, I picture to myself such a man as you say my grandfather was—such a one as Dr. Carson must have been; a person knowing a great deal more than I do ..." (591). The male John Smith can uplift the female Pocahontas through marriage, but the female Virginia can only uplift her Native American neighbors by *not* marrying any of them. When women are portrayed as the Lost Colony's survivors, they are imagined as living alongside their Native American neighbors, not among them, their European identity intact.

It should be noted that, like Robertson, both Cushing and Tuthill get lots of historical facts wrong, despite Tuthill's claim that her narrative "is founded on Bancroft's account of the Colony of Roanoke" and that "the real names of the principal persons have been preserved" (585). As just one example, the names of Virginia Dare's family members are all over the map. In 1837, Cushing doesn't give first names, using just Governor White, Mr. Dare, and Mrs. Dare. When she adds a name in 1840, it is to misname Virginia's mother as Alicia Dare. Tuthill does get Eleanor Dare's name right, but Virginia's father is George, not Ananias, and her grandfather is Philip White, not John White, and he is differentiated from the person who made "the drawings of With" (587).

While neither Cushing nor Tuthill strictly adheres to historical fact, they express an early nineteenth-century sense of what colonization was and should have been—that familial ties and responsibilities are the major motivations of human beings, that women want and need strong men to guide them, and so on. In doing so, they reflected and possibly even shaped the assumptions that would underlie later studies of the 1587 colony.

By turning the 1587 planters into *The* Lost Colony, into a mystery, these writers "solved" the mystery through fictions, turning the blank slate of what actually happened into pictures of what should have happened. As Henry says when he realizes who Virginia, Eleanor, and Dr.

Carson are in Tuthill's story, "Can it be ... that I have discovered the long lost colonists of Raleigh?" (592). Henry has *discovered* the survivors, has solved the mystery, even if he cannot bring the information back to the English world. But the fictional discoveries allow belief in the possibility of historically discovering what happened to the colonists. At the same time, they set up what would be the expectations of—or at least the questions about—what to look for in order to find the Lost Colony in history, not just in imaginative literature. The fictions move past the "starved or killed by Indians" presumptions about the 1587 colonists.

From the 1850s to the Present

By the 1850s, various other texts—both fiction and nonfiction—began to reflect what the first fictions set up. For example, in his 1851 *The North-Carolina Reader,* Calvin Henderson Wiley is one of the earliest writers to suggest that the inscription *Croatoan* could mean the colonists had "become the guests of the hospitable and generous Manteo, and, through his influence, amalgamated with the Indians" (98–99). Wiley notes that earlier historians presumed all of the 1587 colonists died. However, reflecting the new narratives of writers like Robertson, Cushing, and Tuthill, he adds, "it is possible that a majority only met this tragic fate, while a few escaped and formed permanent connections with the original owners of the soil" (99). Wiley, writing in a form that combines narrative history and essay, admits that the Lost Colony's fate is a mystery that cannot be solved:

> The historian cannot lift the veil of mystery and gloom that shrouds the fate of this colony; but a lively imagination can indulge in conjectures and weave a thousand probable stories. Here is a fair field for the poet and novelist; and facts and fancies might be woven into ideal creations that would give a deeper and more enduring interest to history and render more sacred and classic the spot where the Anglo-Saxon, under the auspices of the great Sir Walter Raleigh, began his career in America [99].

For Wiley, the Lost Colony is a work of the imagination but not a lie. It is a way to recuperate firsts and express ideals important to nineteenth-century European Americans, that "here was the soil first pressed by the foot of an Englishwoman, and here was born the first offspring of that race which was destined to possess and rule this mighty continent" (99), ideals based in family and progeny as much or more than in raw power.[14]

Two 1857 publications illustrate how much the ideas developed by Robertson, Bancroft, Cushing, and Tuthill had taken hold in both the popular and the academic literature by the mid–nineteenth century. The first is "The Piny [sic] Woods," the second installment of Porte Crayon's four-part travelogue "North Carolina Illustrated" in *Harper's New Monthly Magazine*. (On the heels of *Harper's* publishing Crayon's travelogue, it would publish Edward C. Bruce's two-part travelogue "Loungings in the Footprints of the Pioneers" [1858, 1860], the first part of which would briefly introduce the Roanoke colonies as part of Bruce's travels through Virginia and North Carolina, but the second of which would give the description of the purported remains of the 1580s fort on Roanoke Island discussed in Chapter 3.)

Porte Crayon was the pen name of David Hunter Strother, who writes how one night, while in Plymouth, North Carolina, he dreams about a Native American encampment in a grove of live oaks. There, from "a lodge whose superior size and decorations proclaimed the dwelling of a chieftain ... a maiden of exquisite beauty came forth" (742). Of course it turns out to be Virginia Dare, something Crayon doesn't realize until the end of his dream. Virginia's clothing consists of a "tunic ... of woven bark tissue, white as paper and light as silk, curiously and beautifully wrought with many-colored shells," along with "embroidered moccasins" and "wrists and ankles clasped by bands of shining gold"; in addition, a "richly-ornamented sash bound her delicate waist, and a necklace of gold and white coral hung about her neck" (742).

Though dressed as "an Indian princess," Virginia's "skin was of dazzling whiteness, and her dimpled cheek flushed with the freshest rose. Her round, wondering eyes were of a tender blue, and the plumy circlet on her head rested on a luxuriant mass of flaxen hair, that fell in wild ringlets over her graceful shoulders, and downward until it became entangled with the shell-wrought fringe of her girdle" (742–43). The trope of European and thus European American virtue overpowering any regressive Native American wildness had become central to the idea of what happened to the Lost Colony.

However, that trope is nearly compromised. As in Cushing's and Tuthill's stories, Virginia is threatened by an inappropriate Native American suitor, though here it is an "aged man ... who, by his dress, might have been a priest or prophet" (743). Unlike Cushing and Tuthill, Crayon allows for the possibility of an acceptable Native American suitor, "a princely youth" who "[w]ith a look full of idolatrous love, he bowed himself; but she raised him up, and ere long her flaxen tresses were nestled lovingly upon that manly breast" (743). However, "the ring-nosed prophet" leads a band of warriors to break up the lovers, and it is at this point Crayon wakes up from his dream. The possibility of an appropriate Native American suitor is not allowed to play out.

But just before he wakes up, Crayon realizes the woman is Virginia Dare, stating, "She was saved—saved, sweet, exotic flower! to bloom so gloriously in the far wilderness amidst these savage weeds of humanity—to reign a queen over these rude beasts—to be worshiped, perhaps idolized!" (743). The dream ends with Crayon lamenting, "Could I but speak now, to claim kindred with her—first-born of English blood upon this mighty continent—Virginia Dare—to hear, mayhap, from her sweet lips, something of the fate of that lost colony; something to fill that mournfulest blank in the pages of history" (743).

While Crayon illustrates the popular vision of Virginia Dare and the Lost Colony, Francis Lister Hawks' 1857 *History of North Carolina* illustrates how the same concerns became part of academic history.[15] Hawks' *History* includes both the major Roanoke colonization-related documents and a historical narrative. Hawks shows an interest in issues that might help solve the mystery of the Lost Colony, including discussion of where the colonists' intended remove "fifty miles into the main" would be, connecting that move to Croatoan (1:203). Hawks ends up developing a full argument about what happened to the 1587 colonists. He asks, "What had become of them? No man can, with certainty, answer; but any man can readily conjecture what must have been the misery of these poor creatures, as sickening under 'hope deferred,' they looked from day to day, but looked in vain for the return of White" (1:228).

Based on Lawson's information about the Hatteras Indian tradition of gray eyes and ancestors who "could talk in a book," Hawks argues that only the 1587 colony could account for the tradition. He concludes:

> We are inclined to think that, driven by starvation, such as survived the famine, were merged into the tribe of friendly Indians at Croatoan; and, alas! lost, ere long, every vestige of christianity [sic] and civilization; and thus those who came to shed light on the darkness of paganism, in the mysterious providence of God, ended by relapsing themselves into the heathenism they came to remove. It is a sad picture of poor human nature [1:228–229].

Paralleling Wiley's uplifting Romantic idea that imaginative literature can provide an idealized truth about the 1587 colonists' fate, Hawks gives a Dark Romantic view, a gloomy picture of the colonists being forced to regress into a wild state. Contrasting the 1587 colonists with the earlier ventures, Hawks writes:

> And here are women and children. Daily life, we may imagine, was somewhat different now. The men are probably not so rough-visaged and so untidy. They have been partially humanized by the gentleness of woman

and the caresses of children. True, they have a hard battle to fight, but they have also a stake to fight for. But, alas! here is an enemy more to be dreaded than even the vindictive and treacherous savage—*starvation*! And now the father wishes that wife and children were but in safety in the land whence he brought them. He can suffer himself, but it unmans him to see them suffer. That skeleton child for whom the mother has starved herself in vain; he has laid it in its coffin and buried it in the ground, and he turns sadly away from the task of comforting its desolate mother; for his own heart is breaking: that mother must go next [1:251].

Hawks does not return to the idea of cohabitation with the Hatteras, but instead to the idea that starvation drives people to extreme emotional ends. In his conjectured portrait of the 1587 colonists, Hawks includes the themes that were growing in importance—that family was at the core of the Lost Colony's story and that while what happened to the Lost Colony was a mystery that could only be solved by conjecture, it should be solved.

Writing about the Lost Colony had just begun by the midpoint of the nineteenth century, and to cover more would take a book of its own. Robert Arner's 1985 booklet *The Lost Colony in Literature* (revised from his 1978 *Southern Literary Journal* article) still stands as an excellent overview of the subject, especially when supplemented by Kelley Griffith's "The Genteel Heroine: Virginia Dare One Hundred Years Ago" (2003), which highlights how the Lost Colony story continued a Romantic vision during the late nineteenth and early twentieth centuries when Realism was at its height. But it would be wrong to think that the Lost Colony story was told in a singular way from then to the present day. Two works often brought up when discussing the Lost Colony help illustrate the point—Sallie Southall Cotten's *The White Doe: The Fate of Virginia Dare, an Indian Legend* (1901) and Paul Green's *The Lost Colony* (1937), a drama still produced every summer on Roanoke Island.

The White Doe uses already familiar plot elements: Virginia Dare is one of only a few survivors saved by Manteo from an unfriendly Indian attack. Growing up among the Croatoan, she is admired for both her beauty and moral judgement. She has two Indian suitors—a good-hearted young brave and an old magician who wants to possess her. Cotten, however, adds a new twist—the supernatural. The old magician transforms Virginia into a White Doe. The good brave learns how to break the enchantment with a magical arrowhead, but just as he shoots the White Doe, Wanchese shoots her with a silver-tipped arrow he received from Queen Elizabeth. The two arrows are shot moments apart, the magical arrowhead transforming the White Doe back to Virginia Dare a fraction of a second before the silver-tipped arrow kills her.

Cotten did not originate Virginia Dare as the White Doe story. Someone identified only as Mrs. M.M. published "The White Doe Chase: A Legend of Olden Times" in an 1875 issue of the pro–Confederate, Lost Cause magazine *Our Living and Our Dead*. These early versions of the White Doe story are unlike Tuthill's 1840 "Virginia Dare," in which Virginia's line about marrying Manteo's son Arcana, "Oh no! ... He is an Indian, and I am an Englishwoman," meets with Eleanor's reply, "That confers no superiority upon you" (591). In Tuthill, Virginia agrees, giving her explanation about gender and intellectual superiority without reference to race. Both M. M.'s and Cotten's White Doe narratives are about what a true woman should be *and* about racial superiority. Cotten writes, "For we know the silver arrow, fatal to all sorcery, / Was the gleaming light of Progress speeding from across the sea, / Before which the Red Man vanished, shrinking from its silvery light..." (78). The silver-tipped arrow came from Queen Elizabeth and mystically saved Virginia from the evil of interracial marriage.

While the story has these beginnings, it has been retold in various contexts. In their 2003 children's history, *Roanoke: The Lost Colony: An Unsolved Mystery from History*, Jane Yolen and Heidi Elizabeth Yolen Stemple make it one of the suggested "theories" about the Lost Colony. In *White Doe in the Mist: The Mystery of the Lost Colony* (2012), Faith Reese Martin writes about two young people having a vision of a white doe, leading them to the Lost Colony mystery and to understanding the English intruded on Native American lands. Virginia Dare is portrayed as a vampire Slayer in Christie Golden's 2001 *Buffy the Vampire Slayer*-inspired short story "The White Doe, London, 1586." And in "The Story of the White Deer Named Virginia Dare," part of his 1993 collection *Tunkashila: From the Birth of Turtle Island to the Blood of Wounded Knee*, Gerald Hausman tries rewriting Cotten's narrative from a Native American point of view. Whether or not these reworkings can remove all of the story's racist elements, it is no longer strictly a tale about the horror of interracial marriage. But even with supernatural elements, these variations of the White Doe story push people to think about what the survival of one or more of the 1587 colonists would look like. Would the colonists retain their Englishness or assimilate into Native American culture or something in between?

The literary work most associated with the Lost Colony, though, may be Paul Green's 1937 drama *The Lost Colony*, produced every summer since except during World War II and the 2020 COVID crisis. Ironically, the one thing Green's drama doesn't do is imagine what ultimately happened to the Lost Colony. The first half of the play presents the history of Roanoke colonization from the 1584 Amadas and Barlowe expedition to the 1587 colonists' sailing from England. After intermission, the colonists arrive on Roanoke Island, Virginia Dare is born, and John White returns to England. Only the last part of the drama is speculative, imagining what leads the colonists to leave the City of Raleigh, but not what happens when they do. Tensions grow between the colonists and Native Americans, but the drama ends with a Spanish ship arriving and the colonists heading out of the settlement to escape from the Spanish. What happens to the colonists from there is not part of the story. Instead, "In the cold hours before dawn they began their march into the vast unknown" (1980:102). Green chose to make the ending ambiguous, unresolved.[16]

However, the Lost Colony and *The Lost Colony* do not end there. In 2021, for the first time, *The Lost Colony* hired Native American actors to play the Native American roles (Hampton 2021). And the role of the Historian, originally a Renaissance scholar narrating the story, has been revised to the Storyteller, played by a Native American woman. To hire Native American actors, the Roanoke Island Historical Association, producers of *The Lost Colony*, has partnered with the Lumbee Tribe of North Carolina in Robeson County. One of the earliest Lost Colony hypotheses, and a problematic one as discussed in the next chapter, is that the 1587 colonists joined with the Croatoan Indians, ultimately migrating inland to become what is today the Lumbee Tribe. Working with the Lumbee helps make the production of *The Lost Colony* more authentic, having Native Americans portray Native Americans rather than having White actors perform in redface. At the same time, the decision tacitly reinforces the problematic idea that Lumbee origins have a significant European connection.

Both usefully and problematically, the line between historical imagination and literary imagination has blurred, with imaginative literature helping set the agenda of what to look for and why when researching the fate of the Lost Colony. In historical and imaginative literature from the seventeenth to the nineteenth centuries, and even into the twenty-first century, the 1587 colonists weren't lost, just abandoned to Native American attack and starvation, but then were mysteriously lost but could be found in imagined stories. The power of these works of imaginative literature is to say we don't know what happened to the Lost Colony ... but we do.

5

The Prevailing Hypotheses

The Scenarios

So far we have examined what is known about the Lost Colony through the historical record and archaeology. There really isn't very much that we can say we know for certain. That they were gone when John White returned seems fairly certain. Did they fortify their settlement? John White said they did. Did they carve a notice of where they were heading on a post and indicate it was done peacefully? John White said they did. Did they leave Roanoke and go down to Croatoan (Cape Hatteras)? John White thought they did.

So what's the mystery? John White said it, I believe it, that settles it, at least for some researchers. However, a decade of digging at Cape Hatteras has turned up no definitive evidence that the colonists went, *en masse*, to Croatoan. Sites X and Y along the Chowan River are similarly disappointing in regard to hard evidence. Tom, the English professor, has the advantage here because, as he's been known to say, "Whether it's true or not, it's a good story—or stories!" And the nineteenth century produced many ripping yarns. Good Indians, bad Indians, damsels in distress, magical transformations. The way things SHOULD have happened.

But researchers in the social sciences, soft as they are, do need stories to be based on some sort of hard evidence. Two important historiographic concepts become central from this point on: *hypothesis* and *theory*. In popular parlance, any idea expressed to answer a question can be called a theory. But in the sciences, and in academic study as a whole, *hypothesis* and *theory* have specific and very useful meanings.

A hypothesis is often described as an educated guess—it has to be based on what is already known. But it also needs to be testable. One way of thinking about a hypothesis being testable is that it can be checked against new evidence. It could be tested against the sorts of

111

archaeological evidence indicating a European-style settlement given at the end of Chapter 3. In other words, not only does a hypothesis fit what is currently known, but it can be checked against additional evidence. When tested against additional evidence, one of three outcomes can occur: (1) the hypothesis remains valid, (2) the hypothesis can be revised to take into account the new information, or (3) the hypothesis can be rejected.

If a hypothesis explains new evidence better than other hypotheses, if it is more predictive and has withstood repeated testing, it can rise to the level of a theory—an idea generally accepted as explaining something, such as what happened to the Lost Colony. As we have seen and will see in even greater abundance, when there is little factual evidence, you can come up with a number of equally plausible hypotheses. We will discuss several published hypotheses, ranging from everyone dying, to colonists hunkering down on Hatteras, to their heading inland and merging with the local population. So which scenario is the correct one? Are any of them completely correct? And perhaps most important, is there enough evidence to test the hypotheses so that any of them rise to the level of being a theory?

Perhaps we should start with what COULD have happened and then proceed to various scholars' hypotheses proposed about what actually did. There are not a large number of possible scenarios out there. In fact, when you get right down to it, these scenarios fall into two groups, either (1) they died or (2) they survived and stayed out of sight of later Europeans.

Scenario Type 1: They Die

Let's begin with the first type of scenario, that they all died. Realistically, this is the most probable outcome and certainly one believed by colonists in Jamestown, even if they didn't say it explicitly. As discussed in Chapter 2, while the idea that some of the 1587 colonists were still alive lasted into the 1620s, the searches for survivors before and after the founding of Jamestown were not especially rigorous. And almost all the early historians worked on the assumption that there was no mystery about the fate of the 1587 colonists—they were dead. But if they died, how might they have died? Thomas Salmon's 1737 line from his *Modern History; or, the Present State of All Nations* sums up almost all the possibilities, "they were famish'd, or cut in pieces by the Indians, or perish'd in attempting to get home by Sea" (1724–1738:30:412). There is one other scenario that might be suggested as well, that they were killed in an attack by the Spanish, one that we have not found a record of—yet.

So, let us count the ways.

Of Exposure/Famine

The first set of scenarios are built around exposure, sickness, and starvation. These scenarios would certainly have been no surprise to the colonists' contemporaries. This explanation starts with the colonists sending John White to get supplies, just as Richard Grenville had the same mission for the 1585–1586 colony. Early settlers always fell short on supplies, and the 1587 settlement on Roanoke Island was not the most conducive for agriculture. Perhaps that was why they were prepared to move "50 miles into the mayne" upon John White's departure.

The Outer Banks are not inhospitable during the warmer months unless, of course, there is a hurricane or other stormy weather. The narratives of the colonists were replete with such storms, which may well have been tropical storms, hurricanes, or nor'easters, as they wreaked havoc on Francis Drake's ships and later John White's. The Jamestown colony found that even their inland town was difficult to supply, and the first winter of their settlement became known as the "starving time," to the point that there is evidence they resorted to cannibalism (Kelso 2017).

Had the 1587 colonists elected to remain on Roanoke, feeding themselves through agriculture would have been challenging as there is good evidence that they had arrived during a catastrophic drought (Blanton 2003). Couple this with the fact that they landed late in the growing season, and it seems unlikely that the colonists could have had much initial success with their own crops.

The profile of the average English colonist many of us learned in the 5th grade was that they were all gentle people and not used to the hard work of farming or the strange soils of the New World. If it wasn't for friendly Indians like Manteo (or Squanto for the later Pilgrims), the colonists would have been doomed. The lessons we learn in 5th grade stick with us, even as we take history in college. However, by all accounts, the colonists knew what they were about and worked very hard to provide for themselves. In an unfamiliar climate, especially experiencing a significant drought, no amount of effort would have been successful. Additionally, their Native American neighbors, whom they were depending on for food until the resupply ship arrived, may have had little to share. This actually gives some insight on the next scenario for demise: native attack.

Of Indian Attack

All of the Roanoke narratives talk of trouble with the Native Americans. Ralph Lane was especially disparaging of the native inhabitants and thought them treacherous. As Lane wrote concerning his spring 1586 interactions with the Algonquian (Chowanoke) and Iroquoian (Mangoak) people living at the end of the Albemarle Sound and further west:

> But this confederacie against us of the Choanists and Mangoaks was altogether and wholly procured by Pemisapan himselfe, as Menatonon confessed unto me, who sent them continuall worde that our purpose was fully bent to destroy them: on the other side he tolde me that they had the like meaning towards us [Quinn 1991(1955):1:265–266].

During the fall and winter of 1587, was there simply a clash of cultures or did the presence of over 100 additional mouths to feed during a terrible drought make conflict inevitable? Quite possibly both factored into the equation. From the beginning, the English Roanoke colonists were always wary of the neighbors and probably with good cause. Several of the Englishmen were recorded as being killed by hostile Natives (for example, George Howe was shot with arrows while out crabbing, and John White learned from the Croatoan Indians that the 15 men Grenville left behind to secure the colony had been set upon by hostile natives from Secotan, Aquascogoc, and Dasemunkepeuc), but were disgruntled neighbors responsible for the annihilation of the entire colony? Strachey, as discussed in Chapter 2, alluded to it, writing that Powhatan "doth often send vnto us to temporize with vs, awayting perhapps but a fitt opportunity (inflamed by his bloudy and furious priests) to offer vs a tast of the same Cuppe which he made our poore Countrymen drinck off at *Roanoak*..." (1953[1612]:58).

However, this may have been Powhatan trying to intimidate the Jamestown colonists at the time or Strachey whipping up sentiment against Powhatan. And it is a Native American tribe from the Chesapeake Bay region killing the 1587 Roanoke colonists, not any of the Native American people from the Roanoke Island region where the colonists had been last seen.

So, if the native inhabitants didn't kill all the colonists, then who did?

OF SPANISH ATTACK

The Spanish are another possible candidate for executioners of the colonists. Spain had claimed most of the New World for themselves (with their claims bolstered by Pope Alexander VI in the Treaty of Tordesillas in 1494), and the Spanish viewed any other Europeans as intruders or, worse, as pirates. These they did not tolerate, as the obliteration of the French at Fort Caroline and the survivors of the wrecked

Ribault fleet south of St. Augustine in 1565 testify (Quinn 1975:254–259). Spanish concerns about the bad intentions of other European powers were not unfounded, as the English took Spanish prizes on every trip to the New World and may have been considering the Carolina colony as a base for privateering operations on Spanish shipping (Jones 2001).

Spain learned of Grenville's plans to establish a colony somewhere up the coast from Florida; however, a reconnaissance in 1588 led by Vicente Gonzalez overshot the Carolina coast and reached the Chesapeake area. This area was reconnoitered, but the ships turned back to St. Augustine when no trace of the English colonists was found. They did explore the Outer Banks on their return to St. Augustine and found evidence of a slipway, that is, a boat ramp, likely at Port Ferdinando, where English boats had passed between the ocean and Roanoke Island. Curiously Gonzalez made no further exploration of the sound, perhaps due to inclement weather. Pedro Menéndez, governor of St. Augustine, did receive information that there was an English colony on Roanoke Island and started to mount an expedition to destroy it in 1589 (Hoffman 1987). However, after the Spanish Armada debacle, Spain's interest in its unprofitable North American colony waned and the expedition was called off (Quinn 1975:299–303). No records have as yet been found suggesting the Spanish reactivated the plan and were successful. It is possible that such documents have yet to be located or that the massacre was never recorded, though given the Spanish proclivity for recording everything, this seems unlikely.[1]

LOST AT SEA

Finally, there is the last lethal possibility. Like the preceding Lane colony that returned to England when given the opportunity by Drake, perhaps the colonists had had enough of waiting for John White to come back with supplies and decided to leave for England or at least somewhere better than where they were. This would have been a desperate gamble, indeed. They had a pinnace, that is, a small sailing vessel, as well as two or more even smaller ship's boats at their disposal, which White noted as missing when he returned:

> From thence wee went along by the water side, towards the point of the Creeke to see if we could find any of their botes or Pinnisse, but we could perceive no signe of them, nor any of the last Falkons and small Ordinance which were left with them, at my departure from them [Quinn 1991(1955):2:614–615].

However, the pinnace, being a small seagoing vessel, would not have accommodated many of the colonists, and the smaller boats would not have been viable for open ocean sailing. Perhaps by the time they decided to leave, only a few were left alive or maybe they even built another boat to take the surplus. Either way, there is no record of them making it to wherever they were going. This scenario has the disadvantage, however, of being nearly untestable unless a shipwreck with fantastic preservation is found somewhere beneath the Atlantic.[2]

So, famine, exposure, warfare, or lost at sea? It could even have been a combination of any of them. Certainly by 1620, when Jamestown was fully established and other settlements were being planted up the Atlantic coast, England had written off the Roanoke colony as just another failed venture in an inherently risky business. And the early historians who wrote about the 1587 colonists were emphasizing their being "famish'd, or cut in pieces by the Indians, or perish'd in attempting to get home by Sea" (Salmon 1724–1738:30:412).

Scenario Type 2: They Assimilate

By the mid–nineteenth century, the next set of scenarios are what most people started to emphasize, what it seems people wanted to believe. The Lost Colonists did not all die. They survived by going native and adapting to the New World or by joining one of the local Native American groups. In this scenario, their DNA is still circulating around Eastern North Carolina. But if they survived, where did they go?

Virtually all the published theories concerning the Lost Colony have them hooking up with native groups at some point before either assimilating into the tribe or being killed (for an exception see McMullan 2014[2010]). The destinations are Hatteras Island (Dawson 2020), the Chesapeake (Quinn 1985), northeastern North Carolina, especially around the western end of the Albemarle Sound (Parramore and Parramore 1984, Horn 2010, Evans et al. 2015), various locations in southeastern North Carolina (Dial and Eliades 1975, Fullam 2017), and even the Piedmont along the North Carolina and Virginia border (Miller 2001). All of these hypotheses will be explored further in this section, and all of the authors make their cases based on the available historical evidence because there is not much archaeology to bolster the hypotheses.

So how could there be so many different destinations if everyone is using the same data? At the risk of being repetitive, there really isn't that much solid data with which to work. We have a brief report by John White on his initial days on Roanoke and his abortive reconnaissance mission to check out his colony. After that there are a couple of reports out of Jamestown that are, at best, hearsay evidence of maybe some Europeans down in what would later become Carolina. In the next few sections we will examine the cases made by the researchers for their respective hypotheses.

Hypothesis 1—The Original Hypothesis: The Lumbee and the Lost Colony

In 1857, Francis Lister Hawks wrote that he was "inclined to think that, driven by starvation, such as survived the famine, were merged into the tribe of friendly Indians at Croatoan," that is, Hatteras, but that "[n]o man can, with certainty, answer" what had happened to the 1587 colonists (1:228). However, by 1888, the first fleshed out hypothesis appeared and was presented with a tone of certainty—that Hatteras Indians from Croatan Island combined with the 1587 colonists then moved inland to the area around the Lumber River in southeastern North Carolina. The major proponent of the hypothesis, Hamilton McMillan, served as representative from Robeson County to the North Carolina General Assembly from 1885 to 1887,[3] during which time he was able to get legislation passed recognizing the Native American people of Robeson County as the Croatan Indians, a tribe that ultimately became the Lumbee.[4]

In 1888, McMillan published the pamphlet *Sir Walter Raleigh's Lost Colony: An Historical Sketch of the Attempts of Sir Walter Raleigh to Establish a Colony in Virginia, with the Traditions of an Indian Tribe in North Carolina.* As a major source, McMillan used an 1864 speech by George Lowrie, whose sons had been killed by a White man while in custody:

> We have always been the friends of white men. We were a free people long before the white men came to our land. Our tribe was always free. They lived in Roanoke in Virginia. When the English came to Roanoke our tribe treated them kindly. One of our tribe went to England in an English ship and saw that great country. When English people landed in Roanoke we were friendly, for our tribe was always friendly to white men. We took the English to live with us. There is the white man's blood in these veins as well as that of the Indian. In order to be great like the English, we took the white man's language and religion, for our people were told they would prosper if they would take white men's laws. In the wars between white men and Indians we always fought on the side of white men. We moved to this land and fought for liberty for white men, yet white men have treated us as negroes. Here are our young men shot down by a white man and we get no justice, and that in a land where our people were always free [McMillan 1888:16–17].[5]

For McMillan, Lowrie's speech tells how the Indians of nineteenth-century Robeson County came to be, beginning with the assumption that the Native American people of Robeson County lived in such relative isolation that they still referred to the area of Eastern North Carolina around the Pamlico Sound as Virginia, the name used by the English from 1585 to 1663. With this assumption, Lowrie's story tells how the English arrived, Manteo went to England, and when he came back, the Indians took in the English colonists, intermarried with them, learned to speak the English language, became Christian, and even lived according to English law.

McMillan's *Sir Walter Raleigh's Lost Colony*—along with Raleigh-based newspaperman and historian Frederick A. Olds' "An American Mystery: Colonists of Roanoke Lost in 1587" (1887), relating McMillan's ideas before McMillan's pamphlet came out—were the main sources for historian Stephen B. Weeks' 1891 academic article "The Lost Colony of Roanoke: Its Fate and Survival" in the *Papers of the American Historical Association* (1891a), as well as a shortened version in the *Magazine of American History*, "Raleigh's Settlement on Roanoke Island: An Historical Survival" (1891b). Weeks took what McMillan had presented and organized it by first tracing the route of the Lost Colony, with the 1587 colonists going from Roanoke Island to Croatan, where they joined with Manteo's people, later known as the Hatteras Indians. For Weeks, the combined Hatteras and English community migrated inland to the Lumber River area of Robeson County sometime around 1650. To back up the idea that the Croatan/Lumbee are this admixture of the 1587 colonists and the Native Americans of Hatteras Island, Weeks highlights three points:

1. The Lumbee have a tradition—an oral history—that their ancestors came from Roanoke.
2. Many surnames common among the Croatan/Lumbee are surnames of some of the Roanoke colonists.
3. The English spoken by the Lumbee when encountered by European colonists in the early 1700s, and well into the nineteenth century, reflected sixteenth-century English.

Over time, the Lumbee–Lost Colony hypothesis was reviewed and sometimes modified to consider the possibility of other groups in the Lumbee admixture, including the Iroquoian Cherokee and Tuscarora as well as the Siouan Cheraw, Waccamaw, and Waccon. For example, O.M. McPherson concluded in his report *Indians of North Carolina* (1915:9–23), that he had "no hesitancy in expressing the belief that the Indians originally settled in Robeson and adjoining counties in North Carolina were an amalgamation of the Hatteras Indians with Gov. White's lost colony," along with some later inclusion of Scotch and Scotch-Irish settlers "together with a small degree of amalgamation with other races," including various Native American tribes (17).

The last major proponent of the Lumbee–Lost Colony hypothesis was Adolph Dial, a member of the Lumbee Tribe as well as a professor of history and founder of the American Indian Studies program at Pembroke State University (now the University of North Carolina at Pembroke). Dial's fullest presentation appears in *The Only Land I Know: A History of the Lumbee Indians* (1975; reprinted 1996), a book-length history of the Lumbee Indians written with fellow Pembroke State history professor David K. Eliades. For Dial and Eliades, the isolated swamps of Robeson and surrounding counties "brought together in one community remnants both of the 'Lost Colony' and several Indian tribes, of which the Hatteras and various Eastern Siouan peoples were the most prominent" (13–14). While by the 1970s the Lumbee–Lost Colony hypothesis had transitioned to consider other later influences on Lumbee society, the 1587 Lost Colony and Manteo's people remained at the core.

Examining McMillan and Week's main arguments point by point helps highlight the historiographic issues involved in testing any hypothesis about the fate of the Lost Colony. To begin, the first point in the Lumbee–Lost Colony hypothesis is that Lumbee oral history, labeled as tradition, connects the Lumbee to the Outer Banks of the sixteenth and early seventeenth centuries. McMillan makes a good deal of the line from George Lowrie's speech that the tribe "lived in Roanoke in Virginia." To counter arguments that there are places aside from Roanoke Island and its environs named Roanoke—especially the Roanoke River that runs from the Blue Ridge Mountains of Virginia to Batchelor Bay on the Albemarle Sound in North Carolina—McMillan writes, "They have no tradition as to any river named Roanoke. This name is invariably applied by them to the territory previously described as occupied by their tribe on the Eastern coast" (19).

However, as Melinda Maynor Lowery points out in *The Lumbee Indians: An American Struggle* (2018), George Lowrie's family had Tuscarora ancestry as part of its makeup. His mother was "Celia (or Sally) Kearsey. She was born and raised near a place called Indian Woods, located on the banks of the Roanoke River.... Celia's mother was Tuscarora, but her father, Thomas, probably belonged to the Weyanoke people from Virginia" (Lowery 2018:31). The Lumbee did not live in isolation and had relationships with people connected to the Roanoke River.[6] Not only did some Lumbee ancestors come from near the Roanoke River, but the Lumbee would have had to live in complete isolation between the early eighteenth and the mid–nineteenth centuries to not have some sense of places named Roanoke beyond the island and its nearby mainland.

To further complicate Lowrie's speech and the Lumbee–Lost Colony hypothesis, McMillan's *Sir Walter Raleigh's Lost Colony* appears to be the only source for his speech, given in 1864 but not recorded until 1888. Was McMillan present when the speech was given or is it something he heard or read about? Did McMillan have a transcript of Lowrie's speech or was he recreating it from memory? Oral history can be an important source, one too often overlooked by scholars in favor of written records. But we need to be as mindful of the context of oral traditions as we are of written records. Even if McMillan provides an accurate transcript of the speech, it is the earliest record of a Native American from Robeson County presenting an oral history connected to the Lost Colony. In 1864, interest in the Lost Colony was growing. For approximately 25 years, literature had portrayed Virginia Dare's being rescued by Manteo's people, from Cushing's 1837 short story to Hawks 1857 history. Was Lowrie reflecting Lumbee traditional knowledge or the growing Lost Colony legend that might usefully serve his family and his community? As anthropologist Karen I. Blu noted in 1980:

> Today, most Indians recite McMillan's theory of the Roanoke lost colony origins as fact. They have apparently been doing this since McMillan's theory was advanced in the middle 1880s. Whether they simply adopted this convenient story because it was helpful to their cause or whether it was widely adopted because it fit many features of their own oral tradition, as McMillan claims, or for both reasons, is difficult to say on the basis of evidence now available. There is no known record of an Indian version of their origins before McMillan's.... (2001[1980]:135)

Blu's judgment that "most Indians recite McMillan's theory of the Roanoke lost colony origins as fact" is based on field work done in Robeson County between 1966 and 1975. However, there are signs that Lumbee traditions are changing and the majority opinion among the Lumbee no longer supports the Lumbee–Lost Colony hypothesis. For example, when the History Channel program *Digging for the Truth* filmed segments at a Lumbee powwow for the episode "Roanoke: The Lost Colony" in 2006, University of North Carolina Wilmington ethnohistorian David La Vere was interviewed, but no Lumbee tribal members. The closest thing to Lumbee involvement with the program was when the show's host, Josh Bernstein, claimed that "elders tell me that over 40 surnames of the original 1587 colonists can be found among the Lumbee people" (Bernstein 2006:35:18). The final ten-minute segment of the program is a search in Eastern North Carolina and England for a DNA link between people with the surname Payne (the surname of one of the men and one of the women colonists) without mentioning any Native American connections.

The next repeated clue to a Lumbee–Lost Colony connection concerns surnames found both on the list of 1587 colonists and among the Lumbee. Weeks does a quick calculation based on McMillan's identification of names found among the Indians living in and around Robeson County, noting that some 43 percent of the surnames of 1587 colonists can be found among the Lumbee, "including such names as Dare, Cooper, Stevens, Sampson, Harvie, Howe, Cage, Willes, Gramme, Viccars, Berry, Chapman, Lasie, and Cheven, which are now rarely met with in North Carolina, are reproduced by a tribe living hundreds of miles from Roanoke Island, and after a lapse of three hundred years" (1891a:475). However, as Melinda Lowery observes in *The Lumbee Indians*, though some of the surnames McMillan gives are common among the Lumbee, noting *Sampson, Brooks,* and *Berry,* "most of the similar names are found as much in the English population as in the Lumbee population" (Lowery 2018:26). Added to this are common Lumbee surnames not found among the English colonists, including Oxendine, Locklear, Dial, and, as Melinda Maynor Lowery points out, Lowry/Lowrie/Lowery (2018:26).

The final point of the Lumbee–Lost Colony hypothesis is that the Lumbee dialect is a form of sixteenth-century English, at least into the 1950s according to Dial and Eliades (12). The argument is that the Lumbee lived in isolation so long that their language retained significant elements from the Elizabethan era. Among these language features, Weeks lists, "They begin their salutations with 'mon-n-n,' *i.e.,* man ... pronouncing cow as *cyow,* cart as *cyart,* card as *cyard,* girl as *gyirl,* kind as *kyind....* They regularly use *mon* for man; *mension* for measurement; *aks* for ask; *hit* for it; *hosen* for hose; *housen* for houses: *crone* is to push down; and *knowledge* is wit" (1891a:474–475). Dial and Eliades give what has been a common trope about the Lumbee dialect, that "the Lumbees, prior to the breakdown of their geographical isolation in the mid-twentieth century with the advent of mass media, spoke a pure Old English" (11). They then conclude that "no one has yet offered an alternative explanation as to how these people learned to speak that type of English and made it their natural language, if they were not influenced by settlers from Raleigh's missing colony" (12).

In the 1990s, linguists under the direction of Walt Wolfram of North Carolina State University confirmed that there is a definite Lumbee dialect, "a distinctive, systematic dialect of English that reflects their peoplehood as an American Indian group" (Dannenberg 2006:94).

However, there is nothing in the dialect tying the Lumbee back to the Lost Colony. As Wolfram explains, "Lumbee English has been molded primarily from the available models of English used by the Europeans settled in the area," including coastal North Carolina dialects and both Scots-Irish and Highland Scots along with innovations made within the Lumbee community (Wolfram, 2001:36).

There is a tendency to identify any dialect that seems different as Elizabethan or Shakespearean English, especially if there are recognizable relic forms in it. For example, Wolfram tells how a BBC crew showed up on Ocracoke Island to have residents read passages from Shakespeare as it would have sounded 400 years ago: "The BBC crew seemed disappointed but undeterred by our insistence that the notion that the residents spoke Elizabethan English was a romantic myth and that Outer Banks speech is dynamic and constantly shifting—like any natural language." The BBC went ahead and "aired a story claiming that Shakespearean English had been located on Ocracoke Island in North Carolina" (Wolfram and Reaser 2014:100). Similar assumptions can be seen in how everyone from McMillan to Dial identify Lumbee English as Elizabethan. While all speakers of English use vestiges of Elizabethan English, none speak Elizabethan English any more than any others—at least not since the Elizabethan era.

Are the Lumbee the Lost Colony centuries on? No. Could the 1587 colonists be part of the Lumbee Tribe's ancestral heritage? Maybe, but not necessarily. But for some one-hundred years, from McMillan's first positing a connection between the Lost Colony and the Indians of Robeson County to almost the end of the twentieth century, the Lumbee–Lost Colony hypothesis held sway—until it had to start competing with David Beers Quinn's Chesapeake Bay hypothesis in the 1980s, around the time of the four-hundredth anniversary of the Roanoke colonization.

Hypothesis 2—David Beers Quinn and the Chesapeake

The scholar most associated with studies of the Roanoke colonization efforts would be David Beers Quinn. A professor of modern history at the University of Liverpool, Quinn's interest in Roanoke came from his study of sixteenth-century Anglo-Irish history, seeing a connection between England's colonization of Ireland and its attempt at North American expansion.[7] First and foremost, Quinn edited the most complete collection of documents related to the 1580s English attempts to establish a colony on Roanoke Island, the two-volume 1955 Hakluyt Society collection *The Roanoke Voyages, 1584–1590* (1991 [1955]). As his interest in the overall Roanoke colonization efforts grew, so did Quinn's interest in the specific question of what happened to the Lost Colony.

Quinn's thinking about the Lost Colony got a boost in 1959 when he was brought to Fort Raleigh National Historic Site with three North Carolina historians: Christopher Crittenden, the head of the North Carolina Department of Archives and History; William Powell, curator of the North Carolina Collection at the University of North Carolina at Chapel Hill; and David Stick, local historian of the Outer Banks (Quinn, 1974:432; Stick 1983:244–245). Quinn went on to develop his ideas most fully in three different works. He laid out the groundwork as the chapter "The Lost Colony in Myth and Reality, 1586–1925" in *England and the Discovery of America, 1481–1620* (1974:432–481); gave the argument succinctly in the booklet *The Lost Colonists: Their Fortune and Probable Fate* (1984); and revised the argument one last time for the chapter "A Colony is Lost and Found?" from what remains the most complete history of England's 1580s Roanoke Island enterprises, *Set Fair for Roanoke: Voyages and Colonies, 1584–1606* (1985:341–377).[8]

Quinn develops a multi-prong scenario. He hypothesizes that there were two periods in the fate of the colonists: (1) at first, most of the colonists went to live alongside the Chesepian Indians of southeastern Virginia, though some went to Croatoan to meet John White on his expected return and guide him to the other colonists; (2) over time, the colonists living with the Croatoan fully assimilated, losing their European identity, while the colonists living with the Chesepians retained some sense of their European identity, being killed by Powhatan in 1607 along with their Chesepian hosts.

The first period, Quinn hypothesizes, occurred between John White's leaving the colonists in 1587 and his return in 1590. As he notes in *The Lost Colonists: Their Fortune and Probable Fate*, "What happened to the colonists in the years 1587 to 1590 is almost entirely a matter for conjecture" (15). However, working backwards from "contemporary or near contemporary guesses and assumptions" about the 1587 colonists (1985:342), along with the statement that the colonists intended to remove fifty miles into the main repeated in the narratives of both the 1587 and 1590 voyages, Quinn assumes that *the main* means along the sea and that most of the colonists went where they originally intended to settle, the Chesapeake Bay region.

Quinn postulates that almost immediately after White's return to England, the colonists packed up whatever they could carry in the pinnace that had been left with them and in whatever long boats and canoes they had available. This main body of colonists sailed along the coast and into the Chesapeake Bay or, more likely according to Quinn, sailed to the head of Currituck Sound, then either up Back Bay or North Landing River, using the boats as far as they could go, then travelling overland to the Chesapeake tribe's major town, Skicóac, along the Elizabeth River.

Quinn elsewhere hypothesized that a group from Lane's 1585–1586 expedition—including Thomas Hariot and John White—established friendly contact with the Chesapeake tribe and spent some time living with them that winter.[9] For Quinn, "it can further be supposed that the Chesapeake Indians proved friendly and cooperative, both because they remembered their pleasant dealings with the Englishmen on their earlier visit and because the English brought women and children with them, indicating their peaceful intentions" (1984:16).

The Quinn hypothesis continues that meanwhile a small group of men remained on Roanoke Island to guide any resupply to the main body of colonists. These men—Quinn assumes about twenty in all—built the palisade which White noted in 1590 surrounding where the houses had been. He adds that these men would have lived on Roanoke Island through to the summer of 1588 when, with no resupply arriving and with a Spanish ship coming into Roanoke Sound, they moved to Manteo's village, Croatoan, leaving the CRO and CROATOAN carvings as signposts for resupply ships. According to Quinn's hypothesis, these men would have integrated into Croatoan society and, a long distance from the Chesapeake group of 1587 colonists, never had contact with them again.

Quinn bases the second part of his hypothesis on the rumors—and even rumors of rumors—that popped up in the early seventeenth century before and after the founding of Jamestown. For example, there is circumstantial evidence that Englishmen sailed into the Chesapeake Bay in 1603 (Quinn 1974:427–429) and may have brought back Native Americans with at least second-hand knowledge of the 1587 colonists living with the Chesepians. And Quinn speculates that Chapman, Jonson, and Marston's play *Eastward Ho!* was inspired by rumors of the continued survival of the 1587 colonists making the rounds of London in 1605.

In Quinn's scenario, the colonists he believed went to live alongside the Chesepians met their end in early 1607. Quinn starts with Samuel Purchas's 1625 note in *Hakluytus Posthumous* that Powhatan confessed to John Smith that he had killed Raleigh's planters, then adds William Strachey's statement from *The Historie of Travell into Virginia Britania* that "the men women, and Children of the first plantation at Roanoak were by practize and Comaundement of Powhatan (he himself perswaded therevnto by his Priests) miserably slaughtered..."

(Strachey 1952[1612]:91). According to Quinn's reading, Powhatan killed the Chesepians and the 1587 colonists when the Jamestown colonists arrived in the Chesapeake Bay in April of 1607, twenty years after their arrival at—and departure from—Roanoke Island.

When Quinn states that "[w]hat happened to the colonists in the years 1587 to 1590 is almost entirely a matter for conjecture," we should extend that to everything from August of 1587 on. Quinn advocates the use of historical imagination—the historiographic concept that underlies all of these hypotheses. Even though stated with a tone of almost certainty, Quinn presents what *could have* happened, not what *did* happen. And he does so with the tacit implication that what has been presented is based on the available data, but if more became available, he would be open to revising the hypothesis. Even with all these caveats, Quinn's hypothesis was so influential that it almost gained the status of a theory among many scholars. It was not just historians such as Karen Kupperman, who cites Quinn to round out her overview of the entire 1580s Roanoke colonization efforts in *Roanoke: The Abandoned Colony* (2007:134–135). Quinn's hypothesis became so influential that most hypotheses since have either used Quinn as a starting point or have presented their own hypotheses as counter arguments to Quinn.[10]

Hypothesis 3–50 Miles into the Maine

Both MacMillan's Lumbee–Lost Colony and Quinn's Chesapeake Bay hypotheses are based on oral traditions and written accounts. That is because there is little physical evidence that conclusively relates to Roanoke-colonization settlement despite over a century of searching. Even the earthwork at Fort Raleigh National Site has recently come under question as to its role, if any, in the settlement (Noël Hume 1996). Still, as the only lead in the case, it was the initial focus of everyone's search—where the colonists left from. Given their lack of success in finding the original settlement, many researchers turned their attention to finding where the survivors went, assuming there were any. But where to start? For many people, John White told us where to look, "for at my comming away they were prepared to remove from Roanoak 50 miles into the maine" (Quinn 1991[1955]:2:613). Taking John White's comment literally, researchers dutifully got out their grade school compasses and drew an arc 50 miles from Fort Raleigh. But unlike Quinn, many assumed "into the maine" meant into the mainland rather than along the coast.

Why would the settlers go inland? It seems that there was nothing but hostile Native Americans waiting for them there. White does not tell us the reason, only that it was their plan, and a rather vague one at that. The archaeological explanation discussed earlier is that the region was experiencing a severe drought and summer was ending when White left them in late August of 1587. Winter inland along the estuaries would allow for more foraging opportunities and better shelter than on a small barrier island.

Thomas Parramore, a former history professor at Meredith College, was one of the first to challenge Quinn's hypothesis that the colonists went to the Chesapeake region and were slaughtered by Powhatan's people.[11] He felt that Quinn had misinterpreted the accounts of John Smith and William Strachey, reading more into them than was warranted. He went further by stating that "Far from supporting Quinn's thesis, both sources effectively refute it" (Parramore 2001:68). He also felt that Quinn had misunderstood how Smith and Strachey had used the term *Roanoke* by assigning it to the island, while Parramore felt it actually referred to the tribal territory encompassing the Albemarle and Currituck sounds.

Parramore took stock of the colonists' geographic and political situation and noted that to the south and southwest were swampy lands inhabited by hostile Indians, most notably the Secotans. "But fifty miles northwest," wrote Parramore, "lay the lands, and only these, of the certifiably friendly Weapemeoc tribe" (2001:70). He also felt that this was the area Ralph Lane had declared had the "goodliest soil under the cope of heaven" with "great store of fishe" and "great red grapis very pleasant" (Quinn 1991[1955]:1:207, 215). Friendly neighbors and lots of food, what was not to like?

For Parramore, the accounts of Strachey and Purchas that state that Powhatan had killed the colonists are seen as boasts, but he does think that the colonists were all killed by other native inhabitants. According to Parramore, the previously friendly Weapemeocs may have factionalized; the hostile faction allied with other tribes and massacred the colonists shortly after they relocated to the mouth of the Chowan River. Parramore thought that "the most eligible site in that vicinity for the Roanoke colonists to have settled would have been on the west side of the Chowan River estuary, at or near the village of Metackwem, evidently the only known Weapemeoc settlement west of the Chowan. It lay apparently on the south side of lower Salmon Creek" (2001:79).

Survivors of the attack may have been carried off to the west into Tuscarora territory, and those rumors are what were received at Jamestown. Parramore closed his case by stating that "no study of White's Lost Colonists that disregards the nature and dynamics of the Indian societies among which they dwelt is likely to reveal much that is useful" (2001:83). He urged archaeologists and historians to follow this lead. It is important to note that sizing up the native politics of the sixteenth-century Coastal Plain required some conjecture, as do all of the hypotheses concerning the colonists.

A decade later James Horn, a historian at Colonial Williamsburg, utilized his extensive research into the Jamestown settlement (Horn 2005) as a springboard to investigate where the Lost Colonists may have gone after leaving Roanoke Island. Focusing on the early Jamestown sources of John Smith, William Strachey, and Strachey's informant, the Indian Machumps, Horn believes the colonists were essentially wiped out just after the Jamestown settlement was begun in 1607. He also notes that there were sightings of the survivors in the interior at locations identified by Horn as being along the Chowan River (Salmon Creek at Metackwem), Panawicke (Cashie Creek), Ocanahonan (up the Roanoke River), and Ritanoe (possible in the Appalachians).

From these locations and what he surmises of the local politics, Horn works backwards and deduces their activities over the 20 years after White left in 1587. Like Quinn and Parramore, Horn hypothesizes that the colonists would have left Roanoke Island shortly after White's departure:

> Before the main group left Roanoke Island, approximately two dozen settlers were transported to Croatoan Island. The exact number is uncertain, but it is unlikely that the Croatoans could have supported many more, especially during a time of drought and with winter coming on. The settlers left messages carved on prominent trees and posts at the settlement to tell White where they had gone. They assumed that White would return to Roanoke Island, go on to Croatoan to pick up the settlers there, and then make contact with the main group inland....
>
> Once they had prepared the ground at their settlement at the head of the Albemarle Sound, the settlers could begin the job of constructing their new living quarters using the timbers and materials brought from Roanoke Island (Horn 2010:226–227).

Like Quinn, Horn assumes that a small group was sent to the Croatoan settlement of Manteo's people; Parramore argues that the carvings could have been just directions to get the colonists' final location from Manteo and his people (2001:75). However, Horn posits that the colonists' location was in the same vicinity that Parramore hypothesized as the most logical place to relocate in terms of available resources and friendly neighbors.

According to Horn, when John White returned in 1590, the survivors at Croatoan tried to get his attention with fires and smoke, but to no avail. After a while the colonists simply accepted their fate. Many married into the Chowanoc tribe, while others moved on to other locations.

In Horn's scenario, twenty relatively peaceful years passed and the colonists were assimilated, though still wearing European style clothing and building two-story houses of stone.[12] Then the massacre occurred.

Horn highlights Machumps' telling Strachey that Powhatan had the colonists and their Chowanoc hosts killed in 1607 (2010:230–231). This was presumably to prevent them from allying with the newly arrived Jamestown settlers and threatening Powhatan's power and control of prestige goods trading into the area. For Horn, the only recorded survivors were the seven who were under the protection of chief Eyanoco at Ritanoe. There they worked copper from (the as yet undiscovered) mines in the area.

The Salmon Creek location, which Horn identifies as Metackwem, received a boost when a discovery was made in the archives of the British Museum. In 2012, Brent Lane, one of the executive board members of the First Colony Foundation (FCF), discussed previously, requested a favor from the British Museum. He had noticed two patches on the 1585 "Virginia Pars" map by John White and was curious as to what they might be covering. He asked that the map be examined so that anything drawn under the patch might be exposed. The request was granted, and the simple act of placing the map on a light table revealed a hidden drawing, thus exposing a possible new clue as to the fate of the Lost Colonists (Ambers et al. 2012).

The larger patch at the bottom of the map appeared to cover a variant depiction of the coastline. Perhaps it was easier to simply cover the earlier depiction and draw the newer one over it than to erase the initial draft. The more northerly patch seemed more interesting. It covered what appeared to be a symbol for a four-sided fort with bastions in the corners. It was also noted that there were light impressions of another, similar drawing that had been applied to the top of the patch (Ambers et al. 2012). Was this a secret retreat covered over to hide it from the prying eyes of Spanish spies? Or was it simply an intended construction that might never have been built? Or was it some other cartographic error "erased" from the map? To find the answer required an archaeological investigation.

The area in question was the head of the Albemarle Sound at the confluence of the Chowan River and Salmon Creek. This was the area that both Parramore and Horn believed that the Lost Colonists were headed for and the location of the Native American village of Metackwem.[13] A previous archaeological survey on the north side of Salmon Creek had recorded a large site (31BR246) containing both locally produced and early imported European ceramics (Evans et al. 2015). Researchers from the FCF reexamined the site and determined it to be Metackwem. The archaeologists set about narrowing the area to search.

To focus the excavation efforts, historical maps were consulted, and a variety of remote sensing techniques were employed (e.g., multi-spectral imagery, LiDAR, magnetometry, and ground-penetrating radar [GPR]). Underwater archaeologist Gordon Watts used remote sensing to survey the lower reaches of Salmon Creek. The GPR survey noted anomalies where "Elizabethan-style" pottery had previously been recovered. The European ceramics were re-examined and identified as Surrey-Hampshire Border Ware and North Devon Baluster Jar that were produced from the mid–sixteenth century until the late seventeenth century. This part of 31BR246 was dubbed "Site X," and excavations were undertaken (Evans et al. 2015). Excavations began in 2012, took a hiatus in 2013, resumed in 2014, and then continued annually until the summer of 2017. Each field season typically lasted between one and two weeks and cumulatively excavated 2,282 square feet of the site. So what did they find?

Unfortunately, due to past agricultural practices, there is no intact stratigraphy at the site, which makes teasing out different temporal occupations extremely difficult (Evans et al. 2015). Important parts of sites are what archaeologists call *features*. These are areas of interest to the archaeologist which can include postholes, building foundations, trash pits, and other soil discolorations or constructions that represent past activity at the site. Although there were many features at Site X, all but two of them were associated with the deeper prehistoric occupation. The two historic features could not be interpreted as to time period or function.

Artifacts are what the FCF archaeologists have relied on to make the connection with the Lost Colonists. The 40 Border Ware sherds found appear to account for at least seven different vessels. Other sites in North Carolina and Virginia where Border Ware has been found, dating to the seventeenth century, have comparatively less. The FCF has suggested that Border Ware is most abundant on early sites and decreases in popularity into the seventeenth century. The same goes for the eight sherds of North Devon Baluster Jar that were recovered. Non-ceramic artifacts include two iron tenterhooks, used for stretching canvas or hides, a copper aglet (lacing tip), and a possible Augsburg lead bale seal that may date to the early seventeenth century or before. There were some other historic artifacts recovered, notably pipestems, but these were interpreted as part of a much later occupation (Evans et al. 2015).

The FCF archaeologists considered the geographic location of the site, the artifacts recovered, and the lack of any documented historical presence in the area prior to the trader Nathaniel Batts in 1655 and have hypothesized that at least a portion of the Lost Colony occupied the area for a short time. Certainly worthy of further investigation.

In early 2019, pedestrian and shovel test surveys were undertaken on the western side of the Chowan River north and south of Highway 17. A site discovered by UNC archaeologists in 1977, 31BR49, was revisited and found to contain some of the same types of ceramics as Site X. These included Surrey-Hampshire Border Ware, Frechen stoneware, and Essex fine redware, all dating to the late sixteenth and early seventeenth centuries. This suggested to the FCF archaeologists that there may be another Lost Colonist refugee site in the vicinity. They called it Site Y.

Again, no structural evidence was uncovered. The FCF archaeologists continue to think that this may be due to the deep plowing that has taken place over the centuries, thus removing evidence of postholes (Evans et al. 2020:56). Or it may be that it was a small group, living in a temporary shelter and leaving little evidence of their habitation. As the FCF archaeologists themselves admit, "there is not and probably can never be a Lost Colonist 'smoking gun' at Site Y" (Evans et al. 2020:57).

The case for the headwaters of the Albemarle Sound being the destination of the Lost Colonists makes sense. The problem is that, at some level, all of the hypotheses concerning their whereabouts make sense. As we have stated earlier, with so little evidence to work with, one can make compelling cases for several different scenarios. As Quinn himself said, it will take physical evidence to settle the question. The archaeological evidence for the native village of Metackwem seems convincing. However, the evidence of a sixteenth-century European presence, while tantalizing, is not compelling. The argument of "who else could it be?" ignores the fact that we know little historically about northeastern North Carolina in the early Colonial Period. It is also worth noting that European artifacts do not necessarily equal European settlers. What is well-documented is that the native population desired these goods (the ceramics or what these containers held) and there was a thriving trade network.

HYPOTHESIS 4–50 MILES INTO THE MAINE—AND BEYOND

About the same time Thomas Parramore published his 2001 article questioning Quinn's Chesapeake hypothesis and positing that Salmon Creek at the head of the Albemarle Sound made better sense as the location the Lost Colony people had gone to from Roanoke Island, Lee Miller published *Roanoke: Solving the Mystery of the Lost Colony*

(2001). Miller's was the first book-length study to question the Quinn hypothesis and, as such, garnered quite a bit of attention. Miller uses much of *Roanoke: Solving the Mystery of the Lost Colony* to explain why the 1587 colonists were abandoned in the first place. She creates a scenario of intrigue and conspiracy in which Sir Walter Raleigh is undermined by his rival in Elizabeth's court, Sir Francis Walsingham, with the 1587 colonists becoming victims of the rivalry. Miller then uses the last part of *Roanoke: Solving the Mystery of the Lost Colony* to argue her own ideas about what happened to the colonists.

Like Quinn, Miller assumes a small group went to Croatoan to wait for John White's return—though for Miller, rather than just men, the group was "composed especially of those women who had recently given birth [including Eleanor Dare] and those with infants too young to travel" as well as "a handful of men, perhaps, to keep them company" (2001:322, n.5; 228). In Miller's scenario, the majority of the colonists follow exactly what John White said they planned to do—relocate "fifty miles into the main." For Miller, only one likely place fits that description, the Chowan River just up from the Albemarle Sound. This would be an area Ralph Lane had explored in 1585–1586 and found rich for agriculture, and it was the borderland between two Algonquian peoples, the Chowanocs and the Weapemeocs, people with whom they had relatively good relationships.

While Miller first places the main body of colonists in the same general area as Parramore, Horn, and the First Colony Foundation do, her story of the Lost Colony doesn't stop there. Miller goes on to discuss Michael Sicklemore's report about his 1609 search for the 1587 colonists among the Chowanoc. As noted earlier, John Smith reported in his 1612 *A Map of Virginia* that Sicklemore "found little hope and lesse certainetie of them were left by Sir Walter Rawley" (1986:1:265). However, Miller relies on the same passage as it appears in Smith's 1624 *Generall Historie* rather than in the earlier *A Map of Virginia*, which adds two sentences: "The river, he saw was not great, the people few, the countrey most over growne with pynes, where there did grow here and there straglingly *Pemminaw*, we call silke grasse. But by the river the ground was good, and exceeding furtill" (1986:2:215).

According to Miller, the same European diseases which decimated Native American populations throughout the Americas severely impacted the Chowanoc and Weapemeoc. This in turn created a situation which allowed the Mandoag Indians, whose territory was just west of the Chowanocs and Weapemeocs, to attack their Native American and English neighbors, taking the English women and children as captives—along with any men who surrendered—making them slaves, as they would do with any Native Americans they attacked. The enslaved English men, women, and children, according to Miller, were then distributed among the various Mandoag towns with some sold to other tribes.

For Miller, distributing the captives explains the reports of Europeans among Native Americans from the Coastal Plain to the Piedmont. She identifies the Mandoag as the Siouan tribe the Eno, with a territory bordered by the Chowan, Tar, and Meherrin Rivers on the east, south, and north and going as far west as present-day Randolph County in the North Carolina Piedmont. In Miller's estimation, the Carolina Slate belt in and around Randolph County must have been the furthest reaches where any of the smaller groups of enslaved 1587 colonists ended up, explaining Strachey's report of four men, two boys, and one girl used to beat copper being mined at Ritanoc, with Ritanoc being either near or the same as the legendary copper center Chaunis Temoatan the English had first heard about in 1585–1586. This series of assumptions can explain the various reports of English/Europeans throughout the region given by Native American sources in the early seventeenth century.

In all of this, Miller's hypothesis parallels much of what anthropologist Helen C. Rountree has more recently published in her study of the Carolina Algonquians, *Manteo's World: Native American Life in Carolina's Sound Country Before and After the Lost Colony* (2021). Rountree writes, "There is a strong likelihood—not merely the possibility—that those English families were *not* completely wiped out by the hostile Algonquian speakers nearest them," but would have been taken in by "more distant, friendlier Native people" (102). Rountree adds that no one Native American village could have taken in all of the surviving English colonists, meaning "the 'lost colonists' refugees would have had to split up. Some would have been split off involuntarily, by being captured and taken home by hostile Native people" (102). The difference between Rountree and Miller is that Rountree gives a general sense of what she believes would have happened to the 1587 colonists based on her studies of Tidewater Virginia's and the Carolina Sounds region's Algonquian cultures. Miller hypothesizes a very specific narrative of exactly what happened to the Lost Colony.

Miller's hypothesis depends not only on suppositions about specifically where the 1587 colonists moved to from Roanoke Island, but on suppositions about specific localized effects of European–Native American contact and of Native American politics of the region. Miller's hypothesis also depends on assumptions about what was true, what was misunderstood, and what was deliberately falsified in the reports of English people living with the Native Americans of the region. First and foremost among these assumptions is that when John Smith wrote that Sicklemore "found little hope and lesse certaintie of them were left by Sir Walter Raleigh" and that Nathaniel Powell and Anas Todkill came back with the news that "nothing could we learne but they were all dead" (Smith 1986:1:266), what he wrote "was a lie, pure and simple" (Miller 2001:218). With a sense of certain knowledge, Miller continues: "White's colonists were not dead. Smith knew it. The London Company knew it. Raleigh knew it. So did the Virginia Council at Jamestown. Yet the legal fiction was created—and would stick for nearly four hundred years" (218).

Miller's explanation for the cover-up is that the Jamestown colony was experiencing great difficulties and that to report captured English colonists had been enslaved and could not be rescued would only add to already bad publicity. It would not attract the needed additional backing and colonists. Miller goes on to argue that reports of the 1587 colonists being killed by Powhatan were used as propaganda to portray Powhatan as a villain, sanctioning the Virginia Company to attack Powhatan and his people, making Virginia safe for the English. In such a scenario, Raleigh's colonists no longer needed to be searched for, and any English survivors with the Eno became rumors of generic Europeans heard occasionally over the next half century.

Miller writes a good narrative, one that includes most if not all of the important references to the Lost Colony in the primary and early secondary sources. At issue, though, is that the narrative depends on deductive extrapolation. Miller deductively uses general beliefs about what happened when Native Americans and Europeans encountered one another (e.g., the decimation of Native American populations because of disease) as well as general European behavior (they said they would move fifty miles into the main, so they did) to predict what happened in the specific instance of the 1587 colonists. However, after the first step is deduced, Miller needs to treat what is an untested hypothesis as a proven theory so she can extrapolate the next step in her narrative.

In the opening hypothesis, the 1587 colonists moved from Roanoke Island to the borderland between the Chowanoc and Weapemeoc. Accepting the opening hypothesis as certain, Miller extrapolates to an additional hypothesis that the coming of the English decimated the Chowanoc and Weapemeoc populations, allowing the Mandoag to attack and to enslave the surviving Chowanoc and Weapemeoc along with the surviving 1587 colonists. Accepting this new hypothesis as certain, Miller extrapolates to a third-level hypothesis that the Mandoag (whom she hypothesizes are the Eno) keep some of the enslaved English for their own uses, selling the rest to other tribes.

Having accepted this hypothesis as certain, Miller extrapolates once again to deduce that among those slaves were the four men, two boys, and one girl who were being used to beat copper for the weroance, or chief, of Ritanoc, a place Miller additionally hypothesizes is either the same as or near the legendary rich copper mines of Chaunis Temoatan. After one deduction is made and shown to be possible, it is treated as fact in order to extrapolate the next step, and so on. Even if all of the primary source material fits into the narrative, it does so through the uncertainty of extrapolation—each step is an untested hypothesis built on other untested hypotheses. In the end, Miller's narrative is a string of untested hypotheses.

Which makes Miller's 2007 history for younger readers, *Roanoke: The Mystery of the Lost Colony*, all the more interesting. In the final pages, Miller deals with what happened to the Lost Colony, stating that John Smith was repeatedly told about English captives. However, Miller writes, "Small and weak, Jamestown hadn't the power to bring them home. So they told a lie: The colonists, they said, were all dead. And thus the search ended" (2007:105). For pre-teen readers, Miller's narrative about the Lost Colony is no longer hypothesis—it even passes over the stage of being a tested theory. It is fact.

Hypothesis 5—The Sassafras Conspiracy

Aside from the Chesapeake Bay and the west end of the Albemarle Sound, other locations for where the Lost Colony went have been suggested. A truly intriguing solution to the Roanoke mystery begins with the legend of Beechland. It is oral history that recalls a ghost town out in the middle of swampland on mainland Dare County just west of Roanoke Island. The legend holds that the original inhabitants of Beechland were descendants of the Lost Colonists. Most of the land today is either wildlife refuge or in agricultural production. According to Philip McMullan (2014[2010]:111–112), all that remains of the settlement are a shingle ditch, a well, and an ancient graveyard.[14] Renowned chronicler of North Carolina legends Judge Charles Whedbee wrote in 1966 that within living memory there were fair-skinned blue-eyed Indians with surnames that matched those of the Lost Colonists (30). The descendants of the original residents claim their ancestors came to the area, mixed with local Croatan Indians, and stayed for over two centuries, completely removed from the outside world.

Folklorist Karen Baldwin notes that similar stories of lost places and peoples are found across Eastern North Carolina. She has observed that "[l]ess directly, yet powerfully and pervasively, the 'Lost Colony' of Roanoke Island resonates with the commemorative experiences of vanished and displaced communities throughout the region.... This pervasive experience of lost community, consciously or unself-consciously sustained, must be recognized in reexamining the meaning of the 'Lost Colony'" (Baldwin 2003:13). So, how do the Lost Colonists end up in a remote swamp completely removed from European society for generations?

What makes the Beechland story different from those of other abandoned towns is the discovery of "riven coffins" by a dragline operator in the 1950s. A riven coffin is made from a tree trunk hollowed out and split in half. Again, Judge Whedbee tells it best:

> West Virginia Pulp and Paper Company was doing some excavating for timbering purposes, they had to dig into a rather large mound near Beechland. In this mound, in the heart of the wilderness, they found numerous Indian artifacts, arrowheads, works of pottery, and potsherds. They also found several riven coffins that were made from solid cypress wood.... On the top of each coffin was plainly and deeply chiseled a Roman or Latin cross.... Beneath each cross were the unmistakable letters, I N R I. These were thought to represent the traditional "Jesus of Nazareth, Rex Judaeorum" or, translated, "Jesus of Nazareth, King of the Jews." ... A riven coffin with English carvings in the midst of a wilderness in an Indian burial ground—is that coincidence? [Whedbee 1966:31]

Like so many urban (or in this case rural) legends, we do not hear it from the horse's mouth. It is always from someone who knew the dragline operator or some other unimpeachable source. In other words, it is hearsay, or anecdotal, evidence. Still, there are many who will attest to its veracity—both of your authors have heard the story of the coffins, and a local author, Deborah Dunn (2017), has even published a mystery novel using the coffins as backdrop to her fictional story.

The solution to how the Lost Colonists found themselves so isolated from their fellow countrymen is a conspiracy theory. According to the *Oxford English Dictionary*, a conspiracy theory is a belief that some covert but influential organization is responsible for a circumstance or event ("conspiracy theory, n." 2021). In this case, Sir Walter Raleigh himself suppressed information regarding the true whereabouts of the colonists and the reason for their being there. This was done to hide the source of his secret commodity—sassafras.

The premise of McMullan's *Beechland and the Lost Colony* (2014 [2010]) is that the John White colony was sent to North Carolina expressly to harvest sassafras. What made this plant valuable was that it was thought to possibly cure syphilis and maybe even the Black Death (Manning and Moore 1936). Raleigh had a monopoly from Queen Elizabeth on this herbal remedy and went to great lengths to keep its source secret. According to McMullan, when White left Roanoke to get supplies, he was actually headed to confirm that the colony was well planted and the sassafras source was secure. As McMullan writes:

> The Croatoan then escorted the colonists onto the mainland where sassafras was located. A rear guard remained behind on Roanoke Island to watch for Spanish ships and await White's return. It is likely that the colonists initially separated into several Croatoan villages to limit their impact on the Indian's drought-restricted food supply. One of these villages was near a large grove of sassafras trees that provided this valuable commodity. After a delay because of the Spanish Armada, Ralegh began to send ships to resupply the colonists and bring back sassafras to England. When Ralegh lost his charter and his head, no further voyages were taken to Croatoan Island. The colonists were then truly abandoned [McMullan 2014(2010):8].

The idea that Raleigh wanted to keep the source of his sassafras secret accounts for the lack of and even contradictory evidence concerning the Lost Colony. The claim that the White colony was initially headed for the Chesapeake was a deliberate red herring, according to McMullan, designed to throw off the Spaniards or any competing English investor. The ships that Raleigh sent to find the colonists, but "failed," actually knew where the colonists were and were bringing supplies and receiving the shipments of sassafras. It was not until 1603, when Martin Pring brought back quantities of sassafras from the Cape Cod region, thus breaking the monopoly, that the ties with the Lost Colonists were presumably severed. Raleigh was imprisoned in the Tower by this time, but McMullan says that even then it is unclear whether he continued to send ships until his death in 1618. However, that seems unlikely, as sassafras doesn't travel well and is largely ineffective against syphilis and the plague (Manning and Moore 1936).

The secret of the location of the Lost Colonists apparently died with Raleigh. McMullan claims that "when it was clear that they had been abandoned, the colonists in family groups moved a short distance from their Indian village [where they had relocated 50 miles into the main] to Beechland. There they maintained a semblance of their English culture. Some descendants of these colonists remained in Beechland for 250 years while others drifted away along the migration trail of the Croatoan" (McMullan 2014[2010]:8).

This abandonment is not as catastrophic as one might think. Again, McMullan is clear on their fate, "Like the Pilgrims in New England, they had come to stay on their own land and they would make the best of the hand that fate had dealt them" (2014[2010]:130). These settlers were better off than they had been with their landless lives in England. It was a brave new world, and they were a heroic part of it.

The evidence to McMullan's point is, like most of the Lost Colony hypotheses, circumstantial. For McMullan, some of what the primary sources tell us is true and some is deliberate misdirection. McMullan crafts a narrative that sounds plausible, though unlikely. That a group of over 100 colonists would hide out in the swamps for centuries seems incredible. But is this hypothesis testable? As it turns out, it could be.

McMullan would like to see an archaeological investigation of the Beechland area. He has narrowed the search parameters to several areas within the wildlife refuge. One remembers that this is the area where it was reported the riven coffins were exposed and then later reburied by the dragline operator in the 1950s. "The first priority," McMullan writes, "is to uncover and date the riven coffins on Milltail Road. If the results are promising, the search should continue at the Payne homestead, the graveyard of wooden markers, the shingle ditch and Beechland Landing" (McMullan 2014 [2010]:132).

The area actually had a preliminary archaeological survey in the early 1980s as required before a local farming corporation could conduct land altering activities. This reconnaissance-level survey of the area by Carolina Archaeological Services (1982) found evidence of prehistoric and historic Native American sites and a later historic occupation in the Beechland area, but no sixteenth-century material or riven coffins (McMullan 2014 [2010]:3–4). No other archaeologists as yet have taken the challenge to perform a follow-up investigation.

Hypothesis 6—You Know What Happens When You Assume

Brandon Fullam—in *The Lost Colony of Roanoke: New Perspectives* (2017), one of the most recent attempts to solve the mystery of the 1587 colonists—is dissatisfied with previous interpretations of the documents and, as his subtitle states, claims to bring a fresh perspective concerning the Lost Colony. He "promises to identify and challenge the difficulties and shortcomings of the theories and assumptions contained in virtually all past and present nonfiction books and published material on the Lost Colony" (2017:1). But are his assumptions and interpretations any better than those he is critiquing? His critique of previous theories (really hypotheses) centers around four fallacies to which previous researchers have fallen victim. Fullam labels these *institutionalized assumptions* (2017:5).

The first of these assumptions is that Simon Fernandez was personally responsible for the failure of the 1587 colony by leaving the colonists at Roanoke Island instead of taking them to the Chesapeake, which, John White assured us, was the actual destination. Fullam finds Fernandez to be far from a villain, claiming that the act of leaving the colony on Roanoke was neither unilateral nor unjustified. According to Fullam, the English discovered en route that the Spanish had intelligence that the colony was headed to the Chesapeake and had plans to eliminate it. This is bolstered by the fact that the Spaniards did, indeed, search for the English colony around Chesapeake Bay. There is also recent research that suggests that Fernandez was far from incompetent or a plant by the Spaniards (Isil 2003; Rocha 2017).

The second fallacy is that John Smith's mentions of "men clothed like me" at Ocanahonan and Pakrakanick indicated Lost Colony survivors. Included in this fallacy is the misinterpretation of the Zúñiga map also referring to the "men cloathed" in the Albemarle region.[15] Researchers have assumed that survivors of the Roanoke colony were prowling the coastal plain of North Carolina while Jamestown was being established. Here, Fullam takes a truly fresh perspective by claiming that the European-clothed men that Smith heard about from his native hosts were actually Spaniards from the Juan Pardo expedition that passed through the interior of North Carolina in 1567. The counter assumption is that one European looks like another and the 20-year difference in the expeditions made little difference to the natives.

The third assumption is that chief Powhatan slaughtered the Lost Colonists who had relocated close to the Chesapeake after leaving Roanoke Island. This was the theory favored by Quinn that influenced many subsequent researchers. Again, Fullam finds a fundamental flaw in the interpretation of the information attributed to John Smith and William Strachey. According to Fullam, the "slaughter at Roanoke" did not refer to the 1587 Lost Colonists; rather, it was a reference to the colonists lost in conflict with the local Native Americans from the previous Grenville expedition. The news had traveled to Powhatan and had been embellished with the retelling. There were English deaths, but Strachey and Smith misinterpreted them as relating to the 1587 colony.

The fourth and final institutionalized assumption also deals with Strachey's report of the "slaughter at Roanoke," in which Strachey appears to imply that Roanoke does not refer specifically to Roanoke Island, but rather anywhere between the Albemarle Sound and Jamestown. Reexamining the writings of Strachey, Fullam is unconvinced that Roanoke referred to anywhere else except the island. This is where the Europeans had suffered some early casualties that Grenville records. Fullam then concludes, "Since it can now be said that the basic information related by the Powhatans—including the two slaughter events—was essentially accurate, but misinterpreted by Smith and Strachey, then all versions of the Powhatan–Lost Colony slaughter scenario are invalid" (2017:199–200).

For Fullam, the original misinterpretations of Smith and Strachey, compounded by Quinn, were repeated by later researchers committing a pair of logical fallacies. The first, Fullam claims, is proof by repeated assertion (2017:6). That is to say, if you repeat something often enough in print, it becomes an unchallenged "fact." This reification, he claims, is how Simon Fernandez becomes the villain in the Lost Colony drama. Another logical fallacy is proof by appeal to authority (2017:6). Here, Fullam claims that distinguished historians get away with their flimsy assertions because of their scholarly reputations. This latter is a clear jab at Quinn and other academics, though one could counter that there is nothing that academics enjoy more than challenging each other's ideas.

Having called into question the hypotheses of those that have gone before him, what does Fullam think happened to the Lost Colonists?

To begin with, that they did not go north. The Spaniards supposedly knew that the Chesapeake was their destination and were out to destroy them. That negated the original plan of heading up to the Chesapeake. Instead, the colonists returned to Roanoke to pick up the men Grenville left behind (who were gone when they got there). To the west were the Secotan, which Fullam remarked were decidedly unfriendly given the previous expeditions' experiences. There was also the consideration of having a decent harbor for resupply, a most difficult proposition given their location along the treacherous Outer Banks, aka "the Graveyard of the Atlantic."

In Fullam's analysis, when John White left to get more supplies, the rest of the colonists went south to the only relatively deep and stable inlet, that on the north end of Ocracoke Island. From there they went inland, settling somewhere along the Neuse River. Fullam is not sure exactly where, but he hypothesizes it was probably somewhere in present-day Carteret, Pamlico, or southern Beaufort County (Fullam 2017:226). In Fullam's version of events, as in several other hypotheses, the colonists carved CROATOAN to direct White to an English outpost left at the village of Croatoan to lead White to the colony's new location, and references to Croatoan were left at Roanoke and presumably at other places along the Outer Banks.

Plans changed when White did not return the following year. Fullam figures that the colonists feared that they had been abandoned and decided on drastic measures. The plan was either to return to England or to go to a place the English frequented. Thus, most of the colonists took to the pinnace that had been left behind for them and perhaps built another and sailed for the closest English outpost. Fullam determines that this would have been the cod fisheries along the Grand Banks of Newfoundland (2017:227). Since there is no historical mention of the fishing fleets encountering the Lost Colonists, he concludes that they must have been lost at sea. This *deus ex machina* neatly wraps up the fate of the colonists with an untestable bow. But wait ... there's more!

And if some colonists remained behind? Fullam has a coda for them. He notes from Spanish sources (García-Herrera et al. 2005) that there was a hurricane in the area in 1588, which he feels would have devastated the southeastern Coastal Plain of North Carolina. The few colonists that survived this final blow would have assimilated into the surrounding tribes and within two generations would have, essentially, gone native. Fullam writes, "Other than the periodic occurrence of an unusual eye or hair color, descendants of the 1587 Lost Colonists would have been virtually indistinguishable from the native peoples" (2017:228). He opines that the few surviving colonists, if there were any, became so scattered over the years that current efforts to trace them through DNA analyses would be futile.

Fullam's hypothesis is based on a reinterpretation of the documents and a supposition of what the colonists would have done on the basis of his reinterpretation. Is it better than those that were previously given? Again, it will depend upon what archaeologists can discover. It seems unlikely that the wrecks of the ships that left for Newfoundland will be found, but there is the chance that the brief occupation somewhere along the banks of the Neuse might be discovered. Perhaps the best part of Fullam's work is, as he calls it, the deconstruction of previous assumptions and hypotheses.

Hypothesis 7—They Told Us Where They Went

Of all the published researchers, Scott Dawson is probably the most certain about the fate of the Lost Colonists. According to Dawson, they went where John White said they went, the village of Croatoan on Hatteras Island—"We know not just where they went but also what happened after they got there" (Dawson 2020:16).

Dawson states directly in his book *The Lost Colony and Hatteras Island*, "If truth is what you seek, you will find it here" (2020:18). Dawson lays out, in straightforward fashion, the trials and tribulations and probable fate of the well-meaning colonists who came to Roanoke Island in 1587 and were gone when John White returned three years later. The Colony was not lost, though. According to Dawson, this is just a misconception based on a popular narrative. It was abandoned. In Dawson's view, the popular outdoor drama along with past and present racism has distorted all other interpretations. This warped view has led researchers to view the Lost Colony in an incorrect and unflattering light, missing, as Dawson writes, "a story unlike any other between

Europeans and Natives—a story of brotherhood and friendship rather than violence and hatred" (2020:20).

Unfortunately, although Dawson doesn't equivocate with his interpretations in *The Lost Colony and Hatteras Island*, he also doesn't cite where he gets his information. There is a bibliography, but no footnotes or in-text citations. So the reader is left wondering what is based on the 20 external sources listed in the bibliography and what are Dawson's own insights. This is doubly unfortunate in that his later assertions about the archaeological finds are based solely on his recollections of what transpired during the excavations in which he participated but did not direct.

As an opening point, Dawson states that everything was tempered by the war with Spain. The Grenville/Lane colony was originally envisioned as a privateering base, particularly to attack Spanish ships. However, this was softened during the John White venture when families, rather than soldiers, made up the bulk of the colonists. This was an example of what Dawson calls the Elizabethan Model of Colonization: "Elizabethans such as Thomas Harriot, John White and Sir Walter Raleigh believed Native Americans had been mistreated by the Spanish and pointed out how the Spanish abuse of Natives had led to Spain's downfall in its attempts to colonize the New World. The Elizabethans had a vision of colonizing the New World not by conquest but by trade and friendship" (Dawson 2020:26).

Dawson also chides past researchers for their ignorance about the native inhabitants of Eastern North Carolina:

> Too often, authors and historians from the twentieth century paint the Natives with too large a brush, lumping them all together into one massive tribe and making no distinction between them as separate nations. Instead, they are just referred to in one category as "Indians." These same authors and historians tend to ignore the impact that the Natives had on this time in history and focus solely on the English perspective. It is this kind of dismissive attitude toward the Native tribes and their influence that has made so many "scholars" blind to understanding the fate of the 1587 colony [2020:50].

Dawson sets up a strawman argument as he doesn't specify which researchers are making these generalizations and certainly those cited earlier in this book (e.g., Parramore, Horn) are neither ignorant nor dismissive of the Native polities. In fact, Michael Oberg has written the well-received book *The Head in Edward Nugent's Hand: Roanoke's Forgotten Indians* (2008) examining the Roanoke colonies from the perspective of the various Native encounters with the colonists.

Dawson tells how the Lost Colonists were beset by unfriendly neighbors, principally the Secotan. For Dawson, the Croatoan, Manteo's people, were the only friends the 1587 colonists could count on. With this kind of understanding, it becomes abundantly clear why the refugees went to Hatteras Island after John White's departure:

> Imagine being a colonist. You are in a strange land thousands of miles from home. One of your own has been shot sixteen times with arrows and had his brains knocked out by Indians from the mainland…. The governor instructs you to carve out the name of the place you relocate to, and you do so. You leave the word Croatoan on a palisade you built to protect yourself from the Secotan. These are the facts, and armed with the facts, it is no wonder why Governor John White had no doubt in his mind where the colony had relocated [2020:56–57].

Apparently, everyone knew where the colonists were (except the Spanish) but preferred not to interact with or even speak of them. According to Dawson, "In 1607, it had been twenty years since the colonists were last seen. To the English at this time, they were hearing how the English and Natives were living together as one and had assimilated into an interracial culture. To them, it was a disgrace. They were appalled and did not want to see it or speak of it" (2020:64–65). Apparently, they took the Elizabethan Model of Colonization too far. The Lost Colonists had gone native.

Dawson harbors no doubts that this is what happened. In his view, the archaeology he helped facilitate on Hatteras Island provides proof for what he already knew. Dawson is not trained in archaeology, but he spent time at the digs that were conducted at Hatteras. He glosses over the early archaeology at the Cape Creek site conducted by Haag and Phelps and bemoans the fact that those earlier recovered artifacts left the island and are inaccessible to the average individual. However, as mentioned previously, the real issue with Phelps' dig and later archaeology is that there are no reports and nothing published in academic journals. Dawson focuses on the archaeology conducted by Mark Horton of the University of Bristol, who picked up where David Phelps left off. With nothing published by Horton or his students, the following informal discussion of the excavations is nearly all there is.

Mark Horton and students from the University of Bristol came out in 2009 and were joined by local volunteers from the Croatoan Archaeological Society. The field season was only a couple of weeks long. They initially dug near, but not on, the property where Phelps dug in the 1990s, though it seems likely that it was part of the same site. Like the ECU project, the University of Bristol crew recovered prehistoric items and European artifacts from the seventeenth and eighteenth centuries. The 2010–2012 seasons produced more of the same. Dawson includes an illustration of a bowl, which he identifies as African colonial ware. Although it was in a Late Woodland Period (i.e., Native American) context, he suggests that the Croatoan may have been harboring a runaway slave (Dawson 2020: 104). Still, there was no sixteenth-century occupation layer where they were digging. Undeterred, Dawson claims, "The story of the missing century (1600s) appears to be that the Croatoan were thriving and very well fed based on the middens. They were using iron tools and English guns, wearing pocket watches and drinking brandy. In other words, we had evidence of assimilation going on at least as early as 1650 and possibly earlier" (2020:114). In his interpretation, this was evidence of the Lost Colonists becoming Croatoans.

In 2013, a find was made that solidified, in Dawson's mind, the idea that they had found evidence of the Lost Colonists in Hatteras. He had speculated that "short of the body of a colonist, there was only one thing we could find that would tell us it came in 1587 as opposed to 1584, and that was a sword" (Dawson 2020:129). A rusty chunk of metal was recovered from a seemingly sixteenth-century context. After three days in the electrolysis tank, Dawson and Horton identified it as a swept hilt rapier. Coupled with a glass fragment that had been fashioned into an arrowhead and a writing slate with what may be a faint drawing of a man shooting a gun, Dawson felt he had the validation for his hypothesis.

For Dawson, the Lost Colonists had been abandoned and so they continued to live out their days with the Croatoan. Dawson allows that some of them may have split off and gone elsewhere. Perhaps they went to the mountains to smelt copper (a copper bun had been recovered from an early historical context) or perhaps they had taken one of the pinnaces and tried to return to England. But the majority of them stayed put on Hatteras. Dawson concludes his book by describing a rectangular anomaly discovered by Horton's flying a drone over private property on Hatteras. He writes that this may be the original survivors' camp and will be the focus of future research.

Dawson makes a straightforward case for the fate of the Lost Colonists. He takes John White at his word—they came to Croatoan. The colonists set up camp and, to the horror of their English contemporaries, mixed with the locals and gradually went Native. Rather than seeing the repurposed European artifacts (e.g., the glass arrowhead) as Croatoans acquiring artifacts through trade and repurposing them to their own needs, he sees the Lost Colonists slowly assimilating and changing their own artifacts to conform to their new lifestyle. The seventeenth-century material is explained as coming down from Jamestown and it, too, being nativized as the assimilation is completed.

Epilogue

So there you have it. Seven published hypotheses about what happened to the Lost Colonists that seem to account for most of the data. But they can't all be right. Even employing Occam's Razor is of little help. All of the hypotheses make numerous assumptions—it is unavoidable without more solid data. As valid hypotheses, they could be tested if the data were available, but because the data haven't been found—and may never be found—they are unable to rise to the status of theory, to become the generally accepted idea explaining what happened to the Lost Colony.

We are often asked which hypothesis we favor. After numerous scholarly discussions, we decided that "none of them" was the answer. Or maybe it was all of them? Or perhaps it was parts of some combined with parts of another? We honestly don't have a favorite. As the historian David Quinn reluctantly opined, it may be up to the archaeologists to find the answer, if there is one to be found. But, if like Tom, you like good fiction as much as you like fact, read on. The "theories" are better when you don't let facts get in the way!

6

Fringe "Theories"

How Far Can We Go?

A hypothesis proposes an idea based on what is known, acknowledging what is not known, and having a way to test the idea. So what is an idea based on misinformation, on misreading known information, or on desires? Sometimes referred to as fringe "theories," with the quotation marks highlighting that they are not scientific theories at all, even better is the term *pseudoscience*, including *pseudo-social sciences* such as *pseudo-geography*, *pseudo-history*, and especially *pseudo-archeology*. People who promote these ideas tend to have so much vested in them that they are out to *prove* what they already "know" rather than proposing a hypothesis based on limited knowledge to be tested and revised or rejected according to the results of the testing. Because there is so little real data, the Lost Colony is a draw for pseudoscientific "theories."

As problematic as they are, pseudoscientific propositions are worth examining. They matter because they influence not only popular ideas about what happened to the 1587 colonists, but at times even academic researchers. Just as important, pseudoscience illustrates how and why people become invested in the fate of the Lost Colony. Pseudoscientific propositions tend to fall into two camps: (1) conjectures based on what people would like to believe and (2) propositions intentionally meant to fool people. In other words, pseudoscience presents beliefs based on hope and "beliefs" that are hoaxes. Both types tell us something about human nature even if they don't tell us much about the actual fate of the Lost Colony. Pseudoscience can be attractive because humans are drawn in by *confirmation bias*, that is, by people's tendency to interpret evidence according to their pre-existing beliefs, according to what they want to be true.

Lost Colony pseudoscience began at least as early as the first hypotheses. There are elements of pseudoscience in Hamilton

McMillan's presentation of the Lumbee hypothesis, in particular his major argument about Lumbee traditions. As noted above, according to McMillan, "the tradition is universal among them from infancy to old age, that their ancestors came from 'Roanoke in Virginia.' By Virginia they mean Eastern North Carolina, and the term Roanoke means the territory occupied by the tribe in the vicinity of Pamlico Sound" (26). There is no exploration of other possible ways to interpret George Low-rie's speech, no skepticism that tests the idea. McMillan concludes, "The writer has been much interested in investigating the traditions prevalent among the Croatans and expresses his firm conviction that they are descended from the friendly tribe found on our eastern coast in 1587, and also descended from the lost colonists of Roanoke who were amalgamated with this tribe" (27).

McMillan asserts as truth that the Lumbee moved to the region of the Lumber River from Roanoke Island and the Pamlico Sound region, that Lumbee/Croatan oral history has been continuous on this point since the 1580s, and that the oral tradition says that the Lost Colony had joined with the Croatan Indians when they moved to the Lumber River area. Asserted truth without discussion of potential areas for further research or possible chinks in a hypothesis's armor is a matter of faith rather than of science, a matter of ideology rather than an exploration of possibilities. These are hallmarks of pseudoscience.

A parallel conjecture appeared in 1910 when Collier Cobb published a piece in the February 1910 issue of *The University Magazine*, "Early English Survival on Hatteras Island." Cobb was a professor of geology at the University of North Carolina at Chapel Hill, with a specialization in the movement of sands and coastlines (Eagles 1979:390–391). This work frequently took him to Hatteras Island, which he portrays as very isolated, "three days' journey from almost any point," adding "when you had made the journey you had gone back three centuries in time" (1910:4). Cobb describes the dialect used on Hatteras Island, writing that it is heavy in words that he identifies as sixteenth-century or earlier, such as *canty* to mean "merry, brisk, lively" (6) or *fleech* to mean "to flatter" (7). And he recognizes tunes sung by a congregation in 1895 being "essentially the same as that of Ariel's song in [Shakespeare's] The Tempest ... sung in the days of Queen Elizabeth" (9).

Cobb's explanation of how sixteenth-century English culture was preserved on Hatteras Island is that "there are strong reasons for believing that the lost colony of Roanoke fled to the protection of its friends, the Hatteras Indians" (10). He adds that, as the Graveyard of the Atlantic, "there are records of wrecks off Hatteras from 1558, when a ship was cast away near Secotan, manned by white people, and some of its crew preserved by the natives, and 1590, when Captain Spicer, Ralph Skinner, Hance, the surgeon, and others, eleven all told, were washed overboard from the ship of Raleigh's adventurers" (10). Cobb's is the only suggestion seen so far that these men survived rather than drowned.

Cobb adds, "The language of the island, particularly the older forms of speech found there, is that of the better classes, or at least the middle classes in England in the days of Queen Elizabeth. The Raleigh voyagers having counted among their number gentlemen adventurers from all parts of the kingdom, it is not difficult to imagine that these forms were introduced by them" (10). Cobb only allows for stranded sixteenth-century colonists and sailors in a place isolated from the world to explain the dialect of Hatteras Island—including the interesting new twists that many of the 1587 colonists were of the aristocracy before being named Assistants of the City of Raleigh and that the men John White said drowned in 1590 in fact survived and swam ashore.

What motivates these early forms of Lost Colony pseudoscience? What is at the root of their confirmation biases? For McMillan, an elected representative to the North Carolina General Assembly, helping the Native American inhabitants of his district gain an identity separate from others, especially African Americans, could bring them into the Democratic fold at a time when there was strong Republican and Populist opposition.[1] For Cobb, it is a growing sense of nostalgia for the isolation being lost in his adopted community, where the dialect "will soon be a thing of the past, as the traveler and the tourist, the schoolmaster and the trader, are fast making even Hatteras like the rest of the world" (10).

Cobb's attachment to Hatteras illustrates one of the strongest motivators, pride of place. Two works that appeared shortly after World War II, Melvin Robinson's *The Riddle of the Lost Colony* (1946) and C.K. Howe's *Solving the Riddle of the Lost Colony* (1947), also illustrate pride of place and how it can lead people to fall for pseudoscience, whether the pseudoscience of hope in the case of Robinson or the pseudoscience of hoax in the case of Howe.

Robinson's *The Riddle of the Lost Colony* has become the poster child among people who like to ridicule Lost Colony fringe theories. Robinson first published his ideas in a 1935 three-part series in his home county newspaper, *The Beaufort News*. There and more fully in his 1946 booklet, Robinson argued that the 1587 colonists—as well as the 1584 and 1585–1586 expeditions—were not based on Roanoke Island, but on Cedar Island, 75 miles south in present-day Carteret County. For Robinson, the island marked *Croatoan* on the 1590 Theodor de Bry map

"Americæ pars, Nunc Virginia dicta" ("That Part of America Now Called Virginia") is Ocracoke Island, counter to how most people interpret it as the southernmost part of modern-day Hatteras Island (1946:24–25). From there, Robinson explains how today's Cedar Island could have had the same name as modern-day Roanoke Island, writing that "One can naturally infer that the word Roanoke was the Indian word for Island" (1946:11), with no sense that *roanoke* was an Algonquian word for a type of trade bead ("roanoke, n." 2021).

Robinson then argues that documents from the 1580s English colonization attempts better describe Cedar Island and its environs than they describe Roanoke Island and the area around it. Robinson finally argues that the Lost Colony was not lost but abandoned. In Robinson's version of events, John White accidentally led the 1590 expedition to modern-day Roanoke Island and that what they found there was left by a short-lived Ralph Lane exploring party, explaining why there were no houses found, only a scattering of various items. In Robinson's explanation, the CROATOAN and CRO carvings on the palisade and tree were casually carved by Lane's men in 1585/1586, just to pass the time (1946:34–35). According to Robinson, White knew of his mistake and could have owned up to it, except seven men drowned while going ashore at Roanoke Island. In Robinson's version of events, White did not admit to his mistake in order to cover up for having led seven men to their deaths, preferring to defer his return for the 1587 colonists to a later voyage, one that never happened (1946:39–40).

Robinson, who was from the small Carteret County town of Atlantic, not far from Cedar Island, placed the Lost Colony in his own backyard. And he does what many fringe theorists do; that is, he points out where others, to fit their own beliefs, have argued that the original documents are wrong—and then makes a similar argument himself, most notably when Robinson asserts that John White purposely covered up his own mistake in 1590. Like most fringe theorists, Robinson's "theory" depends on several assumptions that have no basis in the available data. Finally, when Robinson writes about how Cedar Island and the area around it fit what is found in the primary documents, he does so with a local's fervor, with the confirmation bias of someone who can make everything fit his hometown.

If Robinson illustrates pseudoscience based on hope, Howe's *Solving the Riddle of the Lost Colony* illustrates the pseudoscience behind a hoax. Publishing in Beaufort a year after Robinson, Howe presents purported new primary sources: lengthy excerpts from Eleanor Dare's diary that tell about everything from her marriage to Ananias Dare on Christmas Day of 1585 until her death on Christmas Day 1640; two short entries from another diary whose author is not named; and an account by Robert Jordan, purportedly one of the 15 men left on Roanoke Island by Richard Grenville in 1586.

The story created through these texts is that soon after the 15 men were left in 1586, they were attacked by "savage Indians" (1947:39), and the 12 survivors built what they named Fort Croatan along the Pamlico River between two friendly Indian villages. The following year, the colonists left by John White on Roanoke Island were attacked, but the 1586 survivors showed up and took them to Fort Croatan. At this point, the figure of Friend John Jordan becomes central to the story alongside Eleanor and Ananias Dare. He performed marriages for several English couples as well as between 20 Englishmen and Native American women. Friend John Jordan led a group of Englishmen along with several friendly Indians to a site on the Eno River just south of present-day Hillsborough, where they built what they named Friendly Fort.

Even though a group led by Ananias Dare remained on the coast, there was continual contact between Friendly Fort and Fort Croatan. In the meanwhile, more children were born, including a second daughter to Eleanor and Ananias Dare, Esther, born on Christmas Day 1590. Change came in 1609, when Friend John Jordan brought news not only of the Jamestown settlement but also "that Governor John White had visited Roanoke Island in 1591 (?)" (1947:37). Also in 1609, Powhatan's men attacked Fort Croatan, killing Ananias and Virginia Dare among others, after which Eleanor and Esther moved to Friendly Fort, where they lived out their days. The "history" wraps up with the 1616 marriage of Esther to George Howe, Jr., the son of the man killed on Roanoke Island in 1587; Mother Eleanor White Dare's death on Christmas Day 1640; and Esther's death in 1655, two years after burying her husband.

While a fun story, it is also not credible, with all sorts of holes in it. Even so, only once does Howe admit that Eleanor Dare's diary may not be real, labeling it "the purported diary of Eleanor Dare" just before starting to quote from it extensively (1947:31). The only other place Howe seems to allow that the material may not be authentic is near the beginning of his booklet where he writes, "With these related facts, authenticated by historians, Roanoke Island will be recognized as a National Shrine and the place of the First English Settlement on America—the greatest Empire in the history of the world" (1947:3). Howe does admit in passing that the material needs outside authentication. At the same time, his post-war World War II American flag waving reveals at least part of the basis for his confirmation bias. The strong attachment to place seen in Robinson is now attachment to North Carolina and the United States, not the hyperlocal Cedar Island.

Interestingly, Howe's work is an attack on Robinson's. Both were residents of Carteret County, and personal rivalry can be a source for confirmation bias as well.[2] Though Robinson's work is not explicitly mentioned by Howe, hints are dropped throughout, especially by arguing that Cedar Island is not accurately depicted on maps from the 1580s expeditions (1947:44–45). Above all, Howe titles his book *Solving the Riddle of the Lost Colony*, going a step further than Robinson's *The Riddle of the Lost Colony*.

The intertwining of hope and hoax becomes even more complicated in the story behind *Solving the Riddle of the Lost Colony*. Howe gives his source for Eleanor Dare's diary as "Mr. Wm. H. Jordan, editor of the Golden Rule Press," who claimed to be a descendant of the Lost Colony and who had "copies of diaries, papers, bibles, etc., to this effect, compiled by his ancestor, the Rev. Frank Jordan, in Revolutionary War days and handed down to him by his grandfather" (1947:31). Howe later admitted he fell for Jordan's hoax (Stick 1983:237), but Howe wasn't the first person to fall for this hoax. William Henry Jordan had various elements of the story published at least three times between September 1945 and January 1946 in the Burlington, North Carolina, *The Daily Times-News* (*Daily Times-News*, "Families in Reunion" 1945; Jordan 1945; Storey 1946). Jordan was born in January of 1878, making him some 67 years old and a retired Orange County, North Carolina, newspaper publisher when he started getting his story of the Jordan family's connection to the Lost Colony published in *The Daily Times-News* (Manuel 2009; Department of Labor and Printing 1909; Storey 1946). The piece "Families in Reunion," published on November 12, 1945, gives in brief the fictional family narrative that Jordan was selling as fact:

> The fourth Thursday of November 1587 was the first Thanksgiving day celebration to ever be held by Englishmen in North America. For over 150 years these first English settlers held Thanksgiving day at Occoneechee mineral springs just south of Hillsboro.
>
> Robert Jordan, the second son of Benjamin Jordan of Jordans, England, came with 14 other Englishmen to Roanoke Island during the summer of 1586, and he and Benjamin Forrest, Matthew Efland, Robert Murray, James McDade, Benjamin Duke, Joseph Simmons, and Robert Jordan spent several months at Occoneechee mineral springs and purchased one section of land containing 640 acres on which they built that winter a two story log dwelling. The next year 63 single Englishmen and 15 married Englishmen and their children came to Occoneechee mountains and started life in the new found country.
>
> Friend John Jordan came in the summer of 1587 with Gov. John White and the colonists that are claimed to have been lost, and he was private secretary to Gov. John White. He was the first preacher, doctor and teacher

to come to this section of the province of North Carolina.—From Friend
John Jordan's Golden Rule Press and News Recorder [*The Daily Times-News*
1945:9].

Jordan's Orange County community, along with being where the Lost
Colony ended up, now beats out New England for the first Thanksgiving and first printing press in what is now the United States. Other fictional elements of Jordan's story have connections to Orange County
history, such as Friend John Jordan, whose name alludes to the area's
strong Quaker connections, that is, the Society of Friends, though that
religious movement didn't begin until the mid–seventeenth century.
We don't know what Jordan's motives were—whether it was a practical
joke or something else—but his hoax shows how personal desires and
local pride helped an idea take hold, both in Jordan's Orange County
and Howe's North Carolina.

Jordan's hoax, even when perpetuated by Howe, died a quick death.
However, the best-known Lost Colony hoax still has some legs, the
Dare Stones. In November 1937, Louis Hammond of Alameda, California, brought a 21-pound piece of quartzite measuring 14 by 10 inches
with carving on both sides to Emory University in Atlanta. Hammond
said that in August, while vacationing with his wife, he found the stone
along the Chowan River near Edenton, North Carolina. A group of professors deciphered the carving, including Haywood J. Pearce, Jr., who
became the stone's leading proponent. The carvings appeared to be a
message from Eleanor Dare. One side said that Ananias and Virginia
Dare had died in 1591 and gave instructions for anyone who found the
stone to show it to Governor John White. The other side, addressed to
White, said that after he had returned to England, the colonists came
to the Chowan River, where they experienced sickness and war, leaving 24 survivors by 1591. According to the inscription, at that time local
Native Americans saw an English ship and, afraid of revenge, pretended
that the spirits were angry and killed all but seven of the remaining
colonists.

Eleanor concludes by reporting that the murdered colonists were
buried on a small hill four miles east of the river, their graves marked
by one or more carved stones (the number isn't clear), adding only that
the Native American who was to give the stone to John White had been
promised "greate plentie presents." The message is then signed with the
initials EWD, assumed to stand for Eleanor White Dare.[3] The stone
was moved to Brenau College—a private women's college in Gainesville, Georgia—where Pearce's father was president. The Pearces offered
a reward for additional stones, and in May 1939, a Georgia man named

Bill Eberhardt brought them a stone he said he had found close to the Saluda River near Greenville, South Carolina.

Over the next two years, Eberhardt brought in or helped the Pearces acquire from others a total of 47 stones which, when read together, told the story of Eleanor and her fellow survivors coming inland, being attacked by unfriendly Indians, being aided by friendly Indians, and settling along the Chattahoochee River (near Brenau College), with Eleanor dying there in 1599. All 47 of the stones continue to be held at Brenau College, now Brenau University.

The differences between how the first stone and the others came to light—along with the fact that the Eberhardt-related stones are physically different from the original stone—helped determine that the Eberhardt-related stones were definitely a hoax. Their story is entertaining and interesting reading, especially when done through both Boyden Sparkes' 1941 *Saturday Evening Post* article, "Writ on Rocke: Has America's First Mystery Been Solved?," the original piece exposing the Dare Stones hoax, and David La Vere's 2010 *The Lost Rocks: The Dare Stones and the Unsolved Mystery of Sir Walter Raleigh's Lost Colony*, the most recent and fullest history of the Dare Stones. Especially good is La Vere's Chapter 12, "Acid and Extortion" (161–171), about the how the Eberhardt stones were finally revealed as fakes soon after Sparke's article raised serious questions concerning their authenticity. There isn't any question about stones 2 through 47 being fakes, and there shouldn't have been since 1941.[4]

But a trope has developed in relation to the first Dare Stone, one La Vere indulges in at the end of *The Lost Rocks.* He writes, "The historian should always be skeptical, above all, even while tapping the full power of the imagination," but then goes on to say, "I feel the tug of wanting to believe the Chowan Dare Stone to be true," adding that "it might well be as the story it tells is certainly plausible" (199). The trope is that "we know all those other stones are a hoax, but that first stone...." The trope is built on an approach to the first stone that goes back to the Pearces. In the May 1938 issue of *The Journal of Southern History*, the younger Pearce reported about the first stone before any of the others appeared. There Pearce wrote, "The authenticity of this stone can never be fully and finally established without further corroborative evidence. However, it is pertinent to indicate certain particulars in which the message on the stone checks with the available historical records" (1938:161).

Pearce goes on to show how the story on the stone parallels the records of the Lost Colony, including White's statement that the colonists intended to move fifty miles into the main and Strachey's report of seven survivors. Pearce revised the *Journal of Southern History* article for a March 1939 edition of the *Brenau Bulletin*, now including photographs of the stone. The disclaimer now became, "The authorities of Brenau College make no claims as to the authenticity of the stone in their possession.... They believe that the stone is at least credible, that no evidence has yet come to light, during the year in which it has been under examination, which would throw doubt upon its genuineness" (1939a). It is now not up to the Pearces and Brenau to show through the preponderance of evidence that the stone is a genuine artifact; instead, the burden of proof is on others to show that the stone is *not* genuine.

The Pearces took two more steps towards having the stone accepted as genuine by both academics and the general public. At the end of the May 1939 *Brenau Bulletin* piece is an announcement that starts, "According to [the] inscription on the Dare stone, another stone presumably of similar size and character was placed on the grave of the lost colonists.... Brenau College will pay $500 for the recovery and delivery to Brenau College of this second stone with evidence to prove its authenticity" (1939a). The reward is what lead Eberhardt to bring in his faked stones.

With the corroborative evidence of the first Eberhardt stones, the Pearces took a second step toward acceptance. They had replicas made of the stones, including the original Dare Stone, to put on display in the Georgia Building at the 1939 New York World's Fair, and gave the souvenir pamphlet for the display the somewhat equivocating title *Possible Solution of the Virginia Dare Mystery*. But putting the replicas on display showed how firmly the Pearces believed in the stones' authenticity, a belief being sold to a wider public. The souvenir pamphlet states that for those who want to see the real things, "All of these stones are on exhibition without charge, in the museum of Brenau College, Gainesville, Ga" (Pearce 1939b).

The problem is that parallels between the story carved into the stone and known historical documents doesn't authenticate it as a primary source. The story on the stone could easily have come from the historical documents, sources available to any hoaxer. One root of confirmation bias is when people can't help latching onto the possible over the probable. La Vere expresses what many others have in relation to the first Dare Stone: "While the only evidence to support the Chowan River Dare Stone's account is purely circumstantial; so is the only evidence to disprove it. No archaeological discoveries have come to light that prove it genuine—but none, on the other hand, that prove it false, either" (2010:199). However, to be a viable hypothesis, the burden of proof is not on showing that the stone is a hoax but on showing that it is probable that the stone was carved in the sixteenth century.

And there are enough problems with the first Dare Stone to make the assumption that it isn't a genuine sixteenth-century artifact produced by Eleanor Dare more probable than assuming it is authentic. To begin, there are the questions. For example, why would Eleanor stop to carve a rock that is a grave marker on one side and a lengthy, cramped message on the other, all while under great stress—having lost all but seven of her fellow colonists, including her husband and child? Where did the rock come from when quartzite is not naturally occurring on the coastal plain of eastern North Carolina? And while the carved message uses several spelling and orthographic conventions sometimes used in the sixteenth century, there are almost too many. For instance, an extra *e* is added to words at almost every chance ("SOONE," "GOE," "ENGLANDE," "WEE," etc.), a practice allowed but not required by sixteenth-century spelling conventions. If carving under difficult circumstances, why add extra *E*'s? These are just a few of the questions that would need to be answered to accept the first Dare Stone as authentic.

Beyond these questions is the interesting parallel pointed out by Melissa Darby in her book *Thunder Go North: The Hunt for Sir Francis Drake's Fair and Good Bay* (2019: 115–131). In 1936, a year before the first Dare Stone appeared, a brass plate ostensibly left by Francis Drake in 1579 staking England's claim on the area was purportedly found in Northern California. That plate was brought to Herbert Bolton at the University of California, Berkley, in early 1937. There were skeptics about the plate's authenticity at the time, but it wasn't until the 1970s that it was shown conclusively to be a hoax. Darby points out that not only were the Drake plate and the Dare stone found about the same time, but that the signature of Louis Hammond closely resembles that of Bolton student George Hammond. She goes on to argue that Bolton may have been behind both the Drake Plate and the first Dare Stone hoaxes, perhaps with the complicity of the younger Pearce. Darby's evidence is not conclusive, but it does highlight the many loose ends in treating the first stone as authentic.

However, in the world of pseudoscience, possibility carries more weight than probability, and the demand to show probability is often countered with claims of academic narrow-mindedness and/or parochialism. As the stereotype goes, academics won't accept these ideas if they threaten their lucrative (?) academic standing. Nowhere is this better seen than in the History Channel's productions *Roanoke: Search for the Lost Colony* (McCormick 2015) and the follow up *Return to Roanoke: Search for the Seven* (McCormick 2017). The shows follow two Massachusetts stone masons, Jim and Bill Vieira, as they investigate whether the Dare Stones are authentic sixteenth-century artifacts at the behest of "maverick archaeologist" and director of The Lost Colony Center for Science and Research, the late Fred Willard.

Explaining why they are appropriate investigators, the Vieira brothers allude to a stereotype of academics, "We're stone masons, so it's not like we're going to lose tenure" (McCormick 2015 [0:2:45]). Later in the program, the show's narrator says, "But with an artifact as controversial as the Dare Stone, Fred knows the academic establishment won't be forgiving." The cameras then focus on Willard, who says, "When we attempt to do this, you just have to be clear that they are going to come after us. They're going to come after us like gangbusters" (McCormack 2015:[1:00:55–1:01:20]). The implication is that college professors follow the principles of the scientific method not because they have proven to be effective, but to keep their reputations and jobs—and to exclude outsiders. Implied as well is that true discovery will come from the rule breakers, from people who work outside these principles.

We include Fred Willard, one of those colorful characters referred to in the introduction, because no volume on the search for the Lost Colony would be complete without to him. Both Tony Horwitz in *A Voyage Long and Strange: Rediscovering the New World* (2008) and Andrew Lawler in *The Secret Token: Myth, Obsession, and the Search for the Lost Colony of Roanoke* (2018) met with and described Fred as part of their work. After a long and varied career, from high school wrestling coach to marina owner to dirt track racer (where he was known as Fred "Wildman" Willard), he retired and decided to indulge his Lost Colony passion. It was difficult to tell which of his larger-than-life stories were real, but what was real was his obsession with the Lost Colony.

We both met Fred in classes when he matriculated at East Carolina University, doing everything he could to make all of his coursework connect to his preoccupation with the Lost Colony. Charlie was his undergraduate advisor for a year (until he got tired of Fred's not doing anything he was advised to do to finish his degree). Even so, as Fred continued to take classes and haunt our office hours, it was difficult to not try and assist a student who was so driven to learn about the past. He had studied the documents and explored far more of the swampy interior of Hyde, Dare, and Tyrrell Counties than anyone we had ever met. And Fred talked about his ideas with such certitude that it was difficult to dismiss him out of hand. Business owners funded his research. Administrators entertained his research partnership proposals with the university. He persuaded David Phelps to reopen excavations at the Cape Creek site on Hatteras Island (that Mark Horton and Scott Dawson would continue to excavate). So when he announced to us that he had located other archaeological sites almost certainly associated with the colonists, of course we checked them out. They were always real sites, but they were never Lost Colony sites.

When we refused to chase any more of his wild geese, Fred formed the Lost Colony Center for Science and Research and conducted his own field research with a dedicated cadre of volunteers as well as his wife, Kathryn Sugg-Willard. He could recruit people because his enthusiasm was contagious. As one of his cadre said to Horwitz, "Fred's brilliant.... If he was looking for a comet, I'd follow him there, too" (2008:311). But his attraction was his ability to get others enthused rather than an ability to lay out his ideas.

As Horwitz described his meeting with Fred, he was "connecting dots that seemed obvious to him but not always to me" (2008:312). And the member of his cadre who would follow him even "if he was looking for a comet" added, "You got to take Fred on faith.... I don't always get where his thinking is headed, but you know he'll get there in the end" (2008:312). Whether or not Fred really got there in the end, the History Channel featured him alongside the Vieira brothers because of his enthusiasm. He died in a hunting accident in the woods he had explored for over two decades. Although he never found what he was looking for, he enjoyed the search and shared his passion with many that he met along the way.

One of Fred's more memorable adventures was documented in *Return to Roanoke: Search for the Seven*, the sequel to *Roanoke: Search for the Lost Colony*. Fred convinced the producers he knew where the original Dare Stone had been found and that it was near a site with Lost Colony connections—findings hinted at in the original show. Charlie was asked to make a guest appearance as the archaeologist who would assess the evidence. As with most "reality shows," the entire episode was scripted. Artifacts were recovered at a dig the Vieira brothers oversaw. These consisted of an array of late prehistoric pot sherds and a few nineteenth-century historic ceramics.

Fred was ecstatic. Charlie was not impressed and politely said he saw no connection to the Lost Colony. This apparently gave the producers pause. Couldn't there be pertinent material here that hadn't been found yet? Possibly—it's always possible. That was enough, and the segment wound up with the hope that further excavation would recover the evidence they were after. However, once production wrapped, so did the excavation. It had served its purpose by providing some "science" for the show. Fred had publicity which he could point to, and Charlie got a cautionary tale to relate to his students and now to readers of this book.

And the Vieira brothers moved their story away from Fred and the coast, finding a new "sponsor" for their work, Ed Schrader, geologist and president of Brenau University. In *Return to Roanoke*, Schrader accompanies the Vieira brothers to the University of North Carolina at Asheville for an analysis of the first Dare Stone, preliminary results of which showed it to be quartz. While waiting for further results, the brothers follow up the lead that the seven survivors mentioned on the stone were taken inland to work in copper mines. They locate quartz outcroppings near possible (though actually quite unlikely) Native American copper mines in the Piedmont region. When Schrader informs the Vieira brothers that the Dare Stone quartz contains trace amounts of copper in similar amounts as the samples from the quartz outcroppings, everything seems to have fallen into place.

Bill Vieira suggests that it would have taken only a couple of days for a Native American to take the stone Eleanor Dare had carved to the Chowan River, and his brother responds: Jim: "It's a wild idea … but possible." Bill: "And that keeps the story alive." Jim: "That's all I want." [McCormick 2017:(1:16:00–1:16:17)] Confirmation bias, the desire to keep the story alive, allows the first Dare Stone to continue being used as a possible answer to the mystery of the Lost Colony. Hope and desire keep a story going even when the facts make it highly improbable.

The power of Lost Colony hoaxes continues, but the hope of solving the mystery of the 1587 colonists while gaining recognition for oneself or one's community seems to be even stronger than the desire to con people. For example, the 1930s commemorations of the Roanoke expeditions brought to light another supposed Lost Colony gravesite aside from the one associated with the first Dare Stone. *The Robesonian*, published in Lumberton, North Carolina, printed a story on May 18, 1938, about a local legend that Virginia Dare's grave was beneath a hickory tree outside the Robeson County community of Philadelphus. *The Robesonian*, attaching the legend to the Lumbee, reported, "There is … a superstition among the Indians that the Great Spirit will frown upon those who dare molest this sacred soil," adding, "Jordan Revels, 86-year-old Indian patriarch, will not say that the grave is Virginia Dare's, but he readily states that it long has been tradition that this spot be not despoiled" (*The Robesonian* 1938:7). The story could be written off except that it keeps reappearing. *The Robesonian* reprinted the story in 1951 and again in 1970 with an "Editor's Note" that it was a hoax being reprinted just for interest. But newer versions are not introduced in the same way. As recently as 2017, and reprinted in 2020, *The Fayetteville Observer* published a new account including interviews with local Native Americans who believe it is the site of Virginia Dare's grave (Futch 2020). Just a few years ago, Charlie was contacted by a woman in Robeson County who knew where the grave was and wanted him to investigate it.

As an added twist, sometimes pseudoscience draws on the supernatural. Such is the story of the late Samuel S. Sumner, Jr., or Aloha Sam Sumner, as he introduced himself to Charlie. Sumner taught special education in Hawaii but also spent thirty years investigating the Lost Colony (Monasmith 2016). Sumner believed that "fifty miles into the main" wasn't to the south and Hatteras Island, but to the north and present-day Knott's Island. He built his belief on a 1923 map showing a feature similar to an artist's rendering of an earthwork fort in J.C. Harrington's *Search for the Cittie of Ralegh* (Hampton 2010; Harrington 1962:viii). Sumner believed the colonists moved to Knott's Island and built a fort like one on Roanoke Island.

Sumner's fascination with the Lost Colony was not limited to Knott's Island. In October of 1995, he brought the intuitive archaeologist George McMullen to Fort Raleigh National Historic Site to locate previously undetected archaeological features through remote sensing—that is, using psychic abilities to intuit what was there in the past, including "seeing" underground features and artifacts. In 1998, Sumner returned with ground penetrating radar (GPR) to scan locations where McMullen had said there were various features connected to 25 members of the 1587 colony living in a previously unknown fort for protection. McMullen said these features included a longhouse, a well, and three graves—two of adults and one of a child—and that outside the fort were a small house, a tool house, and a temporary structure, the last inside a second, partial palisade.

The ventures with McMullen had Sumner also contacting coauthor Charlie, with whom Sumner shared his unpublished report, one that included the GPR operator's notes saying that there were features in some of the locations McMullen had pointed out, but of what couldn't be said (Sumner 1998). Charlie looked at the report and said he really didn't see much of anything. None of this deterred Sumner. When *Time Team America* aired the episode "The Lost Colony of Roanoke, NC" (Dixon 2009), Sumner posted a press release saying the *Time Team America* crew had excavated and found post holes just where McMullen said they would be (Sumner 2009).

Neither Sumner's hand-drawn maps nor the *Time Team America* excavation footage show precise locations. And the *Time Team America* episode excavated what were potentially post holes from a sixteenth-century European structure, but what sort of a structure is never said (and which later were determined to be tree roots). However, because what was found during the *Time Team America* filming might line up with one McMullen's intuited features, Sumner believed that it did. And while he complained that credit was not given, *Time Team America* provided Sumner with a sense of confirmation about both his beliefs concerning the colonists and his belief in intuitive archaeology.

A final example of the pseudoscience of hope is based on folk traditions concerning the remains of two-masted ships in the Dismal Swamp and also near the entrance to Catherine Creek in Gates County, North Carolina. In the book *In Pursuit of Dorothie, The Lost Colony Ship* (2018), the late Ahoskie, North Carolina, radio announcer and local historian Donald Paul Upchurch tells about reports of these hulks going back to the mid–nineteenth century, with the last of the timbers seen as recently as 1965. To explain the remains, Upchurch lays out how sometime after John White's return to England, some of the 1587 colonist could have fled Roanoke Island and headed up the Chowan River in the pinnace the *Dorothie*, along with two ships' boats.

Upchurch then describes how, around Holiday Island, the fleeing colonists—in a "they-turned-right-when-they-shoulda-turned-left" twist—could have ended up in the river's smaller tributaries and in the Dismal Swamp, where the vessels finally ran aground. Like Lee Miller's hypothesizing that the colonists first moved to the Chowan River, were then captured and enslaved, and then were taken further and further inland, Upchurch's connection of the oral tradition of ships' remains to the 1587 colonists depends on several steps of deductive extrapolation.

While *In Pursuit of Dorothie* is a fun read, at best it gives a potential explanation of how ships' remains might have gotten to where oral traditions said they were to have been—in other words, a lot of *could have*'s and *might*'s. However, Upchurch's explanation is more probable than other variants of the Dismal Swamp mystery vessel, such as that given by Nancy Roberts in *Ghosts from the Coast* (2001:15–24). In the chapter "A New Mystery of the Lost Colony," Roberts tells about a group of colonists leaving Roanoke Island on shipboard rather than waiting for John White's return. They head up the Albemarle Sound and Chowan River, planning to walk the rest of the way to the Chesapeake Bay. However, around Holiday Island, a waterspout lifts their ship and carries it into the Dismal Swamp, where it was found near Acorn Hill in Gates County in the mid–1800s. Roberts even cites Upchurch and argues that a tornado *could* have carried a boat that far. But with each of these stories, the possible moves ever farther from the probable.

Even present authors Charlie and Tom have edged into the Lost Colony Reality Distortion Sphere, seeing the Lost Colony everywhere—though for us, seeing legends rather than solutions to the mystery of the colonists' fate. About the same time Charlie was contacted concerning the Virginia Dare grave in Robeson County, we came across a Civil War–era map of Henrico County, Virginia, with "The Grave of Virginia Dare" marked near Varina, east of Richmond. We showed the map during talks, saying it certainly looked like all sorts of places were claiming to be where the Lost Colony ended up. Tom even drove to the site and took pictures.

Recently, however, we found *Inventory of Early Architecture and Historic Sites* (1978) done for Henrico County by Jeffrey Marshall O'Dell. In that report, O'Dell mentions the Virginia Dare gravesite on an 1864 map, telling how it "remained a mystery until a longtime local resident pointed out that Virginia Dare had been a famous racehorse in the Varina area in the early 19th century. The inclusion of a horse's grave on a military map was not simply a jest; both Confederate and Union records of the Battle of Chaffins Bluff make note of what must have been a highly visible monument" (1978:182). Without O'Dell's report, we almost certainly would have continued to claim that there was a tradition that the Lost Colony had moved up the James River.

That close shave is another reason not to ask us to engage in guesswork, particularly assuming that because we have looked at so many hypotheses, pseudo-hypotheses, and the data that accompany them, we have an inside track on what happened to the Lost Colony. Don't say, "Come on, you've got to have a favorite idea. Where do you think the Lost Colony went?" You won't believe us, let alone like our answer. No matter which of us you ask, we'll say, "I don't know." And mean it.

Conclusion

What We Don't Know
and How We Don't Know It

OK, we've been holding out on you. Coauthors Charlie and Tom do know where to find the Lost Colony. On TV ... and in novels, creative nonfiction, and even the occasional movie. Especially with the arrival of the cable TV era in the 1990s and 2000s, the Lost Colony has become a pop culture cottage industry. In these outlets, what is "known" about the fate of the Lost Colony and what is actually known are often not distinguished from one another in the name of providing definitive answers where none exist.

So what do we actually know? Very little as it turns out, though there are a couple of things about which scholars agree. The 1587 colonists did arrive along the Outer Banks, almost certainly Roanoke Island, in the summer of 1587. They settled there, and about a month later, John White boarded a ship to England, not returning for three years. When he did return, the planters he had left on Roanoke Island were not to be seen. That's pretty much it. Almost everything else has some question about it. One of the Lost Colony's TV appearances helps illustrate the point.

The 2011 program *Birth of a Colony: North Carolina*, produced by UNC-TV (now PBS North Carolina), is a straight-forward history of North Carolina from the time of first European contact to the end of the colonial era (Finkbiner 2011). In its section on the Roanoke colonization efforts, historians David Stick, Malinda Maynor Lowery, William Price, and Karen Kupperman are all interviewed. Kupperman—whose *Roanoke the Abandoned Colony* (1984, 2nd edition, 2007) continues to be a standard reference—talks about the 1587 colonists being left on Roanoke Island rather than along the Chesapeake Bay, where John White says they were to settle:

> We can't actually know why they didn't go to Chesapeake Bay. All we have
> is John White's account. John White was at daggers drawn with the Mas-
> ter of the Ships, and Simon Ferdinando, as they called him, and John White
> couldn't agree on anything. And so John White put all the blame on Simon.
> He said he wanted to go privateering and he just dumped the colonists at
> Roanoke. But that doesn't really make any sense because the fleet stayed for
> a whole month. If Simon was so anxious to get privateering, he wouldn't
> have stayed there for a whole month [Finkbiner 2011:(36:32–37:11)].

Kupperman reminds us of several things. First, that the colonists
ended up on Roanoke Island and that Fernandez stayed for a month
or so after disembarking the colonists are examples of accepted fact
about the 1587 colony. Next is that why they didn't go to the Chesapeake Bay isn't as certain because the hypothesis that Fernandez just
dumped the colonists on Roanoke Island is based on a single source,
John White. Finally, Kupperman reminds us that the full context surrounding a source needs to be examined. In other words, Kupperman
reminds us that much of what we "know" about the 1587 colonists
comes from uncorroborated single sources and/or hearsay evidence.
But this is a rare sort of admission in televised versions of the Lost
Colony, in which little distinction is made between what is known and
what is not known—let alone discussing on what basis we think we
know what happened.

The History Channel programs with the Vieira brothers are just
two of the several nonfiction (often ostensibly nonfiction) televised versions of the Lost Colony. The earliest television episode focusing on the
Lost Colony appears to be the still often cited "The Lost Colony of Roanoke" from the series *In Search of...* (Landsburg 1979). The late 1970s
and early 1980s series, narrated by Leonard Nimoy, explored various
mysteries, often with a pseudoscientific twist, including episodes about
Bigfoot, the Bermuda Triangle, and alien abductions. But there were
historically-based episodes as well, including "The Lost Colony of Roanoke." Using what has become a standard story arc for nonfiction television accounts of the Lost Colony, the first half presents the "known
history" of the 1587 colonists through reenactments. Then, following a
commercial break, ideas of what happened to the Lost Colony are presented through interviews with people like local historian David Stick
and National Park Service historian Phil Evans. Stick and Evans give
some of the more accepted hypotheses before the episode turns to the
Dare Stones.

The stones are filmed in a basement on the Brenau campus, and
Brenau history professor Dr. James Southerland is interviewed, all
leading up to the story of the White Doe. In other words, the story arc

moves from history to historical speculation to pseudoarcheology to pure fiction. And it's worth noting that the people interviewed continued to be associated with the Lost Colony—Stick as a leading historian of the Outer Banks; Evans, who after he left the Park Service went on to become a lawyer and president of the First Colony Foundation; and Southerland, who appeared in *Roanoke: Search for the Lost Colony* (McCormick 2015) some 36 years later. As a cottage industry, there are a few people who keep showing up, including occasional appearances by Charlie and Tom.

And the same stories keep showing up again and again as well, no matter how debunked. After the 1979 episode of *In Search of...*, the Dare Stones have reappeared at least four more times on television, beginning with a 2012 episode of the Travel Channel show *Mysteries at the Museum* (Wildman 2012). Filmed in the Brenau University Library, the Dare Stones segment focuses solely on the first Dare Stone without acknowledging any of the others. Then, just two years before the 2015 and 2017 History Channel shows with the Viera Brothers, a 2013 episode of another History Channel program, *America Unearthed*, has geologist Scott Wolter asserting that all the Dare Stones appear authentic, including the ones that Bill Eberhardt had admitted to faking (Awes et al. 2013). Here is the crux of the Lost Colony on nonfiction television—or in news articles or even in academic histories. The Lost Colony always starts out as an unsolved mystery, but almost always by the end is not allowed to remain an unsolved mystery.

The first cable programs about the Lost Colony did allow for the mystery. "The Riddle of Roanoke" (Naughton and Valcour 1995), on the Discovery Channel's series *Archaeology*, used the Virginia Company digs at Fort Raleigh National Historic Site as its centerpiece. The episode opened and closed with the Lost Colony, included interviews with historian Karen Kupperman and archaeologist Ivor Noël Hume, and showed archaeologist Nick Luccketti digging a test pit. No single hypothesis about what happened to the Lost Colony was given precedence over any other. This was highlighted by the fact that in order to show archaeology being done, the producers used digs at Fort Raleigh— where the colonists would have left from, not where they would have gone to.

Another early cable treatment, the 1998 episode "Lost Colony of Roanoke" from the History Channel program *In Search of History* (Jennings 1998), examined all of the 1580s Roanoke colonization efforts, using the Lost Colony to frame the story. Along with reenactments of encounters between Native Americans and the English, "Lost Colony of Roanoke" included interviews with Teresa Waterlily Morris, identified as the director of One Nation; archaeologist David Phelps; and Roanoke Island historian lebame houston. Near the end of the episode, Houston wraps up the program's Lost Colony theme when she says, "They were not lost. They knew where they were. Our problem is, we don't know where they went because we do not have enough evidence to corroborate the report in the Jamestown settlement. Therefore, this is the stuff of which legends are made" (Jennings 1998:[40:56–41:10]).

However, it took 17 years for another Roanoke colonization-centered program to be made that didn't promote a specific Lost Colony hypothesis. In 2015, Film and Video Production students at East Carolina University produced *A Colony Lost*, which aired on North Carolina Public Television in January 2016 (Clanet 2015). The program was built around interviews with present authors Charlie and Tom, with their colleagues Larry Tise and Christopher Oakley from the Department of History, and with Park Service historian John Hollenbeck.

However, by the time *A Colony Lost* was aired, a different Lost Colony television paradigm had arisen, one that demanded a solution to the mystery be promoted or a new discovery be made. In 2006, the Josh Bernstein hosted History Channel program *Digging for the Truth* aired "Roanoke, the Lost Colony" (Bernstein 2006). *Digging for the Truth* used the premise of Bernstein's investigating the mystery of the Lost Colony rather than just presenting what others had found before. He talked with various people—including Nick Luccketti; National Park Service historian Rob Bolling; James Horn; and Dennis Blanton, one of the lead investigators on the tree-ring study that showed the 1587–1589 drought. As noted earlier, Bernstein interviewed ethnohistorian David La Vere (before *The Lost Rocks* came out) as they walked around a Lumbee powwow, though no Lumbee were interviewed on camera.

This all led to Bernstein's taking DNA swabs from three men with the surname Payne and trying to find a DNA match with Paynes in England. A match was found between one of the American Paynes and a man from Scotland, meaning these two men share a common ancestor from sometime in the past 500 years. "A breakthrough in the case," Bernstein says, adding "*Digging for the Truth* has made a compelling connection" (Bernstein 2006 [0:42:10–44:25]). What really happened was the introduction of pseudoscience. The DNA match only shows that the two men have a common ancestor, not that their shared ancestry has any connection to the Lost Colony. The need to solve the mystery of the Lost Colony within the space of an hour—or at least make a significant dent into the mystery—makes Bernstein's *Digging for the Truth* episode a precursor to shows that followed.

Some shows have worked toward a middle ground between solving the mystery and leaving it totally open-ended. *Time Team America*, the American version of the British program *Time Team*, made its first episode "Fort Raleigh, North Carolina" (Dixon 2009), the title a refreshing break from specifically mentioning the Lost Colony. Meeting up with the First Colony Foundation (FCF) at Fort Raleigh National Historic Site, much as the show *Archaeology* had done with the FCF's precursor the Virginia Company Foundation fifteen years earlier, *Time Team America* framed the fuller Roanoke colonization history with the Lost Colony.

A familiar cast of experts showed up. From the FCF, Nick Luccketti was there to lead the dig along with Mercer University history professor Eric Klingelhofer (who is seen but not identified in the *Archaeology* episode), as well as project archaeologists Clay Swindell, Carter Hudgins, curator Bly Straube, and FCF president Phil Evans. To add context and to kibbitz about the dig were Karen Kupperman, James Horn, and Ivor Noël Hume. The team brought in geophysical survey equipment, locating some of the first European artifacts found near the reconstructed fort in years. The big finds were possible postholes, maybe belonging to a colonist's house.

The postholes are used to talk about what the Lost Colony took with them from Roanoke Island and what was left behind as well as to present the various hypotheses about where they went. The episode ends with a discussion of what life may have been like on Roanoke Island in the 1580s, but the post-show tag line is "There is more to explore at the *Time Team America* website. Find out about new developments in the search for the Lost Colony" (Dixon 2009:[0:52:25]). None of the finds made with the help of *Time Team America* are specifically 1587-related, and definitely none give any clues about where the 1587 colonists went. But the producers felt the need to contextualize what was found, and the episode as a whole, with the Lost Colony.

A 2016 episode from the Travel Channel show *Expedition Unknown*, "The Lost Colony of Roanoke" (Gates 2016), continues in the same vein. Like Josh Bernstein in *Digging for the Truth*, the *Expedition Unknown* host Josh Gates used the premise of doing his own investigation of the Lost Colony. And as with earlier programs, Gates talked with various figures seen before. Tom was there to introduce the Lost Colony. Charlie showed up alongside University of North Carolina–Chapel Hill geography professor Erika Wise to talk about tree ring studies and drought. Gates joined the First Colony Foundation at Site X, and he jet skied with Scott Dawson to look for artifacts in the water around Hatteras Island.

Importantly, Gates met the requirement of at least creating the image of finding new information and not just reviewing past work. Charlie, Gates, and Wise took a tree ring sample from along the Chowan River. Not shown was how surprised and disappointed Gates and his crew were that Wise couldn't point out the drought year tree rings in the field but had to take the sample back to her lab for any analysis. She was, however, able to say that rings indicated wet and dry periods and that seemed good enough for the producers. Better was the use of a drone to take LIDAR imagery over Site X, imagery that showed a possible fort-like feature, though no follow-up ground-truthing was undertaken. And when Gates and Dawson jet skied to the Croatoan dig site on Hatteras Island, they found sherds of Native American pottery in the water and a glass bead at the dig site. While the episode ends by saying all the hypotheses looked at during the show are possible and no one is more probable than the others, the image is given that new Lost Colony–related finds have been made while Gates and his crew filmed.

With reality TV more often than not being "reality" TV, these explorations of the Lost Colony have quite a bit in common with fictional portrayals. The empty space in the historical record ends up being filled in with almost anything—except leaving the story, the history, open-ended. One of the few fictional television productions that allow the mystery to be a mystery is also one of the earliest, *Roanoak*, a 1986 South Carolina ETV production for the PBS series *American Playhouse* (Egleson 1986).[1] Made to coincide with the 400th anniversary of the Roanoke colonization efforts, the three-part series depicts the full Roanoke ventures, with the first episode portraying the encounter between the Carolina Algonquians and the Amadas and Barlowe expedition, the second episode covering the encounter between the Algonquians and the Grenville/Lane expedition, and the final episode portraying the encounter between the Algonquians and the 1587 colonists.

The show attempted to do something other portrayals of the Roanoke ventures had not: emphasize both the Native American and English perspectives, including using Algonquian with English subtitles for the Native American dialogue. Presenting the Algonquian perspective highlights what should have been an important part of the Lost Colony story all along. Instead of being mainly a European story, especially an English one, Native Americans should be more than secondary players. The first episode starts with John White reflecting back on the Roanoke ventures, and the third episode ends by coming back to the same scene of John White's reflecting on his Roanoke experiences, especially not having found the 1587 colonists. Even a production with a strong Native American element like *Roanoak* ends up making the English perspective on the Lost Colony its framing device.

However, as fictional television programming, *Roanoak* is the outlier, both in leaving the mystery unsolved and in presenting it as straight-forward historical fiction. The one thing that ties together most versions of TV's fictional Lost Colony is that the colony's fate has a paranormal explanation. For example, the 1993 episode "The Lost Colony" of the BBC production *Lovejoy* (Sax 1993) has the series' title character solving the mystery of stolen Lost Colony–related items with the help of a young girl who has the gift of a sixth sense, the ability to have objects speak to her and tell their stories. And by solving the mystery, Lovejoy calms the ghost of one of Sir Walter Raleigh's special friends, the fictional Lady Katherine Moresby.

After the *Lovejoy* episode, the paranormal direction of the Lost Colony on television took a darker turn. In Stephen King's 1999 miniseries *Storm of the Century*, the villain, a demon named Linoge, threatens to do to the inhabitants of Little Tall Island, Maine, what he did to the 1587 Roanoke colonists—get them to commit mass suicide by walking into the ocean (King and Carliner 2014 [1999]). In 2007, the SciFi Channel (now SyFy) aired its take on the Lost Colony in the TV movie *Wraiths of Roanoke*, alternately retitled *Lost Colony* and *Lost Colony: The Legend of Roanoke* (Codd 2007). It turns out that the colonists were killed by the trapped spirits of Vikings who had been tortured to death on Roanoke Island several hundred years earlier.

The longest run of the Lost Colony on television may be in the series *Supernatural* (Kripke 2005–2020). While the series ran from 2005 to 2020, the Lost Colony first showed up in the episode "Croatoan" during the second season (2006) and reappeared in five episodes during the fifth season (2009–2010). In the 2006 episode, Croatoan turns out to be a demonic virus that changes people into zombie-like homicidal maniacs for a day, after which they disappear. Of course, this is how the Lost Colony disappeared, and the sixteenth-century carvings on the post and tree—as well as a similar carving on a telephone pole in the episode—name the virus.

In the later *Supernatural* episodes, demons plan to use the Croatoan virus to bring about the end of the world. Add to these the 2013 episode "John Doe" from the Fox series *Sleepy Hollow* (Dickerson 2013): it reveals that the Lost Colony suffered the plague, with Virginia Dare being the first to fall victim. Her spirit leads the rest of the colonists to Purgatory in order to escape Pestilence, one of the Four Horsemen of the Apocalypse, who are returning to earth in the twenty-first century to end the world. In all these television depictions, the Lost Colony was the victim of supernatural evil spirits out and about in the world.

On the other hand, the Lost Colony is not always the victim. In the very first episode of the horror mystery show *FreakyLinks*, Virginia Dare is an evil shape-shifter who killed the 1587 colonists and who comes back in the present day to kill the main character's brother because he discovered her secret (Holland 2000). And in the darkly satirical series *The Heart, She Holler*, which ran on the Cartoon Network's Adult Swim from 2011 to 2013 (Chatman et al. 2011–2013), Virginia Dare, "the first white person born in the Americas," is now the matriarch of a backward Southern town and, as such, "Her cursed presence is a Caucasian cancer on the continent" (Season 3, Episode 1; Chatman et al. 2011–2013:(0:08:08).

The fictional representation of the Lost Colony on television that has received the most fanfare is the 2016 sixth season of the FX series *American Horror Story*, entitled *Roanoke* (Buecker 2016). The multilayered story is set in a farmhouse located where the Lost Colony of Roanoke had presumably moved, given as Martin County, North Carolina (just west of Bertie County and Site X). In 2014, a mixed-race couple— an African American husband and European American wife—buys the farmhouse to escape the violence of Los Angeles. Once they move in along with the husband's sister, they discover their neighbors are a violent, inbred, backwoods family and the house is haunted. The couple's story is told through a TV show within a TV show.

The first several episodes are presented as a docudrama titled *My Roanoke Nightmare* that uses interviews with the couple and the husband's sister intertwined with scenes of actors reenacting their ordeals. The docudrama is so successful that its producers lure the couple and the reenactors back to the house to film a reality show event, everyone spending three days in the haunted house. It turns out that the ghosts haunting the house are spirits of survivors from the 1587 colony, led by the spirit of Thomasin White, the wife of Governor John White. Thomasin was left in charge when her husband returned to England for supplies, but was overthrown and left for dead. She survived and regained power with the help of a witch, for whom Thomasin began sacrificing people, earning her the name "The Butcher." *American Horror Story: Roanoke* and *The Heart, She Holler* are stories of race and gender, used as much or more to explore Black-White relations as to examine relations between Europeans and Native Americans. Because no one knows the actual fate of the Lost Colony, depictions of it can go wherever social trends lead.

The same ability to use the open-ended history as a space for almost any kind of fictional story is found in print well as on television. African American writer Steve Cannon's sexually explicit 1969 radical Black underground novel *Groove, Bang and Jive Around*, depicts Virginia

Dare as an oversexed stewardess on an airplane to heaven, where sex, especially interracial sex, is both empowering and discomforting. In Seth Grahame-Smith's *The Last American Vampire* (2015), the sequel to his *Abraham Lincoln: Vampire Hunter* (2010), vampirism comes to the Americas through the 1587 colony. Focusing on gender, a vampire named Crowley kills all of the colonists except the infant Virginia Dare (so CRO stands for Crowley, not Croatoan).

Crowley saves Virginia to raise her and ultimately have her as his lover. In reaction to this act of male control, Virginia turns into a villainous vampire herself who over almost 400 years attacks the United States and its institutions because, based on her experiences going back to the Lost Colony, she believes that the American experiment in democracy is a failure. Similarly, the 2013 graphic short story "Lost Colony," by Jason Aaron published in *American Vampire Anthology*, has vampires arriving in North America with the Lost Colony, symbolizing the start of European colonization of Native America.[2]

The paranormal Lost Colony isn't used to explore only concerns of race, gender, and colonialism. It has also been used to explore fears about medical procedures, disease, and pandemics even before Covid-19.[3] One of the first in this line was the 1948 short story "Croatan," by Malcolm F. Ferguson, published in the fantasy and horror pulp magazine *Weird Tales*. In Ferguson's story, a brown, disease-causing snow falls over Roanoke, Virginia, and as the main character falls sick, he has a vision of the Lost Colony. But to express the fear of disease, popular media have connected the Lost Colony to zombies as much as any other motif.

In *Supernatural*, the Croatoan virus turns people into zombies, but Lost Colony zombies have had a life outside of television. In his introduction to *The Zombie Survival Guide: Complete Protection from the Living Dead* (2003), Max Brooks includes the Lost Colony on his timeline of zombie attacks throughout world history. To explain the fate of the Lost Colony after the zombie attacks, Brooks writes: "One version describes the eventual infection and destruction of the entire town. Another has the Croatan Nation, recognizing the danger for what it was, rounding up and burning every colonist on the island. In a third account, these same Native Americans rescued the surviving townspeople and dispatched the undead and wounded" (198). Whichever version is "true," disease is the thing to be feared, and the Lost Colony becomes a way to explore the fear of disease.

Zombies as stand-ins for disease, especially pandemics, showed up again in 2009 on Matt Mogk's *Zombie Research Society* website. Mogk posted "Zombie Colony of Roanoke" (2009a) followed by "Roanoke

Zombie Lifespan Test" (2009b), material he revised to include in his 2011 book *Everything You Ever Wanted to Know About Zombies*. Mogk wrote, "Max Brooks included a fictional zombie outbreak on Roanoke in his 2003 bestseller, *Zombie Survival Guide*, and now it seems life is imitating art, as noted Harvard archaeologist Lawrence Stager recently unearthed evidence of mass cannibalism at the Roanoke site" (2011:Kindle edition, location 2696–2698). Mogk then explains that "a sudden undead plague" must have taken the colony, but because the colony was isolated, the bodies of any zombies left must have rotted, leaving no sign of human remains and stopping the plague from spreading.

Mogk argues that knowing the plague must have occurred during the three years from 1587 to 1590 shows that zombies could survive two years at most, allowing enough time for the last zombie bodies "to rot back into the earth" (2011:Kindle edition, location 2700–2701). (By the way, coauthors Charlie and Tom contacted the late Lawrence Stager in 2013 about Mogk's fictional reference "Lawrence Stager, 'An Investigation into the Roanoke Colony,' *Harvard Alumni Magazine*, August 17, 2009" [Kindle edition, loc. 3799–3800]. Stager very nicely replied, in a tone both amused and put off, "This is the first time I have heard about it or anybody has inquired about this bogus article I didn't write for a bogus journal" [Lawrence Stager, personal communication 2013]).

The Lost Colony's open-ended history has made the paranormal a mainstay of Lost Colony–related creative works, but many other approaches have been taken. There are more traditional mysteries, such as Bill Morris's *Saltwater Cowboys* (2004) and Richard Folsom's *Indian Wood: A Mystery of the Lost Colony of Roanoke Island* (2008). There are historical novels, such as Paul Clayton's *White Seed: The Untold Story of the Lost Colony of Roanoke* (2009), Ed Gray's *Left in the Wind: The Roanoke Journal of Emme Merrimoth* (2016), and Deborah Homsher's *The Rising Shore: Roanoke* (2007). There is Angela Elwell Hunt's Christian romance novel *Roanoke: The Lost Colony* (1996), the first of five historical novels set in colonial America in her Keepers of the Ring series. What this list of TV shows, novels, short stories, and movies shows is that not knowing what happens to the 1587 colonists allows them to be *The* Lost Colony, to be a solvable mystery explained in whatever way someone wants.

The genre that leaves the mystery of the Lost Colony most open is literary or creative nonfiction. Some of the best Lost Colony examples of this genre are participatory narratives, that is, works in which authors not only relate the history of the 1580s Roanoke colonies, especially the 1587 colony, but tell their own stories about investigating that history. Andrew Lawler's recent *The Secret Token: Myth, Obsession, and the*

Search for the Lost Colony of Roanoke (2018) includes in its subtitle the admission that many other works don't reveal—that the answers individuals tend to push about what happened to the Lost Colony are often based on myth, on stories repeated so often that they become reified as truths. The subtitle also admits to the fact that it is easy to become obsessive about the Lost Colony.

Lawler quotes Brent Lane, one of the people involved with Site X, particularly examining what is under the patch on the John White's watercolor map: "The Lost Colony has a kind of inexorable pull, like a black hole.... You may think you are immune, but if you get too close to it, it sucks you in" (11). Lawler admits that while researching and writing *The Secret Token*, he too was sometimes sucked in, feeling the "inexorable pull." Making that admission helps readers temper any of Lawler's own speculations.

Similarly, Tony Horwitz in *A Voyage Long and Strange: Rediscovering the New World* (2008) says that while we don't really know what happened to the Lost Colony, he appreciates that, unlike many other colonists left behind, including the three men still ashore when Drake took the rest of Ralph Lane's colony back to England and, even more, the slaves Drake left ashore to create room for Lane's colonists, the 1587 colonists, "at least, were remembered and celebrated," that "people still sought some connection to them" (324–325). For Horwitz, even if the hypotheses can't be tested and the pseudoscientific "theories" are based on questionable assumptions, they serve the important purpose of remembering these people.

Recognizing that there is value in Lost Colony stories, hypotheses, and fringe "theories," even if they are not historically true, becomes a central point in many works of Lost Colony creative nonfiction. In her essay "Lost Colonies" (2018), Nell Boeschenstein describes being put off by some of the people involved in the current searches and, while travelling around Eastern North Carolina, being told interesting but odd ideas about what happened to the Lost Colony. Boeschenstein writes, "I knew now that I could not care less about what happened to the Lost Colony; that what got me is why we invented it in the first place, why we fought about it and got territorial, and what those squabbles tell us about who we are as Americans."

Marjorie Hudson expands on the same idea. Her 2002 *Searching for Virginia Dare: A Fool's Errand* explores the history of the 1587 colonists, tells the story of how Hudson gathered her information (including visits with Charlie and with Tom in our East Carolina University offices), and reflects on losses in her own life. In the "Author Q & A" added to the 2003 paperback reprint of *Searching for Virginia Dare*,

Hudson explains she subtitled the book "A Fool's Errand" because "I wanted people to know right away I wasn't making any astonishing claims" (2003 [2002]:182–183). Hudson then adds, "Although I learned many new and surprising things, the more I learned, the more I saw it was the nature of the search, and the journey, that had the most to tell me" (2003 [2002]:185). These works of nonfiction highlight that any claim to know what happened to the Lost Colony is a fool's claim, but reflecting on why people want to answer the unanswerable is far from a fool's errand.[4]

That people don't often tell the Lost Colony story as an unsolved mystery returns us to one of our important terms, *historiography*, the study of how history is written, that is, how the core beliefs and cultural influences of people writing about history affect what data are deemed important, affect the ways information is researched and presented, and affect the conclusions drawn from that information. Interpretations of events shift over time as a result of many different factors. The historiography of the Lost Colony helps us understand that societal, political, economic, and other issues may alter the recording of history over time. Hypotheses shift over time. There are ambiguous answers, and ambiguity should be treated as a place to start an investigation, not as an endpoint. Ambiguity can help us look at potential other ways to interpret data—including exploring not only other Lost Colony interpretations, but non–Lost Colony related ideas as well.

We all have (often unconscious) assumptions about the world that guide our thinking—*ideologies* is the term frequently used for these assumptions—and because of their influence, we read hints as facts, interpreting hearsay through our confirmation biases. Looking at how television, novels, short stories, movies, and participatory nonfiction narratives have portrayed the Lost Colony reveals what core beliefs and cultural influences seem to have been influencing the way Lost Colony history has been researched and written.

Just as one example, the story of the Lost Colony has been told primarily as a European and European American story. Michael Oberg's ethnohistory of the Roanoke Colonies, *The Head in Edward Nugent's Hand: Roanoke's Forgotten Indians*, focuses on the Roanoke colonization efforts from the point of view of the Native Americans who encountered the English. Near the end of his study, Oberg posits that one group knew what had happened to the 1587 colonists: "The fate of the 'Lost Colonists' was no mystery to the Algonquians of the Carolina Sounds" (2008:125). Oberg then lays out what might have happened if the colonists had joined with one of various of the Algonquian groups in the region, including the Croatoans on Hatteras Island, the Chesapeakes on the south side of the Chesapeake Bay, the Choanoacs at the west end of the Albemarle Sound, and the even the Lumbee of Robeson County.

While Oberg believes that the most likely scenario is that Wahunsonacock (the Native American name for Powhatan) attacked the colonists and the Native Americans they had joined up with (maybe the Chesapeake, but more likely the Choanoacs or another group in the Carolina Sounds region), more important to Oberg is that "they became Algonquians and were no longer English men and women" (2008:146). By recognizing that the "Indian people knew what happened" to the 1587 colonists, "but only small traces of what they knew reached the Englishmen who wrote the documents upon which historians rely" (2008:146), Oberg is able to use the ambiguity in the data available to help readers see what can be learned when that information is not forced to try to show more than it can.

It isn't just the ambiguity in written documents that needs to be recognized. When a European artifact is found on a Native American site—a signet ring, a piece of Border Ware—too often the first assumption is that it indicates the presence of some or all of the Lost Colony. Little attention is given to the possibility that a Native American might have picked it up elsewhere through trade or at an abandoned European site and brought it to its present location. Such bias is understandable. The usual methodology encourages positing answers with a tone of certainty rather than promoting the idea that there isn't enough information to test many hypotheses. The Lost Colony is in our awareness in ways other parts of the past are not, so connecting something to the Lost Colony feels better than saying we don't know who brought the artifact to where it was found and when. Attempts at using the historical imagination can fill in the gap. But that imagination can easily be affected by confirmation bias, by the Lost Colony Reality Distortion Sphere.

One other influence takes people into this Reality Distortion Sphere. We hate to admit that a mystery might never be solved. Parallels to the Lost Colony can be seen in the History Channel's television show *The Curse of Oak Island,* which first aired in 2014 and is still going as of 2024, even though the Lagina brothers and their associates keep getting excited about unearthing new artifacts and yet not finding the treasure purported to be on Nova Scotia's Oak Island. Why does the crew keep going back to look again and again? Near the end of the show's fourth season, local historian Charles Barkhouse says about the Oak Island treasure, "It's here." Rick Lagina asks, "Why are you so convinced, Charles?" Charles replies, "Because they were convinced. All of them were convinced. Why was Fred Blair involved from 1893 to 1951 and he wasn't convinced? Huh? Why was M.R. Chappell? They all had to believe, otherwise what was the point of them being here. Nobody wants you guys to find it more than I do" (Burns et al. 2017:[0:31:12–31:35]).

Like Barkhouse and the Laginas concerning Oak Island, a large number of people focusing on the Lost Colony believe the mystery has to be solvable because, if it isn't, it feels like the search been in vain. It is a matter of moral justice—the universe owes researchers an answer. The belief that moral justice demands an answer leads people to interpret any possible written clue or artifact first and foremost through the lens of the Lost Colony.

The possibility that interpretations other than ones connected with the Lost Colony may be equally—and sometimes more—informative, let alone more probable, can easily get lost. Is the signet ring found at Cape Creek less valuable for understanding the past if it is a common brass ring used as a seventeenth-century European–Native American trade good rather than a gold ring that belonged to one of the Kendalls and came to Cape Creek through the Lost Colony? And John White did write that he found that his armor and other belongings had been dug up by local Indians when he returned to Roanoke in 1590. Is a rapier handle found on Hatteras Island less important if it is an item a Native American may have found on Roanoke after it was abandoned by the 1580s English colonists than if it was brought to Croatoan by an Englishman when the Lost Colony joined Manteo and his people?

So we are back to the point made by lebame houston, "They were not lost. They knew where they were. Our problem is, we don't know where they went because we do not have enough evidence to corroborate the report in the Jamestown settlement." Charlie and Tom would add: or enough evidence to corroborate any of the of the other tantalizing but varied hints that have appeared over the years. As houston concludes, "Therefore, this is the stuff of which legends are made."

None of the hypotheses presented in this book rise to the level of theory. It could be that one of them ends up being proven correct or that they are all misguided. Without unequivocal physical evidence, they are all educated guesses. So, again, don't ask us where we think the Lost Colony went. Both of us will say, "I don't know." And mean it.

Appendix

The Players:
Major Figures in the Roanoke
Colonization Ventures
and Early Searches
for the 1587 Colonists

(I.) Roanoke and Vicinity

Carolina Algonquians

Granganimeo: Brother of Wingina and one of the first to greet and trade with the English in 1584. His death during the winter of 1585–1586 prompted his brother Wingina to change his name to Pemisapan.

Manteo: One of the first two Native Americans encountered by the English to travel to England, accompanying Amadas and Barlowe's on their return voyage in 1584. Based on Hatteras Island, this prominent Algonquian-speaking native was an ally to the subsequent Roanoke colonists, travelling to England again in 1586 with Ralph Lane, and returning home to the Outer Banks with the 1587 colonists.

Menatonon: An influential elder of the Chowanoc confederacy along the Chowan River. In the spring of 1586, Ralph Lane had him held captive to ensure his men's safety while in Menatonon's main village.

Wanchese: Algonquian native from Roanoke Island. Traveled with Manteo to England in 1584. Proved to be an adversary for the 1585–1586 Roanoke colonists.

Wingina/Pemisapan: Algonquian chieftain of the Roanokes. Suspicious of the English colonists, by the spring of 1586, he began plotting against Ralph Lane's 1585–1586 colony and had changed his name to Pemisapan. He was killed and beheaded by Lane's men in June of 1586.

European Travelers to Roanoke Island

Amadas, Philip: English naval commander and explorer. At age 19 he captained the *Bark Raleigh* and explored the North Carolina coast with Arthur Barlowe in 1584. He sailed to Roanoke Island a year later with Richard Grenville and stayed with the colony under Ralph Lane, returning to England with Francis Drake in June of 1586.

Barlowe, Arthur: Second captain to Philip Amadas on the 1584 voyage and author of the report to Raleigh about the expedition.

Dare, Ananais: Prominent colonist of the 1587 Roanoke venture. A tiler and bricklayer by trade, he was the husband of Eleanor Dare and father of Virginia Dare.

Dare, Eleanor: Colonist of the 1587 Roanoke venture. The daughter of John White, wife of Ananais Dare, and mother of Virginia Dare, she is also the alleged author of the Dare Stones.

Dare, Virginia: Daughter of Ananais and Eleanor Dare. She was the first child born of English parents in North America, on August 18, 1587. According to some legends, she was allegedly turned into a white doe by a native sorcerer.

Drake, Francis: English captain and privateer. He sailed to Roanoke Island in 1585 with supplies after sacking St. Augustine but returned the colonists he found to England at their request instead.

Fernandez, Simon (also Simão as well as Fernándes or Fernando): Portuguese navigator who served as the chief pilot for the 1584, 1585, and 1587 Roanoke voyages. He has been portrayed both as a villain and prudent naval commander in historical texts.

Grenville, Richard: English naval commander and leader of the 1585 Roanoke expedition. He planted the first settlement, explored the region in July and August, and then went back for supplies. Grenville returned in 1586 to find the colony deserted as all had left with Francis Drake for England only a few weeks before.

Hariot, Thomas (also Harriot): English polymath with interests in geography, mathematics, astronomy, and anthropology. He was Raleigh's official representative on the 1585–1586 voyage. His *Briefe and True Report* (1588; reprinted with engravings by Theodor de Bry in 1590) chronicled the flora and fauna of the region as well as several events of that early venture.

Lane, Ralph: Soldier and governor of the 1584 Roanoke colony in Richard Grenville's absence. His military approach sowed discord with the native inhabitants.

White, John: Artist and administrator. He was on the 1585–1586, 1587 and 1590 Roanoke voyages. He was governor of the 1587 colony as well as father of Eleanor Dare and grandfather of Virginia Dare. His watercolor paintings from the 1585–1586 voyage are an invaluable source of information concerning the New World and its inhabitants.

Others

de Bry, Theodor: Sixteenth century engraver and editor. Originally from the city of Liège (now in modern Belgium), he lived in London from 1585 to 1588. In 1588, he moved to Frankfurt, where in 1589 he published English, Latin, French, and German editions of Thomas Hariot's *A Briefe and True Report of the New Found Land of Virginia* (1590) using engravings adapted from John White's watercolors of North Carolina.

Gilbert, Humphrey: half-brother of Walter Raleigh. An early proponent of seeking a Northwest Passage to Asia. Made two abortive attempts at colonizing North America (in 1578 and 1583) and died during the second attempt.

Hakluyt, Richard: Editor, geographer, and Anglican minister. Played a key role in publishing Thomas Hariot *Briefe and True Report* (1588) as well as the other main primary documents from the Roanoke voyages in his *Principall Navigations....* (1589 and 1598–1600).

Lawson, John: Early eighteenth-century explorer of the North Carolina Coastal Plain. Claims to have heard rumors of grey-eyed Indians who could "talk in a book" (i.e., read) like the English.

Queen Elizabeth: Ruler of England at the time of the Roanoke voyages. Granted permission and support for the expeditions. Walter Raleigh was her favorite until he wasn't.

Raleigh, Walter (also Ralegh): English courtier and favorite of Queen Elizabeth who funded several voyages to what is now Eastern North Carolina (including 1584, 1585–1586, 1586, and 1587) and, as one early sixteenth-century source says, tried to resupply the 1587 colonists "five severall times." Though he never set foot in North America, he did later voyage twice to Guiana in failed searches for El Dorado. After Elizabeth's 1603 death, he was imprisoned and later beheaded (in 1618).

(II.) Jamestown Colonists and Others Connected to the Early Searches for the 1587 Roanoke Colonists

Mace, Samuel: English captain sent by Raleigh in 1602 to search for Roanoke survivors. He was unable to search in the immediate area of Roanoke Island and the Outer Banks due to adverse weather conditions.

Powell, Nathaniel: Jamestown settler sent in 1609 with Anas Todkill to search the Chowan River area for evidence of the Roanoke colonists. They are supposed to have found some carvings on trees south of Jamestown, but there is no direct evidence.

Powhatan: Powerful leader of the Algonquian-speaking natives of the Chesapeake region. As early as 1610, the Virginia Company reported rumors that Powhatan had killed the majority of 1587 Roanoke colonists, who had moved to the Chesapeake Bay area, in 1607, at the time of the Jamestown colony's arrival.

Purchas, Samuel: Editor and Richard Hakluyt's editorial successor. Especially his 1625 collection, *Hakluytus Posthumus or Purchas His Pilgrimes*, chronicled the Jamestown voyages. Purchas wrote that Powhatan had told John Smith that he had had the surviving Roanoke colonists killed.

Sicklemore, Michael: Sent to the Chowan River from Jamestown in 1609 to find evidence of the Roanoke colonists. He reported no evidence and was himself dead before he could return to England.

Smith, John: Captain and colonial governor of Jamestown. Relaying what the Powell and Todkill as well as the Sicklemore searches from early Jamestown for the 1587 Roanoke colonists, Smith only writes "that was never any of them found, nor seene to this day."

Strachey, William: Secretary of the Jamestown colony during his less than a year there in 1610–1611. He reported, after talking with Machumps, a local Native, that the 1587 Roanoke colonists were killed by Powhatan in 1607, but that two small groups had escaped the slaughter, including several who were said to be living at Ritanoe.

Todkill, Anas: Jamestown settler sent in 1609 with Nathaniel Powell to search the Chowan River area for evidence of the Roanoke colonists. They are supposed to have found some carvings on trees south of Jamestown, but no direct evidence.

Chapter Notes

Chapter 1

1. A bark is a heavily constructed single-decked vessel designed for fishing or coastal trade, usually having two masts and square rigged. A pinnace is a more lightly constructed shallow drafted vessel under 50 tonnes, usually having a single mast but also able to be propelled with oars (National Park Service 2015).

2. John White notes in his 1593 letter to Richard Hakluyt that the 1590 voyage was his fifth and last (Quinn 1991[1955]:2:715), appearing to put him on the 1584 voyage as well as the 1585, 1587, 1588 and 1590 crossings.

3. Those these sites have been sought archaeologically, but only the Chowanoke site (31HF20) has a generally accepted location, along the Chowan River.

4. Phil Jones' *Ralegh's Pirate Colony in America* (2001) posits that the colony's main purpose was to serve as a staging post for piracy in North America.

5. One of the earliest biographies of John White to go beyond what was in the Roanoke-colonization texts appeared in Paul Hulton's *America 1585: The Complete Drawings of John White* (1984:7–9). Hulton points out that limited records and the commonness of the name *John White* make it difficult to know whether any record referring to a John White refers to the John White of the Roanoke voyages. Both the *American National Biography* entry on White (Shields 1999; written by Tom in the early 1990s) and the *Oxford Dictionary of National Biography* entry (Tiro 2004) are based on Hulton's work.

Additional information about White's life appeared in the *Dictionary of North Carolina Biography* (Quinn 1996) and later in *A New World: England's First View of America* (Sloan 2007, p. 24)—particularly that White married Tomasyn Cooper in 1566; that they had a son Thomas born in 1567 and who died in 1568; and that Eleanor White (Dare) was baptized in 1568. Quinn and Sloan attribute the information to personal exchanges with lebame houston (with Quinn also adding Olivia Isil).

John P. Brooke-Little's "The Armorial Identification of Governor John White" (presented at the 1993 Roanoke Decoded conference but not published until 2015) cites personal exchanges with houston along with a source not picked up by academic indexing, "John White of London," from the souvenir program for *The Lost Colony* (houston 1991). Brooke-Little gives much of houston's evidence, but adds that the coat of arms granted to White as governor does not clear up who his family was: "The fact is that John White's origins are a mystery and his heraldry, which ought to give important clues to his family connections, appears to confuse the issue" (121). Even so, Sloan argues White was a gentleman and not "base-born" (25).

6. Foucault's essay, originally in French, has been translated into English and published several times, one of the earliest being in the 1975 volume of *The Partisan Review*.

Chapter 2

1. *Virginia* meant all of the lands claimed by the English in North America and available to Raleigh for potential settlement. As Theodor de Bry defines the region in the 1590 edition of Hariot's *A Briefe and True Report*, Virginia covers the lands from Spanish Florida to Cape Breton Island (Hariot 1590b:3).

2. Quinn suggests the Lane letter was inserted out of order because Hakluyt received a copy only after the 1589 edition was well along in production (1991[1955]:1:207). The placement of the 1589 investors' agreement could be explained similarly, having been made just before the 1589 *Principal Navigations* was published.

3. This line is now most often given by North Carolinians as "the goodliest land under the cope of heaven."

4. Quinn's *The Roanoke Voyages, 1584–1590: Documents to Illustrate the English Voyages to North America Under the Patent Granted to Walter Raleigh in 1584* (1955; rpt. 1991) illustrates the effect of including as well as excluding texts. Quinn's collection, the fullest of Roanoke colonization-related materials, includes 159 source documents compared to Hakluyt's 14. Quinn's collection develops a more complex story than Hakluyt's. Hakluyt's exclusions were not always deliberate; many documents Quinn includes were not available to Hakluyt. However, some choices were conscious, such as omitting materials about the 1588 resupply attempt and the colony's 1589 investment reorganization from the 1598–1600 edition of the *Principal Navigations* that were in the 1589 edition (see below).

5. Similarly, *colony* was applied to early seventeenth-century English territories in Ireland, connoting landed estates and farms in a land controlled by but outside of England, and the term *planter* described the English and Scottish settlers on lands Irish Catholics had been driven from.

6. All of the Roanoke expedition materials appear in the third and last volume, which came out in 1600.

7. Where the Mace expedition spent the month is given as both forty leagues southwest of Hatteras and "in thirtie foure degrees or thereabout" (Brereton and Haies 1966 [1602]:14), making the location anywhere between Cape Fear and Cape Lookout.

8. Two editions of Gerard's *Herball* appeared after his 1612 death, one in 1633 and another in 1636. Both repeat the language about the survival of the 1587 planters.

9. Beyond these published references, David B. and Alison M. Quinn (1983) note that "The Jewel of Artes," George Waymouth's 1604 manuscript treatise on military fortifications and ordnance presented to King James, uses language implying that the 1587 planters are still alive. Waymouth writes about fortifications "in the land of florida in those partes there of which longe haue beene in possession of our English nation ... but weakely planted with the English, and they more weakely defended from the in vasions [sic] of the heathen, Amongst whom they dwell or subiect vnto manifolde perils. . ." (Quinn and Quinn 1983: 233). *Florida* was the name for all Spanish claims from the Florida Peninsula north to the Chesapeake Bay and beyond and west to the Mississippi River and beyond.

10. Dekker and Webster's *Westward Ho* (and their follow-up in response to Chapman, Jonson, and Marston, *Northward Ho*) sympathetically show the rising middle class sometimes playing fast and loose with traditional morality, but ultimately doing the right thing. *Eastward Ho!* is most often read as promoting traditional morality, especially through its satire of inappropriate social ambition seen as prevalent in London.

11. Citations from *Eastward Ho!* are given using act, scene, and line numbers from *The Cambridge Edition of the Works of Ben Jonson* (Chapman et al. 2012:2:529–640). The play's title varies from *Eastward Hoe* on the original 1605 title page to the modernized *Eastward Ho* to the *Cambridge Edition*'s form using an exclamation mark.

12. David Beers Quinn provides a good overview of these reasons in *England and the Discovery of America, 1481–1620* (1974:432–481). Quinn

argues that "the story of the Lost Colony became somewhat tedious by repetition to Londoners, at least, for in 1605 it was guyed on the stage in the play *Eastward Hoe*.... It might appear that in the current propaganda for the revival of the Virginia enterprise ... the story of the allegedly surviving colony had been somewhat oversold" (452).

13. One recent work hypothesizing about what happened to the Lost Colony, Brandon Fullam's *The Lost Colony of Roanoke* (2017), asserts these Europeans "in reality were Algonquian memories of Spanish expeditions into the Piedmont of the present-day Carolinas many decades earlier. They had nothing whatsoever to do with the Lost Colony" (228).

14. Unless otherwise noted, the 1953 edition by Louis B. Wright and Virginia Freund is used. The Wright and Freund edition is based on the manuscript dedicated to the Earl of Northumberland and owned by Princeton University. The 1849 edition by R. H. Major is based on the manuscript presented to Sir Francis Bacon and owned by the British Museum. The third manuscript was presented to Sir Allen Apsley and is owned by the Bodleian library.

15. The only book-length biography of Strachey is S. G. Culliford's *William Strachey, 1572–1621* (1965). Strachey's *A True Reportory of the Wracke, and Redemption of Sir Thomas Gates Knight* is a main source on the Bermuda shipwreck but was not published until after Strachey's 1621 death when Samuel Purchas included it in his 1625 edition of *Hakluytus Posthumus or Purchas his Pilgrimes*.

16. While getting the date wrong here—and in at least one other copy of the manuscript (1849 [1612]:165)—Strachey uses the correct date of 1587 elsewhere throughout the manuscript.

17. For more on Machumps, see Vaughan (2006:42–56, 2018).

18. Lee Miller (2001:250) believes the word *apes* is not the English word implying there are monkeys in Ritanoe, but Strachey's misunderstanding of an Algonquian word meaning "metal," the equivalent in other Algonquian dialects of *apisk* in Cree, *apes* in Pequot, and *tapisco* in Wicocomoco.

19. Symonds wrote *Virginia: A Sermon Preached at White-Chappel, in the Presence of Many, Honourable and Worshipfull, the Aduenturers and Planters for Virginia* (1609), which states on the title page, "Published for the benefit and vse of the colony, planted, and to bee planted there, and for the aduancement of their Christian purpose."

20. In his edition of "The Proceedings," Philip Barbour argues that "The Proceedings" included some material by Smith but was a compilation by Symonds done to accompany the map and "Description" (Smith 1986:1:195–197). On the other hand, Karen Kupperman argues that "it is probable that the book was basically written by Smith," but that various parts of the text discussing events that occurred after Smith left Virginia in October of 1609 were by the others listed on the title page (Smith 1988:25).

21. "Silke of grasse or grasse Silke" is the first marketable commodity that Thomas Hariot lists in his *Briefe and True Report* (1590b:7). Most likely meaning one or more of the yucca varieties indigenous to coastal North Carolina, finding a way to produce silk was another of the impossible tasks that could be used to indicate the Virginia colony's success.

22. The first edition of *Purchas His Pilgrimage* appeared in 1613, but a second, expanded edition was published almost immediately, in 1614.

23. Purchas published a fourth edition of *Purchas His Pilgrimge* in 1626, the year after publishing *Hakluytus Posthumus*; it was effectively the same as the 1617 edition, including the Roanoke-related materials being the same.

24. *36. 20. Aug. 15*: 36 degrees, 20 minutes north on August 20th.

Chapter 3

1. William S. Powell's *Paradise Preserved* (1965) remains the best overview history of these and other actions in the nineteenth and first half of the twentieth centuries to commemorate the 1580s Roanoke colonization efforts on Roanoke Island.

2. The private non-profit Virginia

Company Foundation was a group of archaeologists assembled to work at Fort Raleigh and other sites of interest. Later it morphed into the First Colony Foundation.

3. The Hariot Nature Trail is a one-third of a mile loop walking trail within the Fort Raleigh National Site grounds located just northwest of the earthwork

4. The premise of this PBS program was having visiting archaeologists investigate a working site using various high-tech wizardry over the course of three days.

5. Cultural resource management (CRM) archaeology applies to investigations required by law of sites located on public properties or of projects using federal funding.

6. This designation follows the Smithsonian trinomial system where the first number, 31, is North Carolina's place alphabetically among the states (excluding Alaska and Hawaii). DR is the abbreviation for Dare County and 1 is the sequential number assigned to the sites as they are found.

7. Among these sources are items from local Outer Banks newspapers *The Coastland Times* (Manteo, North Carolina www.thecoastlandtimes.com) and the now defunct *Outer Banks* Sentinel (partially archived at the *Outer Banks Voice* website www.outerbanksvoice. com), and particularly the Croatoan Archaeological Society's own website (www.cashatteras.com, especially its "CAS in the News!" page).

Chapter 4

1. In fact, Oldmixon discusses *The History and Present State of Virginia*, though in the Roanoke sections often to differ with Beverley. For example, Oldmixon states that Beverley must be wrong that Raleigh traveled on the single supply ship sent ahead of Grenville's resupply in 1586 (1708:215).

2. Through the 1820s and 1830s, others who continued to use this trope include Emma Willard in her *History of the United States, or Republic of America* (New York, 1828); John Warner Barber

in his *Interesting Events in the History of the United States* (New Haven, 1832); S. S. Hill in *The Emigrant's Introduction to an Acquaintance with the British American Colonies, and the Present Condition and Prospects of the Colonists* (London, 1837); and Benjamin Eggleston, *The Wars of America: Or, a General History of All the Important Tragic Events That Have Occurred in the United States of North America, since the Discovery of the Western Continent by Christopher Columbus.* (Baltimore, 1839).

3. In one of the few academic articles on the Hatteras, "The Hatteras Indians of North Carolina" (1960), Gary S. Dunbar notes that Lawson is the first writer to use the name *Hatteras Indians.* Dunbar also notes that while people often assume the Croatoan and Hatteras are the same, just having changed names between the 1580s and the early 1700s, "the available evidence does not prove this connection. There is no evidence of continuity through the 17th century" (411).

4. The introduction was reprinted in 1824 as *A History of the Colonies Planted by the English on the Continent of North America.*

5. Other early histories that write about the Roanoke colonies without speculating on the 1587 colonists' fate include the anonymous *A Collection of Voyages and Travels* (Awnsham and John Churchill, London 1704) and *The American Gazetteer* (A. Miller and J.&R. Tonson, London, 1762), the latter translated into Italian as *Il Gazzettiere Americano* (Marco Coltellini, Livorno, 1763); Abiel Holmes, *American Annals; or, a Chronological History of America* (Cambridge, Massachusetts, 1805); James Jones Wilmer, *The American Nepos: A Collection of the Lives of the Most Remarkable and the Most Eminent Men, Who Have Contributed to the Discovery, the Settlement, and the Independence of America* (Baltimore, 1805); Hugh Williamson, *The History of North Carolina* (Philadelphia, 1812); John Wilson Campbell, *A History of Virginia from Its Discovery Till the Year 1781* (Petersburg, Virginia, 1813); the anonymous *History of the United States of America; with a Brief Account of Some of the Principal Empires*

and States of Ancient and Modern Times, signed as by "A Citizen of Massachusetts" (Keene, New Hampshire, 1820); Salma Hale, *History of the United States, from Their First Settlement as Colonies, to the Close of the War with Great Britain, in 1815* (New York, 1825); William Desborough Cooley, *The History of Maritime and Inland Discovery* (London, 1830–1831); John Howard Hinton, *The History and Topography; of the United States* (London and Philadelphia, 1830–1832); Lambert Lilly, *The Early History of the Southern States: Virginia, North and South Carolina, and Georgia* (Philadelphia, 1832); and John Frost, *History of the United States, for the Use of Common Schools* (Philadelphia, 1837).

6. Davis's story was first published as *Captain Smith and Princess Pocahontas, an Indian Tale* (1805a). *The First Settlers of Virginia* was, as stated on its title page, "The second edition considerably enlarged," with the Roanoke material first appearing in the second edition.

7. See, in particular, Arner (1985:12–14) and Lawler (2018:128–129).

8. Other eighteenth- and early nineteenth-century histories that mention Virginia Dare's birth include *The American Gazetteer* (A. Miller and J.&R. Tonson 1762), Marshall (1804 and 1824), Holmes (1805), Wilmer (1805), *History of the United States of America* (A Citizen of Massachusetts 1820), Butler (1821, who doesn't mention Manteo's christening and knighting), Hinton (1830–1832), and Lilly (1832). Histories that don't mention either Manteo's baptism and knighthood or Virginia Dare's birth include *A Collection of Voyages and Travels* (Awnsham and John Churchill 1704), Lawson (1967 [1709]), Hall (1735), Brickell (1753), Douglass (1749–1753), Rogers (1765), Wynn (1770), Jefferson (1787), and Robertson (1799).

9. For background on Robertson, see Shields (2023).

10. Analostan Island is in the District of Columbia and is now called Theodore Roosevelt Island.

11. Robert D. Aner identified Tuthill's story as the earliest treatment of the 1580s Lost Colony "in full and proper fictional form" (1978:17;1985:14). However, Arner was working in the pre-electronic database era; Robertson's poem and Cushing's story were found only through access to online databases such as *Sabin Americana* and the American Antiquarian Society's *American Historical Periodicals* (Shields 2023).

12. There is no full biography of Cushing. The best sources of literary biographical information about her are Trofimenkoff (2020[1982]), Wagner (1990), and Kalbfleisch (2007).

13. For the little available about Tuthill's life, see Hageman (1879:402–403) and Schröder (2015:18–19).

14. For more on Wiley, see Arner (1985:17–18) and Barbara M. Parramore (1996).

15. For Hawks' biography, see Carraway (1998).

16. Green revised *The Lost Colony* several times between 1937 and his death in 1981 with each revision making the ultimate fate of the colonists less and less clear (Shields 2018).

Chapter 5

1. Joseph Hall recently located a previously unknown short account of the 1588 Gonzalez expedition written by one of its members in 1611 (Hall 2015), indicating that there may be more Roanoke colonization-related Spanish documents to be found.

2. One twentieth-century history, *North Carolina: The History of a Southern State* (1954), by Hugh Talmage Lefler and Albert Ray Newsome, is interesting because while it gives one of the theories of assimilation discussed below (joining with Native Americans to become the Croatoan, i.e., the Lumbee), it stresses the scenarios of the 1587 colonists dying, including being killed by Native Americans, being eradicated by the Spanish, or "the most plausible" hypothesis, "though never advanced by writers," that they left in the pinnace "and were lost in the Atlantic" (Lefler and Newsome 11). The same language is repeated in the 1963 and 1973 second and third editions. Few if any other modern historians promote the "they died" hypotheses, especially attack by the Spanish or attempts to sail back to England.

3. For McMillan's biography, see Stacy (1991).

4. While having been legally recognized by several other names, the tribe chose the name *Lumbee Tribe of North Carolina* in the 1950s; therefore, the name *Lumbee* is used throughout, with *Croatan Indians* occasionally appearing because of its connection to McMillan's Lumbee–Lost Colony hypothesis.

5. For more on the context of Lowrie's speech, see Malinda Maynor Lowery, *The Lumbee Indians: An American Struggle* (2018), especially Chapter 1, "We Have Always Been a Free People: Encountering Europeans."

6. The Roanoke River was originally called the Moratoc, but was labeled as the Roanoke River by at least 1737, when Edward Mosely used that name on *A New and Correct Map of the Province of North Carolina* (Cumming and De Vorsey 1998: Plates 50–51).

7. For background on Quinn, see Canny and Kupperman (2003) and Jones (1987, 2003)

8. While the most straight-forward presentation of Quinn's hypothesis is *The Lost Colonists: Their Fortune and Probable Fate*, it does not include the full academic apparatus to make clear the basis for his assertions. As Quinn notes in *Set Fair for Roanoke*, the references set up in *England and the Discovery of America* are not repeated in *Set Fair for Roanoke* except where he has changed his interpretation or new material has been added (1985:438, n. 4). For the full picture, especially to follow Quinn's paper trail, all three versions need to be examined.

9. Much of what Quinn states about the winter expedition and encampment in the Chesapeake Bay region is hypothesized. It comes from Ralph Lane's narrative about the 1585–1586 expedition, in which Lane states, "To the Northward our furthest discovery was to the Chesepians distant from Roanoak about 130. Miles." Lane then gives a short paragraph about "the Territorie and soyle of the Chesepians," followed by a statement that "sundry Kings, whom they call Weroances," from various tribes near the Chesepians "came to visit the Colonie of the English, which I had for a time appointed to be resident there" (Quinn

1991[1955] 257–258). Quinn admits that the location of the exploration party's camp, which colonists were in the party, and how long they were there is speculative (1974:436; 1985:106–109).

10. While acknowledging Quinn's excellent scholarship connected with the 1580s Roanoke expeditions, Gesa Mackenthun published a solid critique of Quinn's reliance on Purchas and Strachey to promote the idea that the main group of 1587 colonists were massacred by Powhatan in her book *Metaphors of Dispossession: American Beginnings and the Translation Of Empire, 1492–1637* (1997). See in particular the section "A Tale of Two Massacres" in Chapter 4, "'A Mortall Immortall Possession': Virginian Battlefields" (217–229).

11. Parramore began laying out his counter to the Quinn and the Chesapeake hypothesis around the time of the 400th anniversary of the Roanoke colonies in the 1980s (Parramore and Parramore 1984) and expanded it in a chapter of his history of Norfolk, Virginia (Parramore et al. 1994). He then laid out his hypothesis most fully in his 2001 *North Carolina Historical Review* article, "The 'Lost Colony' Found: A Documentary Perspective," which is the main source used here.

12. This description of housing seems unlikely as nothing of the kind was actually seen by Europeans or has appeared in the archaeological record, to say nothing of the lack of available stone as a construction material.

13. English spellings of Native American place names varied greatly. *Metackwem* has come to be the most common spelling for this village, but variants include *Mattaquen, Metocuuem, Metakquam*, and *Mettaquem* (Quinn 1991[1955]:2:858; Evans et al. 2020).

14. A shingle ditch is a ditch used to float shingles cut from junipers to where they could be loaded on boats (McMullan 2014[2010]:195).

15. Prior to 1610, colonists at Jamestown sent a map of the region to London which included information obtained from local informants. The original has been lost, but a spy sent a copy to the Spanish court, what has come to be called the Zúñiga map (Farrell 2021).

Chapter 6

1. For the political background of Hamilton's move to recognize the Croatan Indians, see Lowery (2018:96–102) and Oakley (2005: 21–23).

2. C.K. Howe is apparently Charles Kent Howe (1885–1969), born in East Radford, Virginia; married in Beaufort, North Carolina, in 1909; and buried in the Saint Paul's Episcopal Cemetery in Beaufort (Blankenship 2009; *Family Search* 2021)

3. The stone's message has been published in several places, often with a picture of the stone, including La Vere (2010:14).

4. While there should not be any question about the Eberhardt-related stones being a hoax, see Robert W. White's *A Witness for Eleanor Dare: The Final Chapter in a 400 Year Old Mystery* (1991) as an example of how pseudoscience based on hope and desire can continue to promote an idea after being shown to be a hoax.

Conclusion

1. There is at least one earlier fictional television version of the Lost Colony. In 1966, the series *Daniel Boone* aired the episode "The Lost Colony" (Nicol 1966). The episode's history is fictional but takes cues from the 1587 colony. Set in late eighteenth-century Appalachia, Boone encounters descendants of a colony left on Cape Fear in 1667 rather than Roanoke Island in 1587.

However, in both, the resupply is unable to return for three years.

2. Several other recent Lost Colony–related fictions focus on the paranormal. The supernatural element can show up as ghosts or spirits, as in Deborah Dunn's mystery *The Coffins: A Roanoke Island Suspense Novel* (2017) or Dani Jace's sexually explicit eBook romance novel *White Doe* (2013). On occasion, the paranormal isn't about what was, but what might have been. Alterative histories of the Roanoke colonies placing events in the Marvel universe are played out in a series of graphic novels published between 2003 and 2009. The first of these was *Marvel 1602*, a series written by Neil Gaiman, published in 2003 and 2004, and brought together in hardcover in several editions starting in 2004 (Gaiman 2007). To these were added *Marvel 1602: New World* (2005) and *Marvel 1602: Fantastic Four* (first published in 2006–2007), both by Greg Pak and Greg Tocchini (Pak and Tocchini 2010). These were followed by Jeff Parker and Ramon Rosanas' *Marvel 1602: Spider-Man* (Parker and Rosanas 2009).

3. Kitta (2019: 83–84) provides a quick overview of the Lost Colony and its use as a trope for contagion in recent popular culture.

4. Hudson's *Searching for Virginia Dare* came out in a second edition in 2013, with an added section about returning to the search after the book's original publication and with a new subtitle, *On the Trail of the Lost Colony of Roanoke*.

Bibliography

Aaron, Jason. 2013. "Lost Colony." In *American Vampire Anthology*, vol. 1, pp. 8–17. New York: DC Comics/Vertigo.

Abbot, George. 1599. *A Briefe Description of the Whole Worlde....* London: T. Judson for John Browne.

———. 1605. *A Briefe Description of the Whole Worlde....* London: John Browne.

———. 1664. *A Briefe Description of the Whole World....* London: Margaret Sheares and John Playfere.

Ambers, Janet, Joanna Russell, David Saunders, and Kim Sloan. 2012. "Hidden History? Examination of Two Patches on John White's Map of 'Virginia.'" *The British Museum Technical Research Bulletin* 6:47–54.

The American Gazetteer. 1762. 3 vols. London: A. Millar and J. & R. Tonson.

Andrews, Gavin J. 2008. "Historiography." In *The SAGE Encyclopedia of Qualitative Research Methods*, edited by Lisa M. Given. Thousand Oaks, CA: Sage Publications. https://doi.org/10.4135/9781412963909, accessed July 31, 2023.

Arner, Robert D. 1978. "The Romance of Roanoke: Virginia Dare and the Lost Colony in American Literature." *Southern Literary Journal* 10(2):5–45. https://www.jstor.org/stable/20077586.

———. 1985. *The Lost Colony in Literature.* Raleigh: America's Four Hundredth Anniversary Committee, North Carolina Department of Cultural Resources.

Awes, Andy, Ben Krueger, and Todd Cobery, directors. 2013. "Mystery of Roanoke." *America Unearthed*, hosted by Scott F. Wolter, A & E Television Networks.

Baldwin, Karen. 2003. "Remembrance and Renewal: Modern Belief and Legend in the Region of the 'Lost Colony.'" In *Searching for the Roanoke Colonies: An Interdisciplinary Collection*, edited by E. Thomson Shields, Jr., and Charles R. Ewen, pp. 6–15. Raleigh: Office of Archives and History, North Carolina Department of Cultural Resources.

Bancroft, George. 1834. *A History of the United States, from the Discovery of the American Continent*, Vol. 1. Boston: Charles Bowen.

Barber, John Warner. 1832. *Interesting Events in the History of the United States.* New Haven: J.W. Barber.

Barlow, Joel. 1787. *The Vision of Columbus: A Poem in Nine Books.* Hartford, CT: Hudson and Goodwin.

Bernstein, Josh, host. 2006. "Roanoke, the Lost Colony." Directed by Brendan Goeckel and Brian Leckey, *Digging for the Truth*, A&E Television Networks.

Beverley, Robert. (1705) 2013. *The History and Present State of Virginia.* Edited by Susan Scott Parrish. Chapel Hill: University of North Carolina Press.

Blankenship, Barbara Haddon. 2009. "Charles Kent Howe." *Find A Grave*, www.findagrave.com/memorial/34368250/charles-kent-howe, accessed March 21, 2021.

Blanton, Dennis B. 2003. "If It's Not One Thing, It's Another: The Added Challenges of Weather and Climate for the Roanoke Colony." In *Searching for the Roanoke Colonies:*

An Interdisciplinary Collection, edited by E. Thomson Shields, Jr., and Charles R. Ewen, pp. 169–176. Raleigh: Office of Archives and History, North Carolina Department of Cultural Resources.

Blu, Karen I. (1980) 2001. *The Lumbee Problem: The Making of an American Indian People*. Lincoln: University of Nebraska Press. Originally published in *Cambridge Studies in Cultural Systems* 5 (New York: Cambridge University Press).

Boeschenstein, Nell. 2018. "Lost Colonies." *KROnline*, https://kenyonreview.org/kronline-issue/2018-julyaug/selections/nell-boeschenstein-656342/, accessed May 14, 2021.

Brereton, John, and Edward Haies. (1602) 1966. *Discoverie of the North Part of Virginia*. London: Geor. Bishop (1966 facsimile ed.; New York: Readex).

Brickell, John. 1737. *The Natural History of North-Carolina*. Dublin: J. Carson for the Author.

Brooke-Little, John. 2015. "The Armorial Identification of Governor John White." In *Deciphering the Roanoke Mystery: Archaeology and Document Research and On-Stage in Paul Green's* The Lost Colony, edited by lebame houston and Douglas Stover, pp. 120–126. Manteo, NC: National Park Service, Roanoke Island Historical Association.

Brooks, Max. 2003. *The Zombie Survival Guide: Complete Protection from the Living Dead*. New York: Three Rivers Press.

Bruce, Edward C. 1859. "Loungings in the Footprints of the Pioneers." *Harper's New Monthly Magazine*, May, pp. 741–763. *HathiTrust*, https://hdl.handle.net/2027/ucl.b000541564?urlappend=%3Bseq=749%3Bownerid=13510798903206232-819, accessed February 4, 2024.

———. 1860. "Loungings in the Footprints of the Pioneers: II.–Raleigh and His City." *Harper's New Monthly Magazine*, May, pp. 721–736. *HathiTrust*, https://hdl.handle.net/2027/ucl.b000541566?urlappend=%3Bseq=757%3Bownerid=13510798903578382-789, accessed February 4, 2024.

Buecker, Bradley, director. 2016. *American Horror Story: Roanoke*, FX.

Burns, Kevin, Joe Lessard, and Kim Sheerin, producers. 2017. "Of Sticks and Stones." *The Curse of Oak Island*, The History Channel.

Butler, Frederick. 1821. *A Complete History of the United States of America, Embracing the Whole Period from the Discovery of North America, Down to the Year 1820*. Hartford, CT: Frederick Butler.

Byrd, William. 2013. *The Dividing Line Histories of William Byrd II of Westover*, edited by Kevin Berland. Chapel Hill: University of North Carolina Press.

Campbell, John Wilson. 1813. *A History of Virginia from Its Discovery Till the Year 1781*. Petersburg, VA: J.W. Campbell.

Cannon, Steve. 1969. *Groove, Bang and Jive Around*. New York: Ophelia Press.

Canny, Nicholas, and Karen Ordahl Kupperman. 2003. "The Scholarship and Legacy of David Beers Quinn, 1909–2002." *The William and Mary Quarterly* 60(4):843–860. https://doi.org/10.2307/3491701.

Carraway, Gertrude S. 1988. "Hawks, Francis Lister." In *Dictionary of North Carolina Biography*, edited by William S. Powell, vol. 3, pp. 76–77. Chapel Hill: University of North Carolina Press.

Chaplin, Joyce E. 2007. "Roanoke 'Counterfeited According to the Truth.'" In *A New World: England's First View of America*, by Kim Sloan, pp. 51–63. Chapel Hill: University of North Carolina Press.

Chapman, George, Ben Jonson, and John Marston. (1605) 2012. *Eastward Ho!*, edited by Suzanne Gossett and David W. Kay. In *The Cambridge Edition of the Works of Ben Jonson*, 7 vols., edited by David M. Bevington, Martin Butler, and Ian Donaldson, 2: 529–640. Cambridge: Cambridge University Press.

Chatman, Vernon, John Lee, and Alyson Levy, directors. 2011–2013. *The Heart, She Holler*, Adult Swim, Cartoon Network.

A Citizen of Massachusetts. 1820. *History of the United States of America; with a Brief Account of Some of the Principal Empires and States of Ancient and Modern Times*. Keene, NH: J. Prentiss.

Clanet, David, director. 2015. *A Colony Lost*. East Carolina University. https://vimeo. com/114516524, accessed May 14, 2021.

Clarke, Samuel. 1670. *A True and Faithful Account of the Four Chiefest Plantations of the English in America*. London: Printed for Robert Clavel, Thomas Passenger, William Cadman, William Whitwood, Thomas Sawbridge, and William Birch.

Clayton, Paul. 2009. *White Seed: The Untold Story of the Lost Colony of Roanoke*. CreateSpace.

Clippinger, David. 2001. "Trope." In *Encyclopedia of Postmodernism*, edited by Victor E. Taylor and Charles E. Winquist, pp. 406–407. London: Routledge. https://doi. org/10.4324/9780203195635, accessed May 2, 2021.

Cobb, Collier. 1910. "Early English Survivals on Hatteras Island." *The University Magazine* 27(1910):3–10. *North Carolina Digital Collections*, https://digital.ncdcr.gov/ Documents/Detail/early-english-survivals-on-hatteras-island/501435?item= 622722, accessed February 7, 2024.

Codd, Matt, director. 2007. *Wraiths of Roanoke*. SyFy Channel. Calabasas, CA: American World Pictures.

A Collection of Voyages and Travels.... 1704. 4 vols. London: Printed for Awnsham and John Churchill.

"colony, n." 2021. *OED Online*. Oxford University Press, https://www.oed.com/view/ Entry/36547, accessed May 1, 2021.

Columbian Centinel (Boston). 1819. "President's Tour." 24 April, p. 1. *America's Historical Newspapers*, Readex.

"conspiracy theory, n." 2021. *OED Online*. Oxford University Press, https://www.oed. com/view/Entry/39766, accessed May 13, 2021.

Cooley, William Desborough. 1830–1831. *The History of Maritime and Inland Discovery*. 3 vols. London: Longman, Rees, Orme, Brown, Green, and J. Taylor.

Cooper, James Fenimore. (1823) 2014. *The Pioneers, or, the Sources of the Susquehanna*. London: Heritage Illustrated. Kindle.

Cotten, Sallie Southall. 1901. *The White Doe: The Fate of Virginia Dare, an Indian Legend*. Philadelphia: J.B. Lippincott.

Crayon, Porte. 1857. "North Carolina Illustrated: II. The Piny Woods." *Harper's New Monthly Magazine* May, pp. 741–755. *HathiTrust*, https://hdl.handle.net/2027/ ucl.b000541560?urlappend=%3Bseq=755%3Bownerid=13510798903206086-761, accessed February 4, 2024.

"Croatan Fall Season Uncovers Important Finds." 1998. *Roanoke Colonies Research Newsletter* 6(1):1, 7. *North Carolina Digital Collections*, https://digital.ncdcr.gov/ Documents/Detail/roanoke-colonies-research-newsletter-1998-november-v. 6-no.1/2346353, accessed February 7, 2024.

Croatoan Archaeological Society, Inc. 2020. http://www.cashatteras.com, accessed February 12, 2021.

Culliford, S.G. 1965. *William Strachey, 1572–1621*. Charlottesville: University Press of Virginia.

Cumming, William Patterson, and Louis De Vorsey. 1998. *The Southeast in Early Maps*. 3rd ed. Chapel Hill: University of North Carolina Press.

Cushing, Eliza Lanesford. 1837. "Virginia Dare; or, the Lost Colony: A Tale of the Early Settlers." *The Ladies' Companion* 8:80–92. *Proquest*, https://www.proquest.com/ magazines/virginia-dare-lost-colony/docview/137159605/se-2, accessed February 5, 2024.

———. 1840. "Virginia Dare; or, the Lost Colony." *The Literary Garland* 2:310–324. *Google Books*, https://books.google.com/books?id=BWHZAAAAMAAJ, accessed February 5, 2024.

The Daily Times-News (Burlington, NC). 1945. "Families in Reunion." 12 November, p. 9.

Dannenberg, Clare. 2006. "Lumbee English." In *Vol. 5: Language*, edited by Michael Montgomery and Ellen Johnson, pp. 93–94. *The New Encyclopedia of Southern Culture*, edited by Charles Reagan Wilson. Chapel Hill: University of North Carolina Press.

Darby, Melissa C. 2019. *Thunder Go North: The Hunt for Sir Francis Drake's Fair and Good Bay*. Salt Lake City: University of Utah Press.

Darby, William. 1828. *View of the United States, Historical, Geographical and Statistical....* Philadelphia: H.S. Tanner.

Davenport, B[ishop]. 1831. *History of the United States, Containing All the Events Necessary to Be Committed to Memory....* Philadelphia: Uriah Hunt.

Davis, John. 1805a. *Captain Smith and Princess Pocahontas, an Indian Tale*. Philadelphia: Thomas L. Plowman.

———. 1805b. *The First Settlers of Virginia, an Historical Novel*. 2nd ed. New York: I. Riley and Co.

Dawson, Scott. 2020. *The Lost Colony and Hatteras Island*. Charleston, SC: The History Press.

DeGregory, Lane. 1997. "Hatteras Dig May Open Door to Lost Colony Archaeology: Team Unearths Clues Europeans Were There." *The Virginian-Pilot* (Norfolk), 15 June, p. A1.

Department of Labor and Printing (State of North Carolina). 1909. *Twenty-Second Annual Report of the Department of Labor and Printing of the State of North Carolina 1908*. Raleigh: E.M. Uzzell and Company.

Dial, Adolph L., and David K. Eliades. 1975. *The Only Land I Know: A History of the Lumbee Indians*. San Francisco: Indian Historian Press.

Dickerson, Ernest, director. 2013. "John Doe." *Sleepy Hollow*, Fox.

Dixon, Graham, director. 2009. "The Lost Colony of Roanoke, NC." *Time Team America*, Public Broadcasting Service.

Donegan, Kathleen. 2014. *Seasons of Misery: Catastrophe and Colonial Settlement in Early America*. Philadelphia: University of Pennsylvania Press.

Douglass, William. 1749–1753. *A Summary, Historical and Political, of the First Planting, Progressive Improvements, and Present State of the British Settlements in North-America*. 2 vols. Boston: D. Fowle.

Dunbar, Gary S. 1960. "The Hatteras Indians of North Carolina." *Ethnohistory* 7(4):410–418. https://doi: 10.2307/480877.

Dunn, Deborah. 2017. *The Coffins: A Roanoke Island Suspense Novel*. n.p.: Five Rivers Press.

Eagles, Charles W. 1979. "Cobb, Collier." In *Dictionary of North Carolina Biography*, edited by William S. Powell, vol. 1, pp. 390–391. Chapel Hill: University of North Carolina Press.

Eggleston, Benjamin. 1839. *The Wars of America: Or, a General History of All the Important Tragic Events That Have Occurred in the United States of North America, since the Discovery of the Western Continent by Christopher Columbus*. Baltimore: Hazard & Bloomer.

Egleson, Jan, director. 1986. *Roanoak*. South Carolina ETV Network, 1986.

Evans, Phillip, Eric Klingelhofer, Nicholas Luccketti, Beverly Straube, and Clay Swindell. 2016. *2008–2010 Archaeological Excavations at Fort Raleigh National Historic Site Roanoke Island, North Carolina*. Report submitted to the National Park Service. Durham: First Colony Foundation.

Evans, Phillip W., Eric C. Klingelhofer, and Nicholas M. Luccketti. 2015. *An Archaeological Brief for Site X: A Summary of Investigations of Site 31BR246*. Durham: First Colony Foundation. https://www.firstcolonyfoundation.org/documents/site_x_brief.pdf, accessed February 5, 2024.

Evans, Phillip W., Eric C. Klingelhofer, Nicholas M. Luccketti, Anthony W. Smith, Beverly A. Straube, and E. Clay Swindell. 2020. *Interim Report: North Salmon Creek Survey and Testing at First Colony Foundation Site Y (31BR49) Bertie County, North Carolina*. Durham: First Colony Foundation.

Ewen, Charles R., and Erik Farrell. 2019. "'All that Glitters': A Reassessment of a 'Lost Colony' Artifact." *North Carolina Historical Review* 96(4):408–425. http://www.jstor.org/stable/45286353.

"Family Crest on Sixteenth-Century Gold Ring Tentatively Identified." 1999. *Roanoke*

Colonies Research Newsletter 6(2):1, 6. *North Carolina Digital Collections*, https:// digital.ncdcr.gov/Documents/Detail/roanoke-colonies-research-newsletter-1999-may-v.6-no.2/2346359, accessed February 7, 2024.

Family Search. 2021. "Charles Kent Howe." https://ancestors.familysearch.org/en/ LH2W-KV3/charles-kent-howe-1885-1969, accessed March 21, 2021.

Farrell, Cassandra Britt. 2021. "Zúñiga Chart." In *Encyclopedia Virginia*, https:// encyclopediavirginia.org/entries/zuniga-chart/, accessed March 13, 2022.

Ferguson, Malcolm F. 1948. "Croatan." In *Weird Tales*, July: 70–77.

Fincham, Kenneth. 2011. "Abbot, George (1562–1633)." In *Oxford Dictionary of National Biography*. Oxford: Oxford University Press. https://doi.org/10.1093/ref:odnb/4, accessed February 4, 2022.

Finkbiner, Tim, director. 2011. *Birth of a Colony: North Carolina.* UNC-TV. https:// www.pbs.org/video/unc-tv-presents-birth-of-a-colony-north-carolina/, accessed May 14, 2021.

Folsom, Richard. 2008. *Indian Wood: A Mystery of the Lost Colony of Roanoke Island.* Charleston, SC: Booksurge.

Foucault, Michele. 1975. "What Is an Author?" Translated by James Venti. *Partisan Review* 42(4):603–614.

Franklin, Wayne. 1979. *Discoverers, Explorers, Settlers: The Diligent Writers of Early America.* Chicago: University of Chicago Press.

Frost, John. 1837. *History of the United States, for the Use of Common Schools.* Philadelphia: Edward C. Biddle.

Fullam, Brandon. 2017. *The Lost Colony of Roanoke: New Perspectives.* Jefferson, NC: McFarland.

Futch, Michael. 2020. "This Is Virginia Dare's Grave." *The Fayetteville Observer* (Fayetteville, NC), 7 April. https://www.fayobserver.com/story/news/2020/04/07/legend-has-it-virginia-dare-is-buried-in-robeson-county/41815857/, accessed March 24, 2021.

Gaiman, Neil. 2007. *Marvel 1602.* New York: Marvel.

García-Herrera, Ricardo, Luis Gimeno, Pedro Ribera, and Emiliano Hernández. 2005. "New Records of Atlantic Hurricanes from Spanish Documentary Sources." *Journal of Geophysical Research* 110(3). https://doi.org/10.1029/2004JD005272, accessed May 13, 2021.

Gates, Josh, host. 2016. "The Lost Colony of Roanoke." *Expedition Unknown*, Travel Channel, Discovery Communications.

Gerard, John. 1597. *The Herball or Generall Historie of Plantes.* London: John Norton.

Godwin, Brian C. 2006. "The English Snaphance Lock." In *Catalogue*, pp. 28–63. London: London Park Lane Arms Fair.

Golden, Christie. 2001. "The White Doe, London, 1586." In *Tales of the Slayer*, pp. 21–63. Vol. 1 of *Buffy the Vampire Slayer*, 4 vols. New York: Simon Pulse.

Grahame, James. 1827. *The History of the Rise and Progress of the United States of North America, Till the British Revolution in 1688.* 2 vols. London: Longman, Rees, Orme, Brown, and Green.

Grahame-Smith, Seth. 2010. *Abraham Lincoln: Vampire Hunter.* New York: Grand Central.

⸺. 2015. *The Last American Vampire.* New York: Grand Central.

Gray, Ed. 2016. *Left in the Wind: The Roanoke Journal of Emme Merrimoth.* New York: Pegasus Books.

Gray, Nancy. 1997. "Unearthing Clues to Lost Worlds: An Archaeological Dig on the Outer Banks of North Carolina Reveals Evidence of the Croatan Indians and Possible Links to the Lost Colony." *ECU Report* 28(2):3.

Green, Paul. 1980. *The Lost Colony: A Symphonic Drama of Man's Faith and Work: In Two Acts with Music, Dance, Pantomime, and Song.* 400th Anniversary ed. Durham: Seeman Printery.

Greenblatt, Stephen. 1988. "Invisible Bullets." In *Shakespearean Negotiations: The Circulation of Social Energy in Renaissance England*, pp. 21–65. Berkley: University of California Press.

Griffith, Kelley. 2003. "The Genteel Heroine: Virginia Dare One Hundred Years Ago." In *Searching for the Roanoke Colonies: An Interdisciplinary Collection*, edited by E. Thomson Shields, Jr., and Charles R. Ewen, pp. 32–39. Raleigh: Office of Archives and History, North Carolina Department of Cultural Resources.

Grimshaw, William. 1820. *History of the United States, from Their First Settlement as Colonies, to the Peace of Ghent: Comprising Every Important Political Event.* Philadelphia: Benjamin Warner.

Haag, William George. 1958. *The Archeology of Coastal North Carolina.* Louisiana State University Studies No. 2. Baton Rouge: Louisiana State University Press.

Hageman, John Frelinghuysen. 1879. *History of Princeton and Its Institutions: The Town from Its First Settlement, through the Revolutionary War, to the Present Time.* 2nd ed. Philadelphia: J.B. Lippincott.

Hakluyt, Richard. 1589. *The Principall Nauigations, Voiages, and Discoueries of the English Nation....* London: George Bishop and Ralph Newberie.

———. 1598–1600. *The Principal Navigations, Voyages, Traffiques and Discoveries of the English Nation....* 3 vols. London: George Bishop, Ralph Newberie, and Robert Barker.

———. 1903–1905. *The Principal Navigations Voyages Traffiques & Discoveries of the English Nation: Made by Sea or Over-land to the Remote and Farthest Distant Quarters of the Earth at Any Time Within the Compasse of These 1600 Yeeres.* 12 vols. Glasgow: James MacLehose and Sons.

Hale, Salma. 1825. *History of the United States, from Their First Settlement as Colonies, to the Close of the War with Great Britain, in 1815.* New York: Charles Wiley.

Hall, Fayrer. 1735. *A Short Account of the First Settlement of the Provinces of Virginia, Maryland, New-York, New-Jersey, and Pennsylvania by the English.* London: n.p.

Hall, Joseph. 2015. "Glimpses of Roanoke, Visions of New Mexico, and Dreams of Empire in the Mixed-Up Memories of Gerónimo de la Cruz." *The William and Mary Quarterly* 72(2):323–350. https://doi.org/10.5309/willmaryquar.72.2.0323.

Hampton, Jeff. 2010. "He Heard a Calling in the Lost Colony: Former Teacher Is Convinced, and Wants to Prove, Colonists Went to Mackay Island." *The Virginian-Pilot* (Norfolk), 17 October, pp. 1, 5.

———. 2021. "'Let's Do the Real Stuff Here': Outer Banks Production Pledges to No Longer Hire White Actors in 'Redface' for Native American Roles." *The Virginian-Pilot* (Norfolk, VA), 12 April, pp. 1, 4.

Hariot, Thomas. 1590a. *Admiranda narratio, fida tamen, de commodis et incolarvm ritibvs Virginiae....* Frankfort am Main: Joannis Wecheli for Theodoe de Bry. *East Carolina University Digital Collections*, https://digital.lib.ecu.edu/424, accessed July 31, 2023.

———. 1590b. *A Briefe and True Report of the New Found Land of Virginia....* Frankfort am Main: Joannis Wecheli for Theodor de Bry.

Harrington, Jean Carl. 1957. *New Light on Washington's Fort Necessity: A Report on the Archeological Explorations at Fort Necessity National Battlefield Site.* Richmond, VA: The Eastern National Park and Monument Association.

———. 1962. *Search for the Cittie of Ralegh: Archaeological Excavations at Fort Raleigh National Historic Site, North Carolina.* In *Archaeological Research Series.* Washington, D.C.: National Park Service, U.S. Department of the Interior.

———. 1966. *An Outwork at Fort Raleigh: Further Archeological Excavations at Fort Raleigh National Historic Site, North Carolina.* Richmond, VA: Eastern National Park and Monument Association.

Hausman, Gerald. 1993. "The Story of the White Deer Named Virginia Dare." In *Tunkashila: From the Birth of Turtle Island to the Blood of Wounded Knee*, pp. 229–231. New York: St. Martin's Press.

Hawks, Francis L. 1857. *History of North Carolina: With Maps and Illustrations.* 2 vols. Fayetteville, NC: E.J. Hale and Son.

Heath, Charles. 2012. "Postcontact Period European Trade Goods and Native Modified Objects from The Cape Creek Site (31DR1): Nine Artifact Group Studies." Unpublished report, Phelps Archaeology Laboratory, East Carolina University, Greenville, NC.

Hildreth, Hosea. 1831. *An Abridged History of the United States of America.* Boston: Carter, Hendee and Babcock.

Hill, S.S. 1837. *The Emigrant's Introduction to an Acquaintance with the British American Colonies, and the Present Condition and Prospects of the Colonists.* London: Parbury.

Hinton, John Howard. 1830–1832. *The History and Topography; of the United States.* London: R. Fenner, Sears & Co.; Philadelphia: T. Wardle & I.T. Hinton.

Hoffman, Paul E. 1987. *Spain and The Roanoke Voyages.* Raleigh: America's Four Hundredth Anniversary Committee, North Carolina Dept. of Cultural Resources.

Holland, Todd, director. 2000. "Fearsum." *FreakyLinks,* Fox.

Holmes, Abiel. 1805. *American Annals; or, a Chronological History of America from Its Discovery in MCCCCXCII to MDCCCVI.* 2 vols. Cambridge, MA: W. Hilliard.

Homsher, Deborah. 2007. *The Rising Shore: Roanoke.* Ithaca, NY: Blue Hull Press.

Horn, James. 2005. *A Land as God Made It: Jamestown and the Birth of America.* New York: Basic Books.

———. 2010. *A Kingdom Strange: The Brief and Tragic History of the Lost Colony of Roanoke.* New York: Basic Books.

Horwitz, Tony. 2008. *A Voyage Long and Strange: Rediscovering the New World.* New York: Holt.

houston, lebame. 1991. "John White of London." *The Lost Colony 1991 Souvenir Program,* p. 30. Manteo, NC: Roanoke Island Historical Association.

Howe, C.K. 1947. *Solving the Riddle of the Lost Colony.* Beaufort, NC: M.P. Skarren.

Hudson, Marjorie. (2002) 2003. *Searching for Virginia Dare: A Fool's Errand.* Wilmington, NC: Coastal Carolina Press. Originally published 2002 (Wilmington, NC: Coastal Carolina Press).

———. 2013. *Searching for Virginia Dare: On the Trail of the Lost Colony of Roanoke.* 2nd ed. Winston-Salem, NC: Press 53.

Hulton, Paul. 1984. *America, 1585: The Complete Drawings of John White.* Chapel Hill: University of North Carolina Press.

Hunt, Angela Elwell. 1996. *Roanoke: The Lost Colony.* Wheaton, IL: Tyndale House.

Isil, Olivia. 2003. "Simon Fernandez, Master Mariner and Roanoke Assistant: A New Look at an Old Villain." In *Searching for the Roanoke Colonies: An Interdisciplinary Collection,* edited by E. Thomson Shields, Jr., and Charles R. Ewen, pp. 66–81. Raleigh: Office of Archives and History, North Carolina Department of Cultural Resources.

Jace, Dani. 2013. *White Doe.* n.p.: New Dawning Bookfair.

Jefferson, Thomas. 1787. *Notes on the State of Virginia.* London: J. Stockdale.

Jennings, Tom, producer. 1998. "Lost Colony of Roanoke." *In Search of History,* A & E Home Video.

Johnson, Robert. 1609. *Noua Britannia: Offring Most Excellent Fruites by Planting in Virginia. Exciting All Such as Be Well Affected to Further the Same.* London: Samuel Macham.

Jones, H.G. 2003. "David Beers Quinn, the Roanoke Voyages, and North Carolina (Or, 'Trotting Out David Quinn')." *The Hakluyt Society,* October 30. *Internet Archive,* https://web.archive.org/web/20031030164823/http://www.hakluyt.com/hak-soc-tributes-jones.htm, accessed May 13, 2021.

Jones, H.G., editor. 1987. *Raleigh and Quinn: The Explorer and His Boswell.* Chapel Hill: North Caroliniana Society and the North Carolina Collection.

Jones, Phil. 2001. *Ralegh's Pirate Colony in America: The Lost Settlement of Roanake 1584–1590.* Charleston, SC: Tempus.

Jordan, Wm. Henry. 1945. "Jordans England Where the Lost Colony Met before Taking Boats to America." *The Daily Times-News* (Burlington, NC), 26 September, p. 9.

Kalbfleisch, John. 2007. "Women with the Write Stuff: Two Sisters from Boston Lit up Montreal's 19th-Century Literary Scene." *The Gazette* (Montreal), 6 May, p. A16. *Pro-Quest,* https://search.proquest.com/docview/434475486?accountid=10639, accessed May 10, 2021.

Keel, Bennie C. 2003. "Talcott Williams, 'Pinky' Harrington, and Other Searchers for the 'Lost Colony.'" In *Searching for the Roanoke Colonies: An Interdisciplinary Collection*, edited by E. Thomson Shields, Jr., and Charles R. Ewen, pp. 119–131. Raleigh: Office of Archives and History, North Carolina Department of Cultural Resources.

Kelso, William M. 2017. *Jamestown, The Truth Revealed*. Charlottesville: University of Virginia Press.

King, Stephen, and Mark Carliner, executive producers. (1999) 2014. *Storm of the Century*. DVD, Echo Bridge Entertainment, 2014. Originally aired ABC, 1999.

Kitta, Andrea. 2019. *The Kiss of Death: Contagion, Contamination, and Folklore*. Logan: Utah State University Press.

Kozak, Catherine. 1999. "Ring Has No Lost Colony Link: Likely Owner of Ring Found in Dig Visited Outer Banks Before the Settlement on Roanoke Island Disappeared." *The Virginian-Pilot* (Norfolk), May 11, p. B1.

Kripke, Eric. 2005–2020. *Supernatural*. The CW Television Network.

Kuhlemann, Ute. 2007. "Between Reproduction, Invention and Propaganda: Theodor de Bry's Engravings After John White's Watercolours." In *A New World: England's First View of America*, by Kim Sloan, pp. 79–92. Chapel Hill: University of North Carolina Press.

Kupperman, Karen Ordahl. 2007. *Roanoke: The Abandoned Colony*. 2nd ed. Towota, NJ: Rowman & Littlefield.

Landsburg, Alan, producer. 1979. "Lost Colony of Roanoke." *In Search of...*, Alan Landsburg Productions.

La Vere, David. 2010. *The Lost Rocks: The Dare Stones and the Unsolved Mystery of Sir Walter Raleigh's Lost Colony*. Wilmington, NC: Dram Tree Books.

Lawler, Andrew. 2017. "The Mystery of Roanoke Endures Yet Another Cruel Twist." *Smithsonianmag.com*. https://www.smithsonianmag.com/history/mystery-roanoke-endures-yet-another-cruel-twist-180962837/, accessed January 20, 2021.

———. 2018. *The Secret Token: Myth, Obsession, and the Search for the Lost Colony of Roanoke*. New York: Doubleday.

Lawson, John. (1709) 1967. *A New Voyage to Carolina*, edited by Hugh Talmage Lefler. Chapel Hill: University of North Carolina Press. Originally published 1709 (London: n.p.).

Lefler, Hugh Talmage, and Albert Ray Newsome. 1954. *North Carolina: The History of a Southern State*. Chapel Hill: University of North Carolina Press.

Lilly, Lambert. 1832. *The Early History of the Southern States: Virginia, North and South Carolina, and Georgia*. Philadelphia: Key, Mielke and Biddle.

Lowery, Malinda Maynor. 2018. *The Lumbee Indians: An American Struggle*. Chapel Hill: University of North Carolina Press.

Luccketti, Nicholas M. 1996. *Fort Raleigh Archaeological Project 1994/1995 Survey Report*. Virginia Company Foundation-Association for the Preservation of Virginia Antiquities, Richmond, VA. *The First Colony Foundation*, https://www.firstcolonyfoundation.org/archaeology/dig-reports/ (https://www.firstcolonyfoundation.org/documents/fort_raleigh_1994_1995_survey.pdf), accessed February 6, 2024.

Mackenthun, Gesa. 1997. *Metaphors of Dispossession: American Beginnings and the Translation of Empire, 1492–1637*. Norman: University of Oklahoma Press.

Magoon, Dane T. 1999. "'Chesapeake Pipes' and Uncritical Assumptions: A View from Northeastern North Carolina." *North Carolina Archaeology* 48:107–119.

"main, n.1." 2019. *OED Online*. Oxford: Oxford University Press. https://www.oed.com/view/Entry/112514, accessed April 30, 2021.

Manning, Charles, and Merrill Moore. 1936. "Sassafras and Syphilis." *The New England Quarterly* 9(3):473–475. https://doi.org/10.2307/360282.

Manuel, Ellen. 2009. "William Henry Jordan." *Find a Grave*, https://www.findagrave.com/memorial/34623587/william-henry-jordan, accessed February 28, 2021.

Marco Coltellini. 1763. *Il Gazzettiere americano....* 3 vols. Livorno, Italy: Marco Coltellini.

Marshall, John. 1804–1807. *The Life of George Washington, Commander in Chief of the American Forces, During the War Which Established the Independence of His Country, and First President of the United States.* 5 vols. Philadelphia: C.P. Wayne.

———. 1824. *A History of the Colonies Planted by the English on the Continent of North America, from Their Settlement to the Commencement of That War Which Terminated in Their Independence.* Philadelphia: A. Small.

Martin, Faith Reese. 2012. *White Doe in the Mist: The Mystery of the Lost Colony.* Lancaster, PA: American Literary Publishing.

Martin, François-Xavier. 1829. *The History of North Carolina, from the Earliest Period.* New Orleans: A.T. Penniman & Co.

McCormick, Brandon, director. 2015. *Roanoke: Search for the Lost Colony.* History Channel.

———, director. 2017. *Return to Roanoke: Search for the Seven.* History Channel.

McMillan, Hamilton. 1888. *Sir Walter Raleigh's Lost Colony: An Historical Sketch of the Attempts of Sir Walter Raleigh to Establish a Colony in Virginia, with the Traditions of an Indian Tribe in North Carolina. Indicating the Fate of the Colony of Englishmen Left on Roanoke Island in 1587.* Wilson, NC: Advance Presses.

McMullan, Philip S., Jr. (2010) 2014. *Beechland and the Lost Colony.* Nags Head, NC: Pamlico and Albemarle Publishing. Originally published 2010, *Beechland and the Lost Colony,* MA Thesis, Department of History, North Carolina State University, Raleigh, http://www.lib.ncsu.edu/resolver/1840.16/6486, accessed May 13, 2021.

McPherson, O.M. 1915. *Indians of North Carolina.* Washington, D.C.: Government Printing Office.

Miller, Lee. 2001. *Roanoke: Solving the Mystery of the Lost Colony.* New York: Arcade.

———. 2007. *Roanoke: The Mystery of the Lost Colony.* New York: Scholastic Nonfiction.

M.M., Mrs. 1875. "The White Doe Chase: A Legend of Olden Times." *Our Living and Our Dead* 3(6): 753–771. *Internet Archive,* https://archive.org/details/ourlivingourdead03sout/, accessed February 7, 2024.

Mogk, Matt. 2009a. "Zombie Colony of Roanoke." *Zombie Research Society,* https://zombieresearchsociety.com/archives/2190, accessed May 14, 2021.

———. 2009b. "Roanoke Zombie Lifespan Test." *Zombie Research Society,* https://zombieresearchsociety.com/archives/2461, accessed May 14, 2021.

———. 2011. *Everything You Ever Wanted to Know About Zombies.* New York: Gallery Books. Kindle.

Monasmith, Allen. 2016. "Samuel Shirley 'Sam' Sumner Jr." *Find a Grave,* 18 April 2016. https://www.findagrave.com/memorial/161260250/samuel-shirley-sumner, accessed May 14, 2021.

Moran, Michael G. 2007. *Inventing Virginia: Sir Walter Raleigh and the Rhetoric of Colonization, 1584–1590.* New York: Peter Lang.

Morris, Bill. 2004. *Saltwater Cowboys.* Wilmington, NC: Coastal Carolina Press.

National Archives. 1936. "Fort Raleigh Restoration—Block House—With Monument to Virginia Dare in Foreground." Records of the Work Projects Administration [WPA], Negative 13451-C, 69.4.3, National Archives, College Park, MD.

National Park Service, U.S. Department of the Interior. 2011. *Secrets in the Sand: Archeology at Fort Raleigh, 1990–2010, Manteo, North Carolina: Archeological Resource Study.* Manteo, NC: National Park Service, Fort Raleigh National Historic Site.

———. 2015. "Ships of the Roanoke Voyages." In *Roanoke Revisited,* https://www.nps.gov/fora/learn/education/ships-of-the-roanoke-voyages.htm, accessed May 12, 2021.

Naughton, Tom, and Nicolas Valcour, producers. 1995. "The Riddle of Roanoke." *Archaeology,* Time-Life Video, 1995.

"A New Deal for Fort Raleigh." 2017. *New Deal of the Day* (blog), https://nddaily.blogspot.com/2017/05/a-new-deal-for-fort-raleigh.html, accessed February 20, 2023.

Nicol, Alex, director. 1966. "The Lost Colony." *Daniel Boone,* NBC.

Noël Hume, Ivor. 1969. *Historical Archaeology.* New York: Alfred A. Knopf.

———. 1994. *The Virginia Adventure: Roanoke to James Towne: An Archaeological and Historical Odyssey.* New York: Knopf.

_____. 1996. "Roanoke Island: America's First Science Center." In *In Search of This and That: Tales from an Archaeologist's Quest: Selected Essays from the Colonial Williamsburg Journal*, pp. 96–109. Williamsburg, VA: Colonial Williamsburg Foundation.

O'Dell, Jeffrey Marshall. 1978. *Inventory of Early Architecture and Historic Sites.* Revised ed. County of Henrico, Virginia/ https://www.dhr.virginia.gov/wp-content/uploads/2019/08/HE-011_Inventory_Early_AHHist_Sites_1976_VHLC_Report_public.pdf, accessed May 14, 2021.

Oakley, Christopher Arris. 2005. *Keeping the Circle: American Indian Identity in Eastern North Carolina, 1885–2004.* Lincoln: University of Nebraska Press.

Oberg, Michael Leroy. 2008. *The Head in Edward Nugent's Hand: Roanoke's Forgotten Indians.* Philadelphia: University of Pennsylvania Press.

_____. 2020. "Tribes and Towns: What Historians Still Get Wrong about the Roanoke Ventures." *Ethnohistory* 67(4):579–602. https://doi.org/10.1215/00141801-8579237.

Oldmixon, John. 1708. *The British Empire in America, Containing the History of the Discovery, Settlement, Progress and Present State of All the British Colonies, on the Continent and Islands of America.* 2 vols. London: John Nicholson, Benjamin Tooke, Richard Parker, and Ralph Smith.

Olds, Frederick A. 1887. "An American Mystery: Colonists of Roanoke Lost in 1587." *The Messenger* (Wilmington, NC) July 31, p. 2.

_____. 1908. "A Visit to the Croatan Indians." *Charlotte Daily Observer*, June 21, pp. 2–3, 8.

Olney, J[esse]. 1837. *A History of the United States, on a New Plan; Adapted to the Capacity of Youth.* New Haven: Durrie and Peck.

Pak, Greg, and Greg Tocchini. 2010. *Marvel 1602: New World/Fantastic Four.* New York: Marvel.

Parker, Jeff, and Ramon Rosanas. 2009. *Marvel 1602: Spider-Man.* New York: Marvel.

Parramore, Barbara M. 1996. "Wiley, Calvin Henderson." In *Dictionary of North Carolina Biography*, edited by William S. Powell, vol. 6, pp. 196–197. Chapel Hill: University of North Carolina Press.

Parramore, Thomas C. 2001. "The 'Lost Colony' Found: A Documentary Perspective." *North Carolina Historical Review* 78(1):67–83. https://www.jstor.org/stable/23522231.

Parramore, Thomas C., and Barbara M. Parramore. 1984. *Looking for the "Lost Colony."* Raleigh: Tanglewood Press.

Parramore, Thomas C., Peter C. Stewart, and Tommy Bogger. 1994. *Norfolk: The First Four Centuries.* Charlottesville: University Press of Virginia.

Pearce, Haywood J., Jr. 1938. "New Light on the Roanoke Colony: A Preliminary Examination of a Stone Found in Chowan County, North Carolina." *The Journal of Southern History* 4(2):148–163. https://doi.org/10.2307/2192000.

_____. 1939a. "The Dare Stone and the Lost Colony of Roanoke." *Brenau Bulletin* 30(3). *HaithiTrust*, https://hdl.handle.net/2027/hvd.32044009694472, accessed February 7, 2024.

_____. 1939b. *Possible Solution of the Virginia Dare Mystery.* Gainesville, GA: Breneau College.

Phelps, David S. 1996–1998. Field Notes 31DR1. Records on file, Phelps Archaeology Laboratory East Carolina University, Greenville, North Carolina.

"planter, n." 2021. *OED Online.* Oxford: Oxford University Press. https://www.oed.com/view/Entry/145175, accessed May 1, 2021.

Porter, Charles W., III. 1952. *Fort Raleigh National Historic Site, North Carolina.* National Park Service Historical Handbook, vol. 16. Washington, D.C.: U.S. Government Printing Office.

Powell, William S. 1965. *Paradise Preserved.* Chapel Hill: University of North Carolina Press.

Purchas, Samuel. 1613. *Purchas His Pilgrimage. Or Relations of the World and the*

Religions Obserued in All Ages and Places Discouered, from the Creation unto This Present. London: William Stansby for Henrie Fetherstone.

———. 1614. *Purchas His Pilgrimage. Or Relations of the World and the Religions Observed in All Ages and Places Discovered, from Creation unto This Present.* 2nd ed. London: William Stansby for Henrie Fetherstone.

———. 1617. *Purchas His Pilgrimage, or Relations of the World and the Religions Observed in Al [sic] Ages and Places Discovered, from Creation unto This Present.* 3rd ed. London: William Stansby for Henrie Fetherstone.

———. (1625) 1905–1907. *Hakluytus Posthumus or Purchas His Pilgrimes: Contayning a History of the World in Sea Voyages and Lande Travells by Englishmen and Others.* 20 vols. Hakluyt Society Extra Series, vols. 14–33. Glasgow: J. MacLehose and Sons, 1905–1907. Originally published 1625 (London: William Stansby for Henrie Fetherstone).

———. 1626. *Purchas His Pilgrimage. Or Relations of the World and the Religions Observed in All Ages and Places Discovered, from the Creation unto This Present.* 4th ed. London: William Stansby for Henrie Fetherstone.

Quinn, David B., and Alison M. Quinn, editors. 1982. *The First Colonists: Documents on the Planting of the First English Settlements in North America, 1584–1590.* Raleigh: North Carolina Department of Cultural Resources, Division of Archives and History. Originally published 1973, *Virginia Voyages from Hakluyt* (London: Oxford University Press).

———. 1983. *The English New England Voyages, 1602–1608.* Hakluyt Society Publications, 2nd ser., vol. 161. London: Hakluyt Society.

Quinn, David Beers. 1974. *England and the Discovery of America, 1481–1620.* New York: Knopf.

———. 1975. *North America from the Earliest Discovery to First Settlements: The Norse Voyages to 1612.* New York: Harper Colophon Books.

———. 1984. *The Lost Colonists: Their Fortune and Probable Fate.* Raleigh: America's Four Hundredth Anniversary Committee, North Carolina Department of Cultural Resources.

———. 1985. *Set Fair for Roanoke: Voyages and Colonies, 1584–1606.* Chapel Hill: America's Four Hundredth Anniversary Committee, University of North Carolina Press.

———. 1996. "White, John." In *Dictionary of North Carolina Biography*, edited by William S. Powell, vol. 6, pp. 177–180. Chapel Hill: University of North Carolina Press.

Quinn, David Beers, editor. (1955) 1991. *The Roanoke Voyages, 1584–1590: Documents to Illustrate the English Voyages to North America under the Patent Granted to Walter Raleigh in 1584.* 2 vols. New York: Dover, 1991. Originally published 1955, Hakluyt Society Publications, 2nd ser., vols. 104–105 (London: Hakluyt Society).

Raleigh, Walter. 1596. *The Discouerie of the Large, Rich, and Beuutiful Empyre of Guiana....* London: Robert Robinson.

"roanoke, n." 2021. *OED Online.* Oxford: Oxford University Press. https://www.oed.com/view/Entry/166553, accessed May 13, 2021.

Roberts, Nancy. 2001. *Ghosts from the Coast.* Chapel Hill: University of North Carolina Press.

Robertson, John. 1825. *Virginia: Or, the Fatal Patent.* Washington, D.C.: Davis and Force. *The Pocahontas Archive*, https://history-on-trial.lib.lehigh.edu/trial/pocahontas/bib.php. (https://history-on-trial.lib.lehigh.edu/trial/pocahontas/pdf/1401), accessed February 8, 2024.

Robertson, William. 1799. *The History of America.* Philadelphia: James Humphrey.

The Robesonian (Lumberton, NC). 1938. "Old Indian Legend Puts Virginia Dare's Grave near Philadelphus in Robeson County." May 18, p. 7.

———. 1951. "Grave of Virginia Dare May Be in Robeson Cotton Field." February 26, p. 15.

———. 1970. "Robeson Field May Hold Grave of Virginia Dare." August 16, p. D12.

Robinson, Lorraine Hale. 2003. "John White's Moste Excellente Adventure: A Colonial 'Rule, Britannia.'" In *Searching for the Roanoke Colonies: An Interdisciplinary*

Collection, edited by E. Thomson Shields, Jr., and Charles R. Ewen, pp. 16–24. Raleigh: Office of Archives and History, North Carolina Department of Cultural Resources.

Robinson, Melvin. 1935. "Riddle of the Lost Colony." *The Beaufort News* (Beaufort, NC), July 15, p. 3; July 22, p. 3; and August 5, p. 3.

———. 1946. *Riddle of the Lost Colony.* New Bern, NC: Owen G. Dunn.

Rocha, Gabriel de Avilez. 2017. "Rethinking the Black Legend of 'Simon Fernandez': New Perspectives from the Iberian Atlantic." Paper presented at "Westward Ho! Roanoke, the Map, and X Marks the Spot: Symposium on Sir Walter Raleigh's Lost Colony," The First Colony Foundation, Manteo, NC, October 21, 2017.

Rogers, Robert. 1765. *A Concise Account of North America: Containing a Description of the Several British Colonies on That Continent, Including the Islands of Newfoundland, Cape Breton, &c.* London: Printed for the author.

Rountree, Helen C. 2021. *Manteo's World: Native American Life in Carolina's Sound Country Before and After the Lost Colony.* With Wesley D. Taukchiray. Chapel Hill: University of North Carolina Press.

The Royal Council for Virginia. (1609) 1969. "Instruccions Orders and Constitucions by Way of Advise Sett Downe Declared and Propounded to Sir Thomas Gates Knight Governour of Virginia and of the Colony There Planted, and to be Planted, and of All the Inhabitantes Thereof." In *The Jamestown Voyages Under the First Charter, 1606–1609...*, edited by P.L. Barbour, vol. 2, pp. 262–268. Hakluyt Society, 2d ser, nos. 136–137. 2 vols. London: Cambridge University Press for the Hakluyt Society.

Salmon, Thomas. 1724–1738. *Modern History; or, the Present State of All Nations.* 31 vols. London: J. Roberts.

"Salmon Creek State Natural Area." n.d. North Carolina Coastal Land Trust, https://coastallandtrust.org/lands/salmon-creek-natural-area/, accessed 12 February 2022.

Sanford, Ezekiel. 1819. *A History of the United States before the Revolution: With Some Account of the Aborigines.* Philadelphia: Anthony Finley.

Sax, Geoffrey, director. 1993. "The Lost Colony." *Lovejoy,* BBC Video, 1993.

Schröder, Volker. 2015. "Royal Prints for Princeton College: A Franco-American Exchange in 1886." *The Princeton University Library Chronicle* 76(1–2):13–50. https://doi.org/10.25290/prinunivlibrchro.76.1-2.0013.

Scott, Walter. (1821) 2000. *Kenilworth.* London: Electric Book Company. Kindle.

Shields, E. Thomson, Jr. 1990. "Conquistadors and Englishmen: The Interplay of Language and Culture in English and Spanish Early American Exploration Narratives." PhD diss., University of Tennessee, Knoxville. ProQuest Dissertations & Theses Global (9030736).

———. 1999. "White, John (fl. 1582–1590)." In *American National Biography*, edited by John A. Garraty and Mark C. Carnes, vol. 23, 225–226. New York: Oxford University Press. https://doi.org/10.1093/anb/9780198606697.article.1700924, accessed April 30, 2021.

———. 2005. "The Genres of Exploration and Conquest Literatures." In *A Companion to the Literatures of Colonial America*, edited by Susan Castillo and Ivy Schweitzer, pp. 353–368. Malden, MA: Blackwell.

———. 2018. "'Into the Vast Unknown': The Changing Ending of Paul Green's *The Lost Colony.*" *North Carolina Literary Review* 27:52–71. *Proquest*, https://www.proquest.com/scholarly-journals/into-vast-unknown-changing-ending-paul-greens/docview/2308782837/se-2, accessed February 7, 2024.

———. 2023. "The First Literary Fictions of the 1587 Roanoke 'Lost Colony.'" *ANQ* 36(2):175–182. https://doi.org/10.1080/0895769X.2021.1935682.

Sloan, Kim. 2007. *A New World: England's First View of America.* Chapel Hill: University of North Carolina Press.

Smith, John. 1986. *The Complete Works of Captain John Smith (1580–1631)*, edited by Philip L. Barbour, 3 vols. Chapel Hill: Institute of Early American History and Culture, University of North Carolina Press.

———. 1988. *Captain John Smith: A Select Edition of His Writings*, edited by Karen

Ordhal Kupperman. Chapel Hill: Institute of Early American History and Culture, University of North Carolina Press.

Sparkes, Boyden. 1941. "Writ on Rocke: Has America's First Mystery Been Solved?" *Saturday Evening Post*, April 26, pp. 9–11, 118, 120–122, 124–126, 128.

Special Collections, East Carolina University. 1600–1650. Signet Ring. Croatan Archaeological Site Collection, 1061. *East Carolina University Digital Collections*, https://digital.lib.ecu.edu/927, accessed August 7, 2023.

Stacy, Robin Purser. 1991. "McMillan, Hamilton." In *Dictionary of North Carolina Biography*, edited by William S. Powell, vol. 4, p. 175. Chapel Hill: University of North Carolina Press.

Stick, David. 1983. *Roanoke Island: The Beginnings of English America*. Chapel Hill: University of North Carolina Press.

Stith, William. 1747. *The History of the First Discovery and Settlement of Virginia: Being an Essay Towards a General History of This Colony*. Williamsburg, VA: William Parks.

Storey, Ed. 1946. "Golden Rule Press and Occoneechee Recorder Was First Published in the Year 1631 at Historic Hillsborough." *The Daily Times-News* (Burlington, NC), January 30, p. 5.

Strachey, William. (1612) 1849. *The Historie of Travaile into Virginia Britannia; Expressing the Cosmographie and Comodities of the Country, Together with the Manners and Customes of the People*, edited by R. H. Major. Hakluyt Society Publications, 1st ser., vol. 6. London: Hakluyt Society.

———. (1612) 1953. *The Historie of Travell into Virginia Britania (1612)*, edited by Louis B. Wright and Virginia Freund. Hakluyt Society Publications, 2nd ser., vol. 103. London: Hakluyt Society.

Sumner, Samuel S., Jr. 1998. "The Remote Sensing of the McMullen Site: A Preliminary Report of Field Notes and Radar Profile Interpretations." PDF of typescript, December 1998.

———. 2009. "Lost Colony Site Discovered Through Remote Viewing." *CISION PRWeb*, 18 August 18, 2009, https://www.prweb.com/releases/remote/viewer/prweb2759384.htm, accessed 13 February 2021.

Symonds, William. 1609. *Virginia: A Sermon Preached at White-Chappel, in the Presence of Many, Honourable and Worshipfull, the Aduenturers and Planters for Virginia: 25. April. 1609*. London: Printed by J. Windet, for Eleazar Edgar, and William Welby.

Tiro, Karim M. 2004. "White, John (fl. 1577–1593)." In *Oxford Dictionary of National Biography*. Oxford: Oxford University Press. https://doi.org/10.1093/ref:odnb/29251, accessed April 30, 2021.

Trofimenkoff, Susan Mann. (1982) 2020. "Foster, Eliza Lanesford (Cushing)." In *Dictionary of Canadian Biography / Dictionnaire biographique du Canada*, University of Toronto–Université Laval, http://www.biographi.ca/en/bio/foster_eliza_lanesford_11E.html, accessed May 10, 20201. Originally published 1982, *Dictionary of Canadian Biography*, vol. 11.

Tuthill, Cornelia L. 1840. "Virginia Dare: Or, the Colony of Roanoke." *Southern Literary Messenger* 6(9):585–595. *Making of America*, https://quod.lib.umich.edu/m/moajrnl/acf2679.0006.009/593:2, accessed February 7, 2024.

Upchurch, Donald Paul, and Lucy Rebecca Daniels. 2018. *In Pursuit of Dorothie, the Lost Colony Ship*, n.p.: Lucy Rebecca Daniels.

Vaughan, Alden T. 2006. *Transatlantic Encounters: American Indians in Britain, 1500–1776*. Cambridge: Cambridge University Press.

———. 2018. "Namontack's Itinerant Life and Mysterious Death: Sources and Speculations." *The Virginia Magazine of History and Biography* 126(2): 171-209. Virginia Company of London. 1610. *A True and Sincere Declaration of the Purpose and Ends of the Plantation Begun in Virginia....* London: J. Stepney.

Wagner, Anton. 1990. "Eliza Lanesford Cushing." *Canadian Writers Before 1890*, edited by William H. New. Detroit: Gale, 1990. *Dictionary of Literary Biography, Gale*

Literature Resource Center, https://link.gale.com/apps/doc/H1200005132/LitRC?u=
ncliveecu&sid=LitRC&xid=5670a00d, accessed May 10, 2021.

Watts, Gordon P., Jr. 2008. *2007 Raleigh Colony Investigation: Magnetic Anomaly Identification and Assessment Roanoke Sound and Shallowbag Bay, Roanoke Island, North Carolina*. Electronic document, https://www.firstcolonyfoundation.org/archaeology/dig-reports/ (https://www.firstcolonyfoundation.org/documents/roanoke_report_2007.pdf), accessed March 18, 2022.

Webster, Noah. 1823. *Letters to a Young Gentleman Commencing His Education: To Which Is Subjoined a Brief History of the United States*. New Haven: Howe and Spalding.

Weeks, Stephen B. 1891a. "The Lost Colony of Roanoke: Its Fate and Survival." *Papers of the American Historical Association* 5(4):441–480. *Google Books*, https://books.google.com/books?id=FfwKAAAAIAAJ, accessed February 7, 2024.

———. 1891b. "Raleigh's Settlement on Roanoke Island: An Historical Survival." *Magazine of American History* February:127–139. *Google Books*, https://books.google.com/books?id=YUxIAAAAYAAJ, accessed February 7, 2024.

Welter, Barbara. 1966. "The Cult of True Womanhood: 1820–1860." *American Quarterly* 18(2.1):151–174. https://doi.org/10.2307/2711179.

Whedbee, Charles Harry. 1966. *Legends of the Outer Banks and Tar Heel Tidewater*. Winston-Salem, NC: J.F. Blair.

White, Ed. 2005. "Invisible Tagkanysough." *PMLA* 120(3):751–767. https://www.jstor.org/stable/25486211.

White, Robert W. 1991. *A Witness for Eleanor Dare: The Final Chapter in a 400 Year Old Mystery*. San Francisco: Lexikos.

Wildman, Don, host. 2012. "Lost Colony of Roanoke, Dr. Linda Hazzard, Deep Blue, Greenbrier Hotel Bunker, Death of Edgar Allan Poe, Liberty Bell 7." *Mysteries at the Museum*, The Travel Channel.

Wiley, Calvin Henderson. 1851. *The North-Carolina Reader: Containing a History and Description of North-Carolina, Selections in Prose and Verse, Many of Them by Eminent Citizens of the State, Historical and Chronological Tables, and a Variety of Miscellaneous Information and Statistics*. Philadelphia: Lippincott.

Willard, Emma. 1828. *History of the United States, or Republic of America*. New York: White, Gallaher & White.

Williams, Talcott. 1896. "The Surroundings and Site of Raleigh's Colony." In *Annual Report of the American Historical Association for the Year 1895*, pp. 47–61. Government Printing Office, Washington, D.C. *Google Books*, https://books.google.com/books?id=UMA8AAAAIAAJ, accessed February 7, 2024.

Williamson, Hugh. 1812. *The History of North Carolina*. 2 vols. Philadelphia: Thomas Dobson.

Wilmer, James Jones. 1805. *The American Nepos: A Collection of the Lives of the Most Remarkable and the Most Eminent Men, Who Have Contributed to the Discovery, the Settlement, and the Independence of America*. Baltimore: G. Douglas.

Wolfram, Walt. 2001. "From the Brickhouse to the Swamp." *American Language Review*, July/August, pp. 34–38.

Wolfram, Walt, and Jeffrey Reaser. 2014. *Talkin' Tar Heel: How Our Voices Tell the Story of North Carolina*. Chapel Hill: University of North Carolina Press, Chapel Hill.

Wynne, John Huddleston. 1770. *A General History of the British Empire in America*. 2 vols. London: W. Richardson and L. Urquhart.

Yolen, Jane, and Heidi Elizabeth Yolen Stemple. 2003. *Roanoke: The Lost Colony: An Unsolved Mystery from History*. New York: Simon & Schuster Books for Young Readers.

Index

Aaron, Jason: "Lost Colony" 169
Abbot, George: *A Briefe Description of the Whole World* 40–42, 59, 86
Acorn Hill 159
Albemarle Sound (region) 2, 5, 27, 74–75, 89, 114, 116, 119, 126–131, 134, 138, 159, 173
Algonquian 44, 131, 132, 148, 166, 172–173, 175, 178, 181*n*13, 181*n*18; Carolina Algonquian 76, 78, 132; *see also* Chawanoacs; Chesapeakes; Croatoans; Hatteras; Powhatans; Roanoke; Secotan; Weapemeoc
Amadas, Philip 10–11, 14–15, 31, 35–36, 56, 86, 110, 166, 175, 176
ambiguity 26, 28, 31, 172–173
America Unearthed ("Mystery of Roanoke") 163
The American Gazetteer 182*n*5, 183*n*8
American Horror Story: Roanoke see *Roanoke (American Horror Story)*
Analostan Island 99, 183*n*10
appeal to authority 139
Aquascogoc (town) 18, 114
archaeology (discipline) 13, 29, 60–61, 82; *see also* artifacts; ceramics; features (archaeological)
Archaeology ("The Riddle of Roanoke") 163
aristocracy 14, 23, 42–43, 80, 96–97, 147, 183*n*8
Arner, Robert D. 108, 183*n*11
artifacts 57, 61, 63, 66, 71, 72–75, 77–82, 85, 129–130, 135, 142–143, 153–156, 158, 165, 173–174; brick 64, 71–73, 81; coins 63, 77, 78, 81; glass beads 71, 74, 78, 81; glass bottles 78; gunlock 60, 78; guns 63, 78, 143; iron 61, 63, 66, 71, 78, 82, 129, 143; lead 61, 78, 129; pipe bowls and stems 73, 78, 129; rapier

hilt 60, 81, 143, 174; writing slate 81, 143; *see also* brass; ceramics; features (archaeological); gold; "signet" ring
assimilation 62–63, 82, 101–104, 109, 116, 123, 127–128, 140, 142–144, 149, 183*n*2
Atlantic, North Carolina (town) 148
author function 26

Bahamas 15
Baldwin, Karen 134–135
Bancroft, George: *A History of the United States* 93, 96–98, 100, 102, 104–105
Barber, John Warner: *Interesting Events in the History of the United States* 182*n*2
Barlow, Joel: *The Vision of Columbus* 98
Barlowe, Arthur 10–12, 14–15, 18, 31, 33–36, 86, 175–176
Batts, Nathaniel 130
BBC (British Broadcast Corporation) 122, 167
Beaufort, North Carolina (town) 147–148, 185*ch*6*n*2
Beaufort County, North Carolina 139
Beechland, North Carolina (town) 134–137
Bermuda 48, 50, 86, 181*n*15
Bernstein, Josh: *Digging for the Truth* 120–121, 164–165
Beverley, Robert: *The History and Present State of Virginia* 86–88, 97, 182*n*1
Birth of a Colony: North Carolina 161–162
Blanton, Dennis 164
Blu, Karen I. 120
Boeschenstein, Nell: "Lost Colonies" 171
Bolling, Rob 164
Bolton, Herbert 154

201

Scott Walter: *Kenilworth* 98, 100
Secotan (town) 11–12, 17, 18, 147
Secotan (tribe) 11, 114, 126, 139, 142
Shakespeare, William 122, 146
Shallowbag Bay 73
Shields, E. Thomson (Tom) 3–4, 29, 87, 111, 135, 144, 159–161, 163–165, 170–171, 174, 179*n*5
ships/boats 10–12, 15, 19–22, 30, 41–42, 48, 56, 61, 82, 101, 110, 113, 115, 117, 123–124, 136, 140,-141 146–147, 151, 159, 161–162, 182*n*1, 184*n*14; bark 11, 39, 179*n*1; *Bark Raleigh* 11, 176; *Bonner* 19; canoe 30, 123; *Elizabeth* 15; European style ("shippes like ours") 44–45; flyboat 20, 21, 23, 25, 30; *Lion* 15, 21; makeshift boats 11, 48, 116; pinnace 10–11, 15, 21, 30, 56, 115, 123, 139, 143, 159, 179*n*1, 183*n*2; *Roebuck* 15; ship's boat 30, 115, 159; *Tyger* (1585) 14–15, 18
shipwrecks 11, 48, 50, 78, 116, 181*n*15
Sicklemore, Michael 53–54, 57, 94, 131, 133, 178
"signet" ring 1, 5, 60, 78–80, 173–174
silent movie (1921) 67, 69
silk grass 53, 87, 131, 181*n*21
Siouan 118–119, 132,
Site X (31BR246) *see* First Colony Foundation (FCF)
Site Y (31BR49) *see* First Colony Foundation (FCF)
Skicóac (town) 124
Skiko (person) 19
Skinner, Ralph 147
slaves 43; African 19, 20, 143, 171; European 3, 131–134, 159; Native American 19, 20, 133, 171
Sleepy Hollow ("John Doe") 167
Sloan, Kim 179*n*5
Smith, John 47, 50, 56–59, 62, 85, 94, 98–100, 104, 124, 126–127, 131, 134, 138–139, 178; *The Generall Historie* 50, 55–57, 85, 131; *A Map of Virginia* 48, 52–54, 57, 131, 181*n*20; *True Relation* 44–45
sources 9, 12, 14, 16, 20, 22–25, 29, 33, 48, 54, 87, 118, 120, 135, 137, 141, 148, 153, 162, 180*n*4; primary vs. secondary 13–14, 31, 50, 58–59, 133–134; *see also* Hakluyt, Richard: *The Principall Navigations*; Purchas, Samuel; Smith, John; Strachey, William: *The Historie of Travell into Virginia Britania*
South Sea (Pacific Ocean) 44, 52–54, 57

Southerland, James 162–163
Spain 1, 3, 10–11, 16, 18, 22–23, 38, 46, 49, 77, 90, 101, 110, 112, 114–115, 124, 128, 136, 138–139, 141–142, 180*n*1, 180*n*9, 181*n*13, 183*n*1, 183*n*2, 184*n*15
Sparkes, Boyden 152
Spicer, Edward 147
Stager, Lawrence 170; *see also* Mogk, Matt: *Everything You Ever Wanted to Know About Zombies*
Stemple, Heidi Elizabeth Yolen: *Roanoke: The Lost Colony* 109
Stick, David 123, 161–163
Stith, William: *The History of the First Discovery and Settlement of Virginia* 90, 97
stone/rock 27, 50, 62, 64, 154, 184*n*12; *see also* Dare Stones; houses, European style
Storm of the Century see Carliner, Mark: *Storm of the Century*; King, Stephen: *Storm of the Century*
Strachey, William 48, 178, 181*n*15; *The Historie of Travell into Virginia Britania* 48–54, 56–57, 61–62, 114, 124, 126–128, 132, 138–139, 152, 181*n*16, 181*n*18, 184*n*10
Straube, Bly 165
strawman argument 141
Strother, David Hunter *see* Crayon, Porte
Sugg-Willard, Kathryn 156
Sumner, Samuel S., Jr. 158–159
Supernatural (television series) 167
supernatural/paranormal 108–109, 151, 157–158, 167–170, 185*ch*Concl.*n*2; *see also* vampires; zombies
Swindell, Clay 80, 165
Symonds, William 52, 181*n*19, 181*n*20

Tappahannock River 45
Tar River 132
textual analysis 25, 29, 33–38
theory 4, 91, 125, 133–134, 138, 144, 174; defined 111–112; *see also* hypothesis
Time Team America ("Fort Raleigh, North Carolina") 73, 158–159, 165, 182*n*4
Tise, Larry 164
Tocchini, Greg: *Marvel 1602: Fantastic Four* and *Marvel 1602: New World* 185*ch*Concl.*n*2
Todkill, Anas 52–54, 57, 94, 133, 177–178
tradition *see* oral history (tradition)
Treaty of Tordesillas 114